GREEK RELIGIOUS THOUGHT
FROM HOMER TO THE
AGE OF ALEXANDER

57660

EDITED BY
ERNEST BARKER, M.A., D.LITT., LL.D.
PRINCIPAL OF KING'S COLLEGE, UNIVERSITY OF LONDON

GREEK
RELIGIOUS THOUGHT
FROM HOMER TO THE
AGE OF ALEXANDER

BY

F. M. CORNFORD.

FELLOW AND LECTURER OF TRINITY
COLLEGE, CAMBRIDGE

*Shadows we are and
Like shadows depart*

LONDON
J. M. DENT & SONS LTD.

J. M. Dent & Sons Ltd.
Aldine House · Bedford St. · London

Made in Great Britain
by
The Temple Press · Letchworth · Herts
First published 1923
Last reprinted 1950

TO

WALTER DE LA MARE

A NOTE ON THE AUTHOR

Francis Macdonald Cornford

(Sometime Professor of Ancient Philosophy in the University of Cambridge)

Professor Cornford (as he became in 1931) was born in 1874, and died at the beginning of 1943. His life was spent in the service of Trinity College and the University of Cambridge, and in the pursuit of Greek scholarship. For many years, down to 1931, he was a classical lecturer at Trinity College; for eight years, from 1931 to 1939, he held the office of Professor of Ancient Philosophy in the University; and during his retirement, for the last four years of his life, he still continued to devote himself to the study and elucidation of Greek philosophical writers. He married a granddaughter of Charles Darwin, who was a notable poetess and writer; and he was himself a master of wit and style, as well as of scholarship. He wrote pamphlets as well as works of learning; and one of his pamphlets, originally published in 1908, was again republished, in a fourth edition, as recently as 1949, six years after his death. This was his witty and searching *Microcosmographia Academica*, which analysed the necessary qualities, and suggested the proper tactics, of the budding academic politician, but which went so deeply, and so wittily, into its subject that it may almost be called a vade mecum for any politician of any sort. Witty as he was on paper he was often silent in conversation; but he left with his friends the memory of a fine presence and a deep scholarship.

His writings covered, especially in his early years, the general range of Greek literature. The first of his books, published at the age of thirty-three, won him immediate fame. This was *Thucydides Mythistoricus*, in which he sought to draw a parallel, or establish a connection, between the historic art of Thucydides and the dramatic art of the Greek tragedians in their handling of the ancient myths. His next book showed that his mind was already moving towards those deeper themes which eventually engaged his whole attention: he published in 1912 a work entitled *From Religion to Philosophy: a Study in the Origins of Western Speculation*. But he returned again to literary scholarship and the drama in a work on *The Origin of Attic Comedy*, which was published in 1914. His next work was the present volume, published originally in 1923. But the great and fertile years of his life were the eight years (1931–8) during which he held the university professorship of Ancient Philosophy. In 1932 he published his *Before and After Socrates*. Between 1935 and 1939 he published three different volumes in the International Library of Psychology, all containing translations of and commentaries on the more abstruse and profound of Plato's dialogues—the *Timaeus*, the *Theaetetus* and the *Sophist*, and the *Parmenides*. His last work, published during his retirement, and only a year before his death, was a translation of Plato's *Republic* (published by the Clarendon Press, Oxford), a translation so admirably pithy and lucid, and published in a form so handy and convenient, that it may be said to have already established itself as the classical translation of the *Republic*.

The present volume (which has for its companion Dr. E. R. Bevan's *Later Greek Religion*), attests in its seventeen sections, ranging from Homer to Aristotle, both the range and the depth of his scholarship and the felicity of his style. The Library of Greek Thought was fortunate in beginning with such a volume.

ERNEST BARKER,
Editor of the Library of Greek Thought.

Cambridge, 1950.

INTRODUCTION

THE purpose of this book is to let the English reader see for himself what the Greeks, from Homer to Aristotle, thought about the world, the gods and their relations to man, the nature and destiny of the soul, and the significance of human life. The form of presentation is prescribed by the plan of the series. The book is to be a compilation of extracts from the Greek authors, selected, so far as possible, without prejudice and translated with such honesty as a translation may have. This plan has the merit of isolating the actual thought of the Greeks in this period from all the constructions put upon it by later ages, except in so far as the choice of extracts must be governed by some scheme in the compiler's mind, which is itself determined by the limits of his knowledge and by other personal factors. In the book itself it is clearly his business to reduce the influence of these factors to the lowest point; but in the introduction it is no less his business to forewarn the reader against some of the consequences.

In the first place, it is probable that the development of Greek religion is, in some ways, better understood by us than by the Greeks themselves. It is true that much of the labour of modern scholarship is spent in divining by painful inference truths that do not happen to stand in the literary or monumental record, either because so much has been lost, or because the truths in question were only dimly apprehended, or again because they were so familiar that there was no occasion to mention them. On the other hand, it is also certain that our immensely wider knowledge of other societies, civilised or barbarous, gives us an advantage over the most learned men of antiquity. Within living memory the work of Robertson Smith, Tylor, Lang, Sir James Frazer, and many others has permanently shifted the perspective. The discovery by Sir Arthur Evans of a civilisation in Crete stretching back thousands of years before Homer has finally destroyed the illusion that Homer's world is primitive, and has laid down at least a framework of historical fact in times from which little more than the rumour of a Minoan thalassocracy had reached Thucydides. In so far as this new knowledge goes beyond anything known to the Greeks, it has no place in this volume. In so far as it reveals what the Greeks knew, but do not happen to have mentioned in the surviving literature, the picture here presented is incomplete.

Further, man's attitude towards the divine is most directly expressed in liturgy, in ritual observance, in prayers and hymns of the temple service. If our aim were to understand the religious thought of England in the sixteenth century, we should turn to the Book of Common Prayer before consulting what is commonly called the literature of the time. About the corresponding side of Greek religion we possess a considerable mass of evidence, but it cannot be represented by extracts from contemporary writers. Even if room were found for descriptions of ritual, there would remain the very delicate question how far the liturgy in use at any moment reflected the real beliefs of any part of the population. We know from late sources that, at an ancient festival of All Souls called the Anthesteria, the Athenian householder entertained the ghosts of the dead, who " went about the city " at that season, till they were dismissed with the words: " Out of the doors, ghosts! The Anthesteria is over." When the details of the ritual have been pieced together from indirect allusions and from scraps of lost antiquarian works preserved by late annotators of Greek texts, we seem to make out that the Anthesteria belonged to an order of primitive festivals embodying beliefs about the dead and the gods of the lower world such as scarcely find utterance in the extant literature. They had been overlaid by the Olympian religion of Homer, from which the cult of the dead had almost entirely disappeared. What are we to infer from the perpetuation of the festival custom? What was in the mind of the Athenian who feasted his ghosts and then sped their departure with the curt formula which became a proverb addressed (we are told) to those who " are always demanding a repetition of favours received"? Evidently, there is no simple answer to this question. The belief originally implied in a ceremonial custom may fade as time goes on, till, in extreme cases, no one but an antiquary knows what the custom means. And besides the effects of time, we have to remember that a civilised society is stratified in many layers. In the fifth century there may have been some Athenians who still believed that the ghosts went about the city at the Anthesteria; some who thought that the dead were at a safe distance underground or in the west; others who found no offence in the suggestion that they were permanently consigned to dreamless sleep, or that the spirit, breathed out from the dying frame, was scattered and lost in the impersonal air.

So much for the limitations imposed by the plan of this series. Even within these limits, the translator is faced by the formidable difficulty of finding faithful renderings for the words *theos* ("god") and *theion* ("divine"). The modern Englishman, whether he reads the Bible or not, is nourished on a tradition in which Judaic monotheism, reformed by Christ and St. Paul, is combined with a metaphysical theology derived from Plato and Aristotle. Moses enjoins, and Plato countenances, the belief in a God who is one, a person, good and benevolent, the designer and maker of the universe. Christianity adds that God is love, and a Father who cares for every one of his children. In English the serious use of the word "God" suggests all these attributes. But the Greek word "*theos*" does not necessarily imply any one of them. The issue between monotheism and polytheism, so vital to the Jew, seemed to the Greek a matter of small importance. Even Plato, in a context where the very nature of deity is in question, will speak of "God" or of "the gods" indifferently, and it is still debated whether, and in what sense, he believed in a plurality of personal divinities. In general, the essential attribute of the divine is immortality— exemption from old age, decay, and death. Whatever is immortal is divine; whatever is divine, immortal. Even this definition, however, is too narrow. "Immortal" would naturally be taken to imply some kind of life and consciousness. But the word *theos* can be applied to abstractions such as the most concrete imagination could not really personify or endow with consciousness of any sort. A character in Euripides says that the recognition of friends after long absence is "a god." The sudden onset of unlooked-for joy in meeting is a divine thing. It seems to come from without, as "something not ourselves." In cases such as this, even the expressions "deity," "divinity," "heaven," which I have sometimes employed as renderings of *theos*, are too definite and concrete.

The phrase "something not ourselves" may serve to remind us that, after all, a searching inquiry would disclose a high degree of vagueness in the notion of divinity even among professed Christians in our own age. Two thousand years hence, a student who knew nineteenth century literature only from anthologies and fragmentary quotations, might be seriously misled. He might set down Wordsworth as a pantheist believing only in "something far more deeply interfused, whose dwelling is the light of setting suns," and might have no inkling that the poet sincerely recited the Athanasian creed in Grasmere Church. In a recent article on Louis XI. and Charles the Bold, I find these sentences: "Men do not know of what they are the instruments. Their ambitions, their desires, their fixed objects, have no relation to the things which they are used by higher powers to do. . . It was a God, it was a God, which drove the Capetians and compelled them to remake Gaul." The expression "*a* God," and the neuter "which" would not lead one to suppose that the writer (Mr. Belloc) was one who usually made no secret of his adherence to the Roman faith. The author has lapsed into traditional—really pagan—language, formally irreconcilable with his professed religion. So hard is it to discover what men believe, or what they think they believe, from fragments of what they say.

If "something not ourselves" may be taken as the lowest common measure of the usages of *theos*, we can arrange its other applications along a scale ascending from the barest abstractions, such as the sudden recognition of a lost kinsman, to the completely anthropomorphic gods of Homer. Towards the lower end of this scale there were spirits whose whole being consisted in a momentary or occasional function, *e.g.* the Fly-chaser, whose only business was to drive the flies away from the sacrifice to Athena at Aliphera. Then there are adjectival spirits, like Victory (*Niké*), who is the epithet of a personal goddess (*Athena Niké*), and at the same time is figured in human form with wings. Next there are various kinds of daemons or spirits: vegetation spirits; daemons identified with the souls of an earlier race of mankind; spirits of vengeance (*Erinyes*); the guardian genius of a race or of an individual; and so forth. Next come the heroes or demigods, men of divine parentage on one side or deified for their extraordinary excellence. Finally the Olympian family of Zeus, though rigidly distinguished from man by immortality and superhuman powers, are otherwise endowed with every attribute and passion of the mortal nature.

It is impossible to mark a point in this scale where anything that we should unhesitatingly recognise as personality begins. The Greeks, indeed, had no word for "personality." All we can say is that "god" or "the divine" normally meant something alive, active, imperishable. When this something is enclosed in a human form, it naturally tends to be invested with human passions and an autonomous will; it can then be called a person, or at least a personification. The Greek mind was distinguished from the Roman by its singular power of conceiving the "something not ourselves" as clothed in a form no less definite than its visible and tangible embodiments in the works of plastic art.

Here we touch a fact of central importance—that Greek theology was formulated, not by priests, nor even by prophets, but by artists, poets, and philosophers. The great civilisations of the East were dominated by a sacerdotal caste, and the temple became for them the centre of intellectual, no less than of religious, life. In Greece nothing of this sort ever happened. There was no priestly class guarding from innovating influence a sacred tradition enshrined in a sacred book. There were no divines who could successfully claim to dictate the terms of belief from an inexpugnable fortress of authority. One consequence was that the conception of deity could be dissociated from cult, and enlarged to include beings and things which no one ever dreamed of connecting with the obligation of worship.

The fact that in Greece the prophet's place was filled by the poet explains why it was that the poets were so strictly called to account for their religious and moral sentiments, even when these were merely the appropriate utterances of some character in a drama. Euripides was attacked because, in one of his plays, a character said: "My tongue has sworn, my mind has made no oath." This is an extreme case; and if Euripides' assailants seriously thought he was condoning perjury, they can hardly be acquitted of stupidity. It must be remembered, however, that the poets were looked upon as religious and moral authorities in a degree that is foreign to our notions. It does not seem to us to be the primary business of a dramatist to inculcate religion and morality, and we think that the gallery betrays some lack of culture when it pelts the villain in a melo-drama. I have no doubt, indeed, that someone has written a book called "Shakespeare as a religious teacher," and has been at the pains to reconcile Gloucester's outburst:

> As flies to wanton boys, are we to the gods;
> They kill us for their sport

with Hamlet's

> There's a divinity that shapes our ends.

But most sensible people would hesitate to hold the playwright responsible for either opinion or for both. The position of the Greek poet was different. I doubt if it could be shown that the history of English protestant belief from the seventeenth century onwards would have been appreciably different if Shakespeare had died in infancy. But to the Greek ear " theologian " (*theologos*) meant a poet who sang of the world's beginning and the birth of the gods, and laid claim to the divine inspiration of the Muses. If Homer, Hesiod, and " Orpheus " are to be set against the Bible, the lyric and dramatic poets may be as plausibly compared to the Fathers of the Church. They would have admitted a measure of responsibility which their modern counterparts are seldom called upon to disclaim.

On the other hand they were, to a large extent, merely casting into exact and perfect form the substance of traditional thoughts. The reader will observe the recurrence of such commonplaces in this volume; it would have been easy to multiply them indefinitely. Taken as a whole and as actually existing in the popular mind, no body of religious ideas in any age is either clear or consistent with itself. When various elements in it are distinguished by perfect expression, the inconsistency, till then unnoticed, may become manifest. To reconcile it is not the business of the dramatist, as it might be of the philosopher. When the poets are working in this way, we have no right to put together all the discordant utterances and call them the religion of Aeschylus or of Euripides.

Such being the position of the ancient poet, it was a serious matter for the Greeks that their literature should begin with Homer. In the *Iliad* and *Odyssey* anthropomorphism has attained the furthest limit. Olympus is inhabited by a community of supernatural men and women, whose characters and personal histories are as well known as the details of their appearance and dress. Modern scholars, falling under the poet's spell, are loyally bent upon making the best of his religion. If they were required to believe it, they might be more alive to the depressing aspects of a theology in which the gods hardly reach the standard of morality and dignity set by the best human beings, and no desirable form of immortality is offered to mankind. Not a few of the Greek philosophers and poets felt the need to break with the authority of Homer. Some of them ignored this theology as childish; others denounced it as immoral; others again sought to reform it by expurgating such elements as had become offensive to a genuinely religious mind. Our own view of the Homeric gods is to some extent coloured by these reforming efforts, much as our view of the Mosaic Jehovah is coloured by the prophets and the New Testament. The Zeus of Aeschylus still bears the name of the polygamous father of gods and men, whose temper made his consort an expert in the arts of wifely deceit; but it is clear that Aeschylus did not believe that such a person guided the destinies of the world. A great part of the supreme god's biography had to be frankly rejected as false, or reinterpreted as allegory, or contemplated with reserve as mysterious myth too dark for human understanding. But the very clearness of unmistakable detail in the Homeric picture made it a hard task to distort the contents of the myth in the sense of a revised morality.

Above and beyond the sharply outlined figures of Olympus stands the indefinite presence of Fate. The position assigned to Necessity or inexorable limitation depends partly upon the nature of the gods. The power of man is limited in the first place by death. The overwhelming consciousness of mortality darkens the whole main current of Greek reflection upon life. It lies near the root of the conception of Fate. It is the absence of this shadow that makes the life of the Olympians radiant; though they can feel grief and even bodily pain, they do not grow old and they cannot die.

> Fair Aegeus' son, only to gods in heaven
> Comes no old age, nor death of anything;
> All else is turmoiled by our master Time.[1]

So the fact of death not only puts a term to all man's endeavour, but also sets a barrier between the mortal sphere and the immortal. Even the hopeless wish to transcend this barrier is enough to draw down the jealousy of heaven. Two utterances of Pindar: " O my soul, seek not a life immortal," and " Seek not to become a god," mean the same thing, since "immortal" and "divine" are synonyms. The law of mortality for man operates as a limitation on the power of the gods, who cannot save even their own sons from death; and since the death of princes is linked with the fall of kingdoms and the sacking of cities, there are wider decrees of destiny that the gods may perhaps postpone, but cannot altogether avert.

[1] Sophocles, *Oedipus at Colonus,* translated by Professor Murray.

There is another aspect, too, in which Fate limits the divine as well as the human. If there are many gods, each with a personal will on the human model, these wills are bound to clash, and each must limit every other. The conflict was not, to the Greek mind, anarchical. When Cronos was overthrown and the new dynasty of Zeus established, the gods were allotted their several provinces and prerogatives. The Greek word for Fate (*Moira*) means " lot " or " portion," and the representation stands for this constitutional system of boundaries delimiting the provinces within which the several gods have peculiar rights, not to be lawfully infringed by others. This principle of apportionment is superior even to the will of the father of gods and men. If Zeus claims a monarchy, it is a constitutional monarchy, not a despotism.

This position is clear in Homer, but from the sixth century onwards the reader will discern a drift in the direction of monotheism. Zeus becomes less anthropomorphic; the father of the unruly family of Olympus moves towards the position of the supreme power in the universe. This tendency entails a significant readjustment of the idea of Fate. As soon as the universe comes to be governed by a single will, or even by a supreme will capable of overriding all others, it is possible for Destiny to be merged in this will. For religion this result is of great importance. Destiny or necessity had at first been a negative, impersonal thing, confronting all power and desire with limits that must be accepted because they could not be broken. But when Destiny is absorbed into a personal will, it becomes positive—a direction and government of the world's affairs; and this direction is sure to be regarded as foreseeing and benevolent. Henceforth

B

it is possible for man to fall into the attitude of faith. He can trust this government, however hard it may be in detail to justify its ways. The fusion is complete in Stoicism, whose founder identified Destiny with Providence. But Aeschylus is well on the way towards it. His great trilogy ends with the assurance that " all-seeing Zeus and *Moira* have come to an agreement." Even in Homer there are anticipations in such phrases as "the fate (apportionment) of Zeus."

There is yet another way in which man becomes conscious that his destiny is shaped by constraint. Fate may be experienced, not as an outside barrier confronting the will to power, but no less as the positive compulsion of a violent passion which a man does not identify with his conscious "self," but on the contrary resists with all the force his "will" can command. If this unacknowledged motive proves irresistible, it will seem to him, as to Raskolnikov in *Crime and Punishment*, that he has been driven into sin as the mere tool of destiny. " Going over all that happened to him during those days, minute by minute and step by step, he recalled later how each event always seemed to him evidence of the predetermination of his fate."

Among the extracts from Euripides I have included Hecuba's speech in the *Trojan Women*, where Helen is told that, when she lays the responsibility for her sin on Aphrodite, the simple truth is that " Aphrodite " is only a name for the passion fired in her by the beauty of Paris. If Aphrodite had been a real person, the motives ascribed to her would be absurd and she could have gained her ends by much simpler means. Here Euripides seems to see, as clearly as Dostoyevsky, how an unacknowledged passion is projected or objectified as " fate "

or as the will of a divinity, just because it is disowned
and resisted by the conscious self. In Marlowe the two
conflicting parts of Faustus' nature are externalised as
the good and evil angels, alternately urging him, the one
to lay his damnèd book aside, the other to complete his
contract with the devil. The Greeks also knew of the
daemon or genius, attending a man from his birth and
guiding his destiny. A family might have an hereditary
genius carrying a taint of crime from generation to
generation. So Clytemnestra, defending herself for the
murder of Agamemnon, at one moment casts the blame
upon the daemon of the House of Tantalus. In these
ways a compulsion of internal origin may be identified
with the external will of a supernatural being, or with
the impersonal and blind constraint of Destiny.

In Greek a special name denoted the state of a man
dominated by an unacknowledged and irresistible motive
which drives him to destruction. *Atê* means "infatua-
tion" or moral blindness; it also means the "ruin" that
results. This condition was believed specially to afflict
men of high station whose exceptional prosperity lifted
them too near the felicity that is the prerogative of
jealous gods. It is the state of those who are "above
themselves" and flown with insolence (*Hybris*). They
provoke the justifiable anger (*Nemesis*) of the gods,
whose province they threaten to invade. Thus *Atê*, to
men thinking in anthropomorphic terms, is the minister
of *Nemesis*; and she has her own child or instrument,
Temptation or Persuasion (*Peitho*), who personifies the
promptings of the unacknowledged motive.

> Child of designing Atê's deadly womb,
> The wretch Temptation drives him to his doom.[1]

[1] Aeschylus, *Agamemnon*. See p. 107.

This lying spirit of persuasion suggests the commission of some action — not necessarily in itself a very bad action, but having some fatal aspect of which the man in his state of moral blindness is unaware. So the train of destruction is fired, and the end follows inevitably.

It was in the light of this philosophy of tragic action that Herodotus, as well as Aeschylus, saw the grandiose attempt of Eastern despotism to overwhelm the free cities of the West in the Persian Wars. At this crisis of their history the Greeks could read the judgment of heaven upon pride in the defeats of Marathon and Salamis. The selection of passages from Herodotus' history is designed to illustrate this group of conceptions.

This golden moment was followed by the age of Pericles; and then, to the eyes of the later Greeks as to our own, it seemed that the shadows began to fall thickly in the period best known to us from surviving literature. The Peloponnesian War and the disastrous expedition to Sicily exhausted, in fratricidal strife, the strength which had enabled the Greek cities to stand against Persia. In the fourth century they were to become like playthings in the hands of the Macedonian Philip, the father of Alexander. Thucydides, for all the reticence and self-effacement of his record of the Peloponnesian War, shows clearly enough that the tragedy of Athens and Sparta shaped itself to his philosophy on the same lines as the tragedy of Persia.

When we turn from the poets and historians to the philosophers, we observe the curious fact that the movement of thought in the science of nature starts from a point as remote as possible from the full-blooded anthropomorphism of Homer at the head of the poetic tradition. In the sixth century we find anthropomorphism laid bare to the philosophic satire of Xenophanes. Besides this, the earliest school of physical speculation at Miletus tacitly ignores the Homeric pantheon altogether. Taking for its problem the origins of the world-order and of life, this school taught that all things arose out of a primitive living stuff, the intermediate element (water, mist, air) between the fire of heaven and the solid earth. This living stuff, which "encompasses" the ordered world as well as forming its substance, they called "the divine." It possessed the minimum of divine attributes: it was alive, without beginning or end, immortal. What kind or degree of consciousness was attributed to it is a question that remains entirely vague; but it was certainly not personal, even in the lowest sense we can give to that word, nor was it in any way associated with cult.

It is, perhaps, not commonly recognised that, in reducing " the divine " to this impersonal living substance, the philosophers were, without knowing it, reverting to a conception of divinity immensely older than the Homeric anthropomorphism. They were undoing all the work of the poets and the plastic artists, and rediscovering the raw material out of which the humanised gods had been built up.

Setting out from this remote position, the course of philosophy, in the next two centuries, moves towards a point where it converges with the monotheistic tendency of the reforming poets. It is in the philosophic tradition, at its highest pitch of development in the Socratic school, that we encounter for the first time the conception of a benevolent maker of the universe. The Zeus of Homer had never held such a position. He had belonged to the youngest generation of gods, and even the oldest had been the children of Heaven and Earth, and so younger than the world. It was not impossible, on the other hand, for the Zeus of Aeschylus and the later poets to be fused ultimately with the wise and good supreme being of philosophy. The necessary hint was supplied to Socrates and his successors, Plato and Aristotle, by Anaxagoras, a man of typically scientific temper, who introduced the Ionian physical philosophy to Athens in the age of Pericles. His system is of cardinal significance, because it begins to throw into relief the contrast between mind and matter. The earlier Ionians had believed that the ultimate stuff of the world was a living stuff, and therefore endowed with the capacity for self-motion. For Anaxagoras the living and moving force becomes distinct from the body which it moves. It is called Mind or Intelligence. The name suggests not only consciousness, but design; and the function of Mind is to set things in order by causing rotatory motion from which order results mechanically. Anaxagoras' Mind creates nothing—to him, as to all the other philosophers, creation *ex nihilo* is an impossibility; nor is this Mind benevolent. It is precisely the doctrine that the divine Intelligence planned the world-order in every detail *for the best* that Socrates, when he first heard of Anaxagoras, hoped to find in his book, and failed to find there. Socrates himself, and Plato after him, took this further step, and so, for the first time in Greek thought, appeared the belief in a provident and benevolent maker and father of the universe, a belief that always remained a philosophic opinion and never had the force of an obligatory religious dogma.

From the age of Socrates and the sophists onwards, the philosophic schools are divided according as they see in the world the work of design (art, *technê*) or of chance (luck, *tychê*). Chance is the new, scientific name for Fate. Though Chance or Luck may be popularly spoken of as a person or a deity, for reflection chance is the negation, not of necessity, but of will and design; it is the crossing, at haphazard, of independent lines of mechanical causation. The theory that the world is the work of undesigned necessity is perfected in Atomism, the system adopted by the Epicureans and handed on by Lucretius to the Roman world. Their opponents, the Stoics, championed the other alternative and identified Destiny, not with blind mechanical necessity, but with the will of Zeus, the decree of Providence.

In the sphere of morals the fundamental antithesis was between " nature " and " convention." Does the difference between right and wrong, righteousness and unrighteousness, lie in the " nature of things," or is it an arbitrary product of human agreement, of a social contract ? And if it rests on contract, am I, the individual, bound by that contract ? If I am strong and determined enough to assert my self-interest and push the weaker to the wall, what is it to me that the state in which I happen to live was formed long ago by men who agreed, as a matter of convenience, to call individual self-assertion " unjust " ? Why should I not indulge my " nature," by which I understand the instincts that impel me to the fullest assertion of my powers ?

This terrible moral problem emerged in the fifth century, when a growing knowledge of the varying and contrary customs of different lands raised the question whether any custom or law (*nomos*) could claim universal and absolute validity. The problem lies outside the scope of this book, except in so far as customary religion was called in question no less than customary morality, and men began daringly to assign to the gods themselves an origin in social convention. Moreover, the whole philosophy of the main Socratic school—Socrates, Plato, Aristotle—may be seen as a grand attempt to base the laws of human conduct upon the laws of the universe. Plato's central doctrine is that "Justice, Temperance, and all things else that are of value to the soul" are not the product of capricious human convention, but eternal and immutable things which can be known and defined as certainly as the circle, the triangle, and the other concepts of geometry. Virtue is the health of the soul, and no more arbitrary than the health of the body. Virtue is natural, for the "nature" of man is not the tangle of instincts he shares with the animals below him, but the perfection of the divine intelligence he shares with the gods above. His duty is to "follow God" and to "become immortal."

These watchwords reveal Plato as the successor of Pythagoras and the inheritor of the mystical tradition in Greek religion. The characteristic which sets this tradition in sharp contrast to the Homeric theology is that it asserts the unity of all life—divine, human, animal—and accordingly denies that there is any gulf fixed between the nature of the gods and the nature of man. The human soul, though fallen and tainted by association with its bodily prison-house, is of divine origin and able to regain divinity or, in other words, immortality. Immortality in this sense is to be sharply distinguished from the mere continuance, in some unseen region, of a life resembling life on earth.

This belief cannot be said to belong to the main current of Greek thought, but it had its source far back before the beginnings of history in the cult of Dionysus—a popular cult barely mentioned by Homer. In the sixth century B.C. it was revived by a religious society known as the Orphics at Croton in South Italy. Thence, towards the end of that century, it spread to central Greece. The doctrine was adopted by Pythagoras who migrated from Samos to Croton about the year 530 B.C., to found a school which existed for some two hundred years, though its members were dispersed from its original home in the latter half of the fifth century. Before Plato we can trace this doctrine back through the fragments of the Sicilian philosopher Empedocles and certain passages of Pindar. But the earlier Orphics and Pythagoreans have left no literature. I have accordingly departed from the plan of this book so far as to include a few extracts from late authors describing the rituals of ecstasy and sacramental communion with the divine and the corresponding myths. Though the descriptions are late, the rituals and myths themselves are of unknown antiquity. Plato's adoption of the Pythagorean religion raised it to a position of incalculable importance in the whole subsequent history of European theology. It made possible the alliance of Platonism with the religion of Christ and of St. Paul.

But many centuries were to pass before the conversion of the western world to Platonised Christianity. For the contemporaries and pupils of Plato his own saying proved true: " It is a hard task to find the maker and father of this universe; and, if we had found him, it would be impossible to declare him to all men." In a letter written near the end of his life Plato confesses that the same had proved true for himself. He speaks as if there were moments when his own mind, the greatest mind ever given to philosophy, could attain, or almost attain, to a vision of the world as it is ordered in every part by Truth, Beauty, and Goodness. But he expressly declares that such a vision is incommunicable, and that he had never even tried to communicate it in writing or in speech.

In the gigantic system of Aristotle the God of Plato ceases to be either the maker or the father of this universe. He is identified with the Final Cause, the object of the world's desire. But he is himself incapable of any passion; his being consists in the unwearying activity of the pure intellect and nothing more. We are still exhorted to achieve the immortality of divine life by the imitation of God; but aspiration is chilled by a doubt whether this metaphysical ideal—pure Form without matter—may not be as unreal as the abstraction that balances it at the opposite pole—pure Matter without form.

Here we reach the term of our period and of the creative age of Greek religious thought.

In grouping the extracts into sections I have adopted a compromise between three simpler principles of arrangement: by strict chronological order, by authors, and by affinity of subject. Adherence to any one of these principles would destroy all sense of development, and I have preferred to hold out a reward to the perfect reader who will begin at the beginning and persevere to the end.

I have, of course, consulted many existing translations. In rendering poetry I have not ventured to use metre, because prose that is tolerable prose is easier to read than tolerable verse that is not poetry. Moreover, the proper object of this volume is the faithful reproduction of ancient thought, and the translator who employs metre can rarely avoid sacrificing the exact expression of the sense in the attempt to preserve an emotional atmosphere. The metrical versions by other hands which are included have been chosen because they seem to me to recall the poetical quality of the original without misleading the reader who is ignorant of Greek. In my own renderings I have taken some liberties. I have, for instance, omitted some of the conventional epithets in epic poetry, which in English become merely grotesque; and I have sometimes substituted a name for a descriptive phrase used by the poet for no other reason than that it scans conveniently. Thus it seemed simpler to put " Hermes " in the text rather than in a footnote to " the Conductor of Souls, the Slayer of Argos." In the passages from Plato marked " abridged," I have, in a few places, ventured still further and run together speeches which are interrupted by expressions of assent on the part of the minor interlocutors. Certain features of Platonic dialogue become tedious and unnatural in English, and for our present purpose I see no advantage in retaining them everywhere.

I have spelt Greek names without the smallest regard for consistency. For centuries English scholars have been content to speak of " Thucydides " ; nothing will induce me to write " Thoukudides." On the other hand, to latinise Keleos into Celeus is to invite the unlearned reader to call him *Seel-yeus*.

The numbering of the fragments of the philosophers is that of Diels, *Fragmente der Vorsokratiker* (1922). I have constantly consulted Professor Burnet's renderings in his *Early Greek Philosophy* (1920). The tragic fragments are numbered according to Nauck's *Tragicorum Graecorum Fragmenta*, Ed. II, except in the case of Sophocles, where I have followed Professor Pearson's edition.

I thank the authors and publishers of the following works for permission to make extracts: Sir James Frazer, *Apollodorus* (Loeb Classical Library, Heinemann), and *Pausanias' Description of Greece* (Macmillan); Mr. A. D. Godley, *Herodotus* (Loeb Classical Library, Heinemann); Mr. A. O. Prickard, *Selected Essays of Plutarch*, II (Clarendon Press); Mr. A. B. Cook, *Zeus* (Cambridge University Press); Professor Gilbert Murray, *Appendix on the Orphic Tablets* in J. E. Harrison, *Prolegomena to the Study of Greek Religion* (Cambridge University Press), and *The Rise of the Greek Epic* (Clarendon Press); Mr. E. R. Bevan, *Aeschylus, Prometheus Bound* (D. Nutt); Walter Headlam, *A Book of Greek Verse* and *The Agamemnon of Aeschylus* (Cambridge University Press); Professor A. C. Pearson, *The Fragments of Sophocles* (Cambridge University Press); Professor J. Burnet, *Early Greek Philosophy* (A. and C. Black); Mr. R. D. Hicks, *Aristotle, de Anima* (Cambridge University Press); B. Jowett, *Thucydides* (Clarendon Press); B. B. Rogers, *The Clouds of Aristophanes* (G. Bell & Sons); H. G. Dakyns, *The Works of Xenophon* (Macmillan); Mr. W Miller, *Xenophon* (Loeb Classical Library, Heinemann); R. C. Jebb, *Attic Orators* (Macmillan).

F M. C.

Trinity College, Cambridge.

CONTENTS

I. HOMER

CONTENTS

VI. THE ITALIAN PHILOSOPHY

VII. HERACLEITUS AND XENOPHANES

X. PINDAR, BACCHYLIDES, SOPHOCLES

XI. THE IONIAN PHILOSOPHY AT ATHENS

XII. RATIONALISM. THE AGE OF THE SOPHISTS

C

XV. PLATO

XVI. ARISTOTLE

XVII. POPULAR THOUGHT

GREEK RELIGIOUS THOUGHT

I. HOMER

Olympus

ODYSSEY VI. 41.

So saying, grey-eyed Athene departed to Olympus, where, they say, is the seat of the gods established for ever. It is not shaken by winds nor ever wet with rain, and the snow comes not nigh ; but the clear air spreads without a cloud, and the white light floats over it. There the blessed gods take their pleasure for all their days.

The Division of the World among the Three Sons of Cronos

ILIAD XV. 185. Zeus, awaking one day, finds the Trojans hard pressed in battle by the Greeks, assisted by Poseidon. He sends Iris with a threatening message to Poseidon, bidding him withdraw from battle, and go to Olympus or to the sea (his proper sphere). Poseidon is very angry and protests:

" Alack, strong though he be, these words are past all bearing. Will he constrain me by violence against my will, though I am his equal in rank ? For we are three brothers, born of Cronos and Rhea, Zeus and I and Hades, the lord of the dead. And in three lots were all things divided, and each took his appointed domain. When we cast the lots, to me fell the hoary sea, that I should dwell therein for ever; and Hades drew the misty darkness, and Zeus the broad heaven among the bright air and the clouds: the earth and high Olympus are yet common to all. Therefore never will I walk after the will of Zeus; no, masterful though he be, let him stay quiet in his own third part."

Reminded by Iris that the avenging spirits (*Erinyes*) come to the aid of the elder-born, Poseidon thinks better of it and angrily retires to the sea.

Zeus and Fate

ILIAD xvi. 431. Patroclus and Sarpedon are about to fight.

And seeing them the son of Cronos was moved to pity and he spoke to Hera, his sister and wife: " O me, it is fated that Sarpedon, whom I love beyond all men, shall be subdued by Patroclus, son of Menoetius. In my heart I am in two minds whether I shall snatch him up alive out of the sorrowful battle and set him down in the rich land of Lycia, or whether I shall subdue him at once under the hands of the son of Menoetius."

Then the ox-eyed lady Hera answered: " Dread son of Cronos, what is this word thou hast spoken? Is it thy will to deliver from ill-sounding death a man that is mortal and long since doomed by fate? So do; but all we other gods shall not approve it. And hear this also, and lay it up in thy heart. If thou shalt send Sarpedon alive to his home, take heed lest, afterwards, some other god also desire to send his own dear son away from the strong battle. For the Immortals have many sons fighting about the great city of Priam, and thou wilt send terrible wrath among them. But if he is dear to thee and thy heart is grieved for him, suffer him indeed to be subdued in the strong battle under the hands of Patroclus, and then, when his life fails and his shade leaves him, send

Death and sweet Sleep to bear him until they come to the broad land of Lycia, and there his kindred and friends will bury him with a mound and a pillar; for that is the due of the dead."

So said Hera, and the Father of gods and men gave heed to her words. But he let fall upon the earth a shower of rain like blood, for the sake of his dear son, whom Patroclus was about to slay in the rich land of Troy, far from his fatherland.

A Battle of the Gods

ILIAD xxi. 385.

And heavy and bitter strife fell upon the other gods, and the spirit in their breasts was distraught. And they came together with a great clash, and the broad earth and the heaven on every side rang as with a trumpet. And Zeus heard where he sat upon Olympus, and his heart laughed with delight, when he saw the gods coming together in strife.

Then they stood off no longer; for Ares, piercer of shields, began, and first ran upon Athene, with his bronze spear, and taunted her:

" Dog-fly, why dost thou match thyself in strife against gods, with stormy daring unleashed by thy proud spirit? Dost not thou remember how thou didst send Tydeus' son Diomede to wound me, and thyself in the sight of all didst take a spear and drive it straight at me, piercing through my fair skin? Now, therefore, I think thou shalt pay for all thou hast done to me."

So saying, the murderous Ares smote her with his long spear on the fringed aegis, that not even the lightning of Zeus can overcome. But she, giving back, caught up in her strong hand a black stone, huge and rugged, that lay upon the plain, set there by men of old time for a landmark.   Therewith she struck Ares on the neck, that his limbs gave way.   He fell, covering seven roods, and his hair was fouled with dust, and his armour rang about him.   And Pallas Athene laughed and boasted over him with winged words:

"Fool, that hast not even yet learnt how far better I am than thou, that thou dost match thy strength with me.   Thus shalt thou satisfy in full thy mother's curses, who plots evil in her anger against thee, because thou hast left the Greeks to give help to the haughty Trojans."

And with that she turned away her shining eyes. And Aphrodite, daughter of Zeus, took him by the hand and led him away, groaning heavily, for hardly could he collect his spirit within him.   But when Hera, the white-armed goddess, perceived her, straightway she spoke winged words to Athene:

"Alack, thou child of Zeus who bears the aegis, thou warrior unwearied, yonder dog-fly is leading Ares, destroyer of men, out of the battle through the press.   Nay, but go after her."

Then Athene, glad at heart, made after her, and falling upon her smote her on the breast with her strong hand, so that her knees gave way and her heart was faint.   So there they both lay upon the bountiful earth, and Athene boasted over them with winged words:

"So may it be with all the helpers of Troy, when they fight with the mailed Argives.   May they be as bold and stout of heart as Aphrodite, when she came to succour Ares and encounter my strength!   So should we long since have had rest from war and sacked the well-built city of Ilium."

And the white-armed goddess Hera smiled at her words.

Then Poseidon, lord of the earthquake, spoke to Apollo:

"Phoebus, why stand we two apart? It is not fitting when the rest have begun; shame it were that we should go to the bronze-floored house of Zeus upon Olympus without having fought. Begin, for thou art younger; it is not meet for me, who was born before thee and know more. Fool, how dull is thy wit! Thou hast forgotten all that we two, alone of all the gods, suffered at Ilium, when we were sent by Zeus to proud Laomedon to be his hired servants for a year at a fixed wage, while he told us what we should do. Then I built for the Trojans a fair broad wall about their city, that it should not be broken into; and thou, Phoebus, didst herd the cows with their curled horns and swinging feet in the wooded valley-folds among the spurs of Ida. But when the seasons brought the happy term of our hiring, the terrible Laomedon robbed us of all our wage and sent us away with threats, that he would bind us hand and foot and sell us into the isles, far off beyond the sea; and he swore that he would shear off the ears of us both. So we went home together with wrathful hearts, angry for the promised wage he had not paid. His are the people to whom now thou showest favour, instead of seeking with us to bring evil and utter destruction upon the haughty Trojans and their tender wives and children."

And the archer Apollo answered him:

"Lord of the earthquake, thou wouldst not call it wisdom in me to fight with such as thou, for the sake of miserable mortals, who are like the leaves; to-day the flame of life burns bright in them, and they eat the fruits of the ground, and to-morrow they are withered and die away. Nay, let us even now take our rest from fighting, and let them do battle by themselves."

So saying, he turned away, for he had respect unto his father's brother, that he should not come to blows with him. But his sister, the huntress Artemis, the queen of the wild creatures, sharply upbraided him with taunts:

"So then, thou fliest, archer, and hast yielded to Poseidon a victory that he may brag of at no cost. Fool, why dost thou bear a bow that is good for naught? Never again let me hear thee in our father's house boast as before among the immortal gods that thou wouldst match thy strength in battle against Poseidon."

So said she, and the archer Apollo answered her not. Nevertheless, the wife of Zeus rebuked Artemis with taunting words:

"Art thou now minded, shameless vixen, to set thyself against me? Thy strength were an ill match for mine, for all thou bearest a bow, since Zeus made thee as a lion against women and gave thee to slay them at thy will. Thou shouldst rather be killing the wild beasts and the deer upon the mountains than fighting with thy betters. But if thou wouldst know war, have thy will, and learn by how much I am the stronger, since thou wilt match thy force with mine."

Then Hera with her left hand caught Artemis by both wrists, and with her right took the bow and quiver from her shoulders, and with them beat her about the ears, smiling; and as Artemis turned and twisted, the arrows fell fast out of the quiver. And the goddess, weeping, fled from her as a dove flies from a falcon to the hollow cleft of a rock, when she is not destined to be caught. So fled Artemis weeping, and left her bow and arrows where they lay. . . . And she came to Olympus, to the bronze-floored house of Zeus, and sat upon her father's knees, and her immortal raiment was shaken with her weeping. And her father took her to him, and asked her, laughing gently: "Which of the sons of Heaven, dear child, had done this to thee?"

And the fair-crowned lady of the clamorous chase answered: "Father, it was thy wife that mishandled me, the white-armed Hera, from whom strife and contention have come upon the Immortals."

The Gods observe Human Conduct

ODYSSEY xvii. 483. One of the wooers of Penelope rebukes Antinous for insulting a poor stranger (the disguised Odysseus).

"Antinous, it was dishonourable to strike an unfortunate wanderer; thou wilt come to a bad end, if there is a god in heaven. Indeed, the gods, in the likeness of strangers from far countries, put on all manner of shapes and visit the cities of men, beholding their violence and their righteousness."

The Gods love Justice

ODYSSEY, xiv. 80. Eumaeus, the swineherd, entertains Odysseus on his return to Ithaca, without recognising him.

"Now eat, sir, of this sucking-pig—all that a servant has to offer; the fatted hogs are meat for the wooers, and little they care for the eye of heaven or for other men's troubles. It is certain the blessed gods love not unkindly deeds; they have respect to justice and fair dealing among men. Why, even bitter enemies, when they land on a strange coast and Zeus suffers them to plunder it, and they fill their ships before they set out for home—even their hearts are smitten with a strong fear of the eye of heaven. But be sure these wooers know that my master has come to a sad end—they have had some word from a god—seeing how they will not either do their wooing fairly nor yet go home; but they take their ease and devour our living insolently, and spare nothing."

Atê

ILIAD xix. 83. After the death of Patroclus, Achilles offers to lay aside his quarrel with Agamemnon and to fight again with the Greeks. Agamemnon replies:

"I will declare my mind to the son of Peleus. Take heed, ye other Argives, and each mark well what I shall say. Often have the Achaeans spoken thus to me, upbraiding me continually; but it is not I that am the cause, but Zeus and Destiny (*Moira*) and Erinys that walks in darkness, who put blind fury into my heart at the assembly on that day when I robbed Achilles of his rightful spoil. But what could I do? It is heaven that accomplishes all things. The eldest daughter of Zeus is Atê, who blinds all men, a power of evil. Delicate are her feet; for she treads not upon the ground, but walks rather over the heads of men, making mankind come to harm: over one and another she casts her snare.

"For once indeed even Zeus was blinded, who, they say, is greatest among gods and men; yet even he was deceived by Hera, with her womanly cunning, on that day when Alcmena was to bring forth the mighty Heracles in the city of Thebes with fair walls crowned. For then he spoke solemnly among all the gods: ' Hear me, all ye gods and goddesses, that I may speak what the spirit in my breast bids me. This day shall the birth-goddess who helps women in travail bring forth to the light of day a man who shall rule over all that dwell round about him, even one of those men that are sprung of my blood.' And Queen Hera, in the subtlety of her heart, said to him: ' Thou wilt belie thy words, and not crown them with fulfilment. Come now, Olympian, swear me a strong oath that in very truth he shall rule over all that dwell round about him, whosoever, of all men that are of thy blood and lineage, shall this day fall between a woman's feet.' And Zeus perceived not her subtlety, but sware a great oath, and therewith sore blindness came upon him. And Hera darted from the peak of Olympus and swiftly came to Achaean Argos, where she knew that the comely wife of Sthenelus, son of Perseus, was great with child, and her seventh month was come. And Hera brought her son to the light of day, though his tale of months was not fulfilled; and she stayed Alcmena from her bearing and held back the birth-goddesses. And she herself brought the tidings to Zeus, and said: ' Father Zeus, god of the bright lightning, take heed to the word that I shall speak. Now is there born a man of valour who shall rule among the Argives, Eurystheus, the child of Sthenelus, son of Perseus. He is of thy lineage; it is not unseemly that he should rule among the Argives.' And at her words Zeus was smitten with sharp pain to the depth of his heart, and immediately he took Atê by the bright hair of her head, in the anger of his heart, and swore a strong oath that never again should Atê, who blinds all, come to Olympus and the starry heaven. And, when he had so said, he whirled her round with his hand and flung her from the starry heaven; and quickly she came down among the fields of men. And he continually lamented against her,

whensoever he saw his beloved son Heracles put to
unseemly labours under his task-master Eurystheus.

"So I also, when great Hector of the glancing helm
was slaying the Argives at the sterns of the beached ships,
could not forget Atê, by whom I was blinded at the first.
But since I was blinded and Zeus took away my wits,
I am willing to make amends again, and to give recompense
without stint."

Atê and Prayers

ILIAD ix. 496. The aged Phoenix appeals to Achilles.

"But do thou, Achilles, subdue thy proud spirit; it
is not right for thee to have a heart without compassion.
Even the gods themselves can bend, although they be
greater and more excellent in honour and might. Their
hearts are turned by the prayers of men, with incense
and vows and libation and burnt-offering, whensoever
any one transgresses and is in fault.

"For Prayers are daughters of great Zeus, lame and
wrinkled and squint-eyed, and they attend upon Atê and
follow after her. But Atê is strong and swift of foot;
wherefore she far outruns them all, and before they can
come up with her she goes over all the earth causing men
to come to harm. Prayers follow behind and bring
healing. And whosoever shows respect unto the daughters
of Zeus when they draw near, him they profit much and
hear his petitions; but when one denies them and harshly
says them nay, then they go to Zeus, the son of Cronos,
and pray to him that Atê may attend that man, so that he
may come to harm and pay the penalty. Now, Achilles,
see thou also to it that the reverence that bends the heart
of all good men be paid unto the daughters of Zeus."

Zeus repudiates Responsibility for Human Sin

ODYSSEY i. 26.

And the other gods were gathered together in the hall of Olympian Zeus; and among them the Father of gods and men began to speak, for he bethought him of the noble Aegisthus, whom the renowned Orestes, son of Agamemnon, slew. Thinking upon him, he spoke among the Immortals:

" Alack, see now how mortals lay blame upon the gods. For they say that evils come from us; but it is they who, from the blindness of their own hearts, have sorrows beyond that which is ordained. Even so now Aegisthus, beyond that which is ordained, married the wedded wife of Agamemnon, and slew him at his home-coming, although he knew that ruin and destruction would befall him. For we had sent Hermes and warned him that he should not kill Agamemnon nor woo his wife; for the son of Atreus should be avenged by Orestes when he came to man's estate and desired to see his own land. So Hermes told Aegisthus, but, for all his good-will, he persuaded him not; and now Aegisthus has paid for it once for all."

The arbitrary Dispensation of Zeus

ODYSSEY vi. 187. Nausicaa to Odysseus:

" It is Olympian Zeus himself who gives prosperity to men, whether they be good or bad, to each one as he wills; and doubtless thy lot is given by him, and thou must bear it."

The Two Urns of Zeus

Iliad xxiv. 518. Priam comes to Achilles to ransom the dead
body of Hector. He reminds Achilles of his father Peleus, now
grown old. They weep together, Priam for Hector, and Achilles
for Peleus and his dead friend Patroclus. Achilles takes Priam's
hand and says:

" Ah, unhappy man, how great a burden of evils has
thy spirit borne. How couldst thou dare to come alone
to the ships of the Achaeans to look me in the eyes, who
have slain so many of thy valiant sons ? Surely thou hast
a heart of iron.

" But come, sit down upon a seat, and we will let
our sorrows lie quiet in our hearts, for all our grief;
weeping is cold comfort and nothing comes of it. For
such is the destiny that the gods have laid upon miserable
men, that they should live in grief, while the gods
themselves have no cares. For there stand upon the floor
of Zeus two urns full of gifts such as he gives, evils in
the one and blessings in the other. And when Zeus gives
to a man a mixture of both, then he meets sometimes
with ill, sometimes with good; but when he gives only
of the evils, he puts him to scorn, and fell hunger drives
him over the divine earth, and he goes to and fro un-
honoured of gods or men. So was it that the gods gave
to Peleus glorious gifts from his birth; for he surpassed
all men in prosperity and wealth, and was king among
the Myrmidons; and, though he was mortal, they gave
him a goddess to wife. Yet even upon him heaven laid
a burden of evil, in that no princely sons were born to
him in his house, save one only, whom he begat to die
untimely; and now that he is growing old, I am not there
to tend him, seeing that I sit here in the land of Troy
far from my own country, vexing thee and thy sons.

" And thou also, old man, we have heard how thou wast once in prosperity, richest in wealth and in sons of all that dwell within the bounds of Lesbos towards the north and the further parts of Phrygia and the great Hellespont. But ever since the lords of heaven brought this trouble upon thee, there have been battles around thy city and man slaying man. Have patience, and let not thy spirit sorrow without ceasing, for all thy grief over thy son will avail nothing: thou wilt not raise him up again, before some new evil comes upon thee."

The feeble State of Man

ODYSSEY xviii. 125. Odysseus, disguised as a beggar, acknowledges the courtesy of one of the wooers of Penelope.

" Amphinomus, thou seemest to me a man of understanding. . . . Therefore I will tell thee; listen to my words and mark them well. Of all things that the earth nourishes and that breathe and move upon the face of the earth, none is feebler than man. So long as heaven gives him prowess and his limbs move lightly, he thinks that no evil will ever befall him in the days to come; but when the blessed gods fill his cup with sorrow, that also he bears, as he must, with a steadfast heart. For the spirit of men upon the earth is even as the day that the Father of gods and men brings upon them. Even so I also once was like to have been prosperous among men, but I did much foolishness, giving way to the might of my own strength and putting my trust in my father and my brethren. Therefore I would have no man be altogether lawless, but hold his peace and keep whatsoever gifts the gods may give him."

D

The Ghost of Patroclus

ILIAD xxiii. 59.

The son of Peleus, upon the shore of the sounding sea,
lay groaning heavily, amid the Myrmidons, on the clean
sand where the waves were washing on the beach. And
when sleep took hold upon him, sweet sleep that poured
about him and set free his heart from care (for right
weary were his glorious limbs from setting upon Hector
towards windy Troy), then came to him the ghost of
unhappy Patroclus, in all things like himself, in stature
and fair eyes and voice; and the garments about his
body were the same. He stood above Achilles' head
and spoke to him:

"Thou sleepest, Achilles, and hast forgotten me.
Now I am dead thou hast no care for me, as when I was
alive. Make haste and bury me, that I may pass the
gates of Hades. The spirits, the shadows of the dead,
keep me far off and suffer me not yet to mix with them
beyond the river, but I wander idly about the wide gates
of the house of Hades. Also give me thy hand, I entreat
thee; for never again shall I come from Hades, when
once ye have given me my meed of funeral fire. No more
as living men shall we sit apart from our companions
and take counsel together; for the chill fate that was
appointed at my birth has swallowed me up, and thou
too, godlike Achilles, art doomed to die beneath the wall
of rich Troy. Another thing I will say and charge thee,
if thou wilt obey. Lay not my bones apart from thine,
Achilles, but together, even as we were brought up
together in your house, when Menoetius brought me,
a child, from Opoeis to your country because of a woful
man-slaying on the day wherein I slew the son of Am-

hidamas, not willing it, in childish anger at the dice.
Then Peleus received me in his house and reared me with
good care and called me thy squire. Even so also let
me coffin hold the bones of us both together."

And swift-footed Achilles answered him and said:

"Why, O my brother and my lord, hast thou come
hither to lay all these commands upon me ? Surely I
will obey thy bidding and perform them all. But come,
draw nearer; let us put our arms each about the other
and satisfy ourselves with grief and lamentation."

Then Achilles reached forth his hands, but clasped
him not; for, like a vapour, the spirit was gone beneath
the earth, shrieking. And in amazement Achilles sprang
up and smote his hands together and spoke sorrowfully:

"Alack, there is then even in the house of Death a
spirit or a shade, though the wits dwell in it no more.
For all night long the spirit of hapless Patroclus stood
over me weeping and making lament, and told me all
that I should do; and it was marvellously like to the
man himself."

Elysium

ODYSSEY iv. 561. The only mention in Homer of an Elysium
to which heroes who are demi-gods are translated. Proteus,
after describing the fortunes of Agamemnon and Odysseus on
their return from Troy, says to Menelaus:

"But for thee, Menelaus, son of Zeus, it is not ordained to die and meet thy fate in Argos the pasture-land
of horses, but the Immortals will convey thee to the
Elysian Plain at the ends of the earth, where is fair-haired
Rhadamanthys. There life is easiest for men; there is
no rain, nor snow, nor winter storm, but always Ocean
sends the breath of the high west wind, blowing cool upon

men. For thou hast Helen to wife, and in the eyes of th
Immortals thou art the son-in-law of Zeus."

Odysseus' Visit to the Land of the Dead

ODYSSEY xi. 11, 264, 475. Odysseus tells how he went t
learn his fate from the spirit of the dead seer, Teiresias.

All day long the ship's sails were taut as she made he
way over the sea; and the sun set and all the ways wer
darkened. And she came to the deep stream of Ocea
that bounds the earth. There are the land and city o
the Cimmerians, covered with mist and cloud; th
shining sun never looks down upon them with his rays
neither when he climbs toward the starry heaven, no
when he turns back from heaven earthwards, but deathl
night is outspread over miserable mortals. Thithe
coming we ran the ship ashore, and took out the sheep
and ourselves went along the stream of Ocean, unti
we came to the place that Circe had told us of.

There Perimedes and Eurylochus held the victims
and I drew my sharp sword from my thigh and dug
trench as much as a cubit's length each way, and poure
about it a drink-offering to all the dead, first with mea
and afterward with sweet wine, and for the third tim
with water; and I sprinkled white meal thereon. An
I besought the strengthless heads of the dead with man
supplications, saying that, when I should have come t
Ithaca, I would sacrifice in my house a barren heife
the best I had, and heap rich gifts upon the fire of sacri
fice, and I would offer for Teiresias, apart from the rest,
black ram without spot, the fairest of our flocks. An
when I had besought the nations of the dead with vow

nd prayers, I took the sheep and cut their throats into
ae trench, and the dark blood flowed.

And the shades of them that are dead and gone began
) gather themselves out of Erebus, brides and unwedded
ouths, and old men that had endured much, and tender
aaidens with their grief yet fresh at heart, and many
rounded with bronze-pointed spears, men slain in battle,
rearing their blood-stained arms.   A great multitude
ame from every side about the trench with a strange
rying, and pale fear took hold upon me.

Then I called to my companions and commanded
aem to flay the sheep that lay slaughtered with the
ruel knife, and to consume them with fire, making
rayer to the gods, to mighty Hades and dread Persephone;
nd myself drew the sharp sword from my thigh and sat
aere, not suffering the strengthless heads of the dead
) draw near to the blood until I should have word
f Teiresias.

(Among the shades, Odysseus' mother Anticleia comes, but
e keeps her away from the blood until Teiresias has appeared
ad, after drinking of the blood, has prophesied of his return
) Ithaca.   Then Anticleia drinks and describes her own death
ad what is happening at his home.)

And I mused upon her words and desired to embrace
ae shade of my dead mother.   Thrice I started forward to
mbrace her as my heart bade me, and thrice she escaped
om my arms like a shadow or a dream, and the grief
rew ever sharper in my heart.   And I cried aloud,
»eaking to her winged words:

" O my mother, why dost thou not stay for me who
»ng to embrace thee, that even in the place of Death
e may put loving arms about each other and find cold
»mfort in weeping ?   Is this indeed but a phantom that

Queen Persephone has sent me, that I may grieve an
lament yet the more ? "

And straightway my lady mother answered:

" O me, my child, ill-fated beyond all other mer
Persephone, daughter of Zeus, doth not deceive thee
but this is the way with mortals when they die: th
sinews no more hold together the flesh and bones, bu
they are over-mastered by the force of the strong burnin
fire, as soon as the life has left the white bones, and th
shade hovers like a dream and flits away. But mak
haste with all thy heart towards the light of day, and mar
all these things, that thou mayst tell thy wife hereafter.

(After Odysseus has seen other shades, the spirit of Achill
comes and asks him:)

" How didst thou dare to come down to the house o
Hades, the dwelling of the senseless dead, the phantom
of men outworn ? "

And I answered and said to him: " O Achilles, so
of Peleus, greatest of the Achaeans, I came to see
counsel of Teiresias, how I might return home to rugge
Ithaca; for I have not yet come nigh to the Achaea
land, nor set foot in my own country, but it goes ha
with me continually. But thou, Achilles, art the mo
blessed of men that have been or shall be hereafter; fe
aforetime, in thy life, we Argives honoured thee like th
gods, and now thou art a great prince here among th
dead. Therefore grieve not that thou art dead, Achilles.

And he answered me and said: " Seek not to conso
me for death, glorious Odysseus. I would rather be o
earth as the hired servant of another, in the house o
a landless man with little to live upon, than be ki
over all the dead "

II. HESIOD

The Origin of the World and the Birth of the Gods

THEOGONY 104.

HAIL, daughters of Zeus, and grant the gift of delightful song. Celebrate the holy race of the Immortals who are for ever, who were born of Earth and the starry Heaven, and of dark Night, and those that were the brood of the salt Sea.

Tell how in the beginning the gods and Earth came into being, and the rivers, and the unbounded sea whose waves rage and swell, and the shining stars, and the broad Heaven above; and tell of the gods who were born of these, the givers of good gifts; and how they divided their wealth and apportioned their honours, and how in the beginning they took possession of many-folded Olympus. O Muses, whose home is on Olympus, tell me of these from the beginning, and declare which of them first came into being.

Surely, first of all Chaos [1] came into being; and then Earth with her broad breast, a seat for ever unshaken for all the Immortals who dwell on the snowy peaks of Olympus; and misty Tartarus in the hollow of the wide-wayed Earth; and Love (*Erôs*), who is fairest among the immortal gods: he loosens the limbs and subdues the understanding and prudent counsel in the breast of every god and every man.

[1] Chaos is the "yawning gap" between Heaven and Earth, which in many primitive cosmogonies were at first pressed close together. Cosmogony begins with the lifting-up of the sky from the earth.

19

And of Chaos were born Erebus and dark Night; and of Night the bright Sky (*Aether*) and Day were brought to birth, when their mother had conceived them in loving union with Erebus.

And Earth first brought forth the starry Heaven, equal to herself, to cover her about on every side, that there might be for the blessed gods a seat unshaken for ever. And she brought forth the high Mountains, a habitation well-pleasing to the divine Nymphs who live among the forests of the hills. And she brought forth also the unharvested deep, whose waves rage and swell, the Sea, without the rites of loving union.

And, after that, in marriage with Heaven, she brought forth deep-eddying Oceanos, and Coios, and Crios, and Hyperion, and Iapetos, and Theia, and Rhea, and Themis, and Mnemosyne, and Phoebe of the golden crown, and lovely Tethys. And after these was born Cronos of crooked counsel, the youngest of her children and the most terrible; and he was at enmity with his mighty father

The Dynasties of the Gods

APOLLODORUS, *Library*, i. 1. The following summary, written probably in the first or second century A.D., is mainly based on Hesiod. It is given here for the sake of brevity.

Sky (*Uranus*) was the first who ruled over the whole world. And having wedded Earth, he begat first the Hundred-handed, as they are named: Briareus, Gyes, Cottus, who were unsurpassed in size and might, each of them having a hundred hands and fifty heads. After these, Earth bore him the Cyclopes, to wit, Arges, Steropes, Brontes, of whom each had one eye in his forehead. But them Sky bound and cast into Tartarus, a gloomy place in Hades as far distant from earth as earth is distant from the sky.

And again he begat children by Earth, to wit, the Titans as they are named: Ocean, Coeus, Hyperion, Crius, Iapetus, and, youngest of all, Cronus; also daughters, the Titanides as they are called: Tethys, Rhea, Themis, Mnemosyne, Phoebe, Dione, Thia.

And Earth, grieved at the destruction of her children, who had been cast into Tartarus, persuaded the Titans to attack their father and gave Cronus an adamantine sickle. And they, all but Ocean, attacked him, and Cronus cut off his father's genitals and threw them into the sea; and from the drops of the flowing blood were born Furies, to wit, Alecto, Tisiphone, and Megaera. And, having dethroned their father, they brought up their brethren who had been hurled down to Tartarus, and committed the sovereignty to Cronus.

But he again bound and shut them up in Tartarus, and wedded his sister Rhea; and since both Earth and Sky foretold him that he would be dethroned by his own son, he used to swallow his offspring at birth. His first-born Hestia he swallowed, then Demeter and Hera, and after them Pluto and Poseidon. Enraged at this, Rhea repaired to Crete, when she was big with Zeus, and brought him forth in a cave of Dicte. She gave him to the Curetes and to the nymphs Adrastia and Ida, daughters of Melisseus, to nurse. So these nymphs fed the child on the milk of Amalthea; and the Curetes in arms guarded the babe in the cave, clashing their spears on their shields that Cronus might not hear the child's voice. But Rhea wrapped a stone in swaddling clothes and gave it to Cronus to swallow, as if it were the new-born child.

But when Zeus was full-grown, he took Metis, daughter of Ocean, to help him, and she gave Cronus a drug to swallow, which forced him to disgorge first the stone and then the children whom he had swallowed, and with their aid Zeus waged the war against Cronus and the Titans. They fought for ten years, and Earth prophesied victory to Zeus if he should have as allies those who had been hurled down to Tartarus. So he slew their gaoleress Campe and loosed their bonds. And the Cyclopes then gave Zeus thunder and lightning and a thunder-bolt, and on Pluto they bestowed a helmet and on Poseidon a trident. Armed with these weapons the gods overcame the Titans, shut them up in Tartarus, and appointed the Hundred-handers their guards; but they themselves cast lots for the sovereignty, and to Zeus was allotted the dominion of the sky, to Poseidon the dominion of the sea, and to Pluto the dominion in Hades.

J. G. Frazer.

Prometheus and Pandora

Works and Days 42. Man is born to toil for the fruits of earth.

For the gods have hidden away the bread of man's life; if it were not so, a day's work might easily have won thee store enough to live idle for a year; the rudder might be hung up in the smoke, and the labour of oxen and patient mules be as nothing.

But Zeus hid it away in the anger of his heart, because the cunning Prometheus had deceived him; therefore Zeus devised for man labour and sorrow. And he hid away fire; but the good Prometheus, son of Iapetos, stole fire again for men from Zeus, hiding it from the Lord of the Thunder in a hollow stalk of fennel.

And the Cloud-gatherer spoke to him in anger: "Son of Iapetos, surpassing all in cunning, thou art glad that thou hast outwitted me and stolen fire, bringing thereby great trouble both upon thyself and upon men in the days to come. In requital for fire, I will give to men an evil thing, wherein the hearts of them all shall rejoice, and they shall lovingly entreat their own plague."

And the Father of gods and men laughed aloud. And he commanded glorious Hephaestus to make haste and mix earth with water, and to put therein a human voice and strength, and to give it the lovely form of a fair maiden, like unto the immortal goddesses to look upon. And he commanded Athene to teach her handiwork, to weave the web of many colours, and Aphrodite to shed golden grace about her head, and beauty that wastes the longing heart with weariness and pain. And he charged Hermes to put in her a shameless mind and ways of deceitfulness.

And they obeyed the word of Zeus, the king. And immediately Hephaestus moulded out of earth the likeness of a tender maiden, as the son of Cronos willed. And grey-eyed Athene clothed her in fine raiment with a girdle, and the Graces and Peitho (Persuasion) put golden chains upon her body, and the fair-tressed Hours wreathed her with the flowers of spring. And in her breast Hermes put lies and beguiling words and ways of deceitfulness, and he called the name of the woman Pandora (All-gifts), because all the dwellers in Olympus had given gifts to her, the plague of men that eat bread.

Now when the Father had accomplished this work of ruinous deceit past all remedy, he sent Hermes, the swift messenger of the gods, to bear the gift to Epimetheus. And Epimetheus heeded not the word of Prometheus, how he had charged him never to take a gift from Olympian Zeus, but to send it back again, lest perchance some evil should come upon mortal men. But he took it, and perceived nothing until the evil had befallen him.

For of old the generations of men lived upon the earth with no evils, or painful labour, or sore diseases that bring death to men. But the woman lifted up the great lid from the jar with her hands and scattered them abroad, and she wrought trouble and sorrow for mankind.

Only Hope abode there within under the lip of the jar in her dwelling that cannot be broken into, for ere she could fly forth the woman set the lid upon the jar. But sorrows innumerable wander abroad among men; for the earth is full of evils, and so is the sea also; and diseases go abroad among men by day, and others by night, coming of themselves to bring evil to mortal men, silently, for Zeus of his wisdom has taken away their voice.

So there is no way to escape the will of Zeus.

The Five Ages

WORKS AND DAYS 109.

First of all, the immortal dwellers in Olympus made a Golden race of mortal men. These lived in the days of Cronos, when he was king in heaven. They lived like gods, with hearts free from care and from painful toil and trouble. And miserable old age came not upon them; but, ever the same in strength of hand and foot, they feasted in delight apart from all evils; and they died as it were overcome with sleep. All good things they had; the earth of herself bore them the harvest of the corn she gives in plenty without stint, and they with good will lived at peace upon their lands with good things in abundance. Now, after that this race was hidden in the earth, by the will of great Zeus they are become good Spirits, above the ground, guardians of mortal men; and they keep watch over the right and over unkindly deeds. Clothed in mist and darkness they go to and fro through all the earth. They give wealth: even that royal privilege is theirs.

Then next thereafter the dwellers in Olympus made a far worse race of Silver, not like to the Golden either in body or in mind. For a hundred years the child was nurtured beside his good mother, playing, a foolish infant, in his home. But when at last they came to the full measure of manhood, they lived but for a little while, and suffered by their folly; for they could not keep their hands from violent outrage one upon another, nor would they do service to the Immortals or make sacrifice upon the holy altars of the blessed gods after the lawful manner of men in every land. Then Zeus in his anger put them away, because they paid not due honours to the blessed gods who dwell in Olympus. Now, after that this race also was hidden in the earth, they are called by men Blessed ones of the underworld, second in rank; yet they too are attended with honour.

And Father Zeus made a third race of mortal men, a race of Bronze, in no wise equal to the Silver. They were born of the Meliai (Nymphs of the ash-trees ?), and they were strong and terrible, and delighted in deeds of dolorous war and in insolence. They ate no bread, but their heart was stout as adamant, unapproachable; their strength was great, and invincible the arms that grew out of the shoulders upon their thick-set frames.

Their weapons and their dwellings were of bronze, and with bronze they wrought: dark iron was not yet. These, slain by their own hands, went to the cold dank house of Hades, nameless. Terrible though they were, black death took them, and they left the bright light of the sun.

Now after that this race also was hidden in the earth, Zeus made yet a fourth race upon the bountiful earth, a divine race, better and more righteous, of Hero men, that are called demigods, the race that was aforetime upon the boundless earth. They were destroyed by evil war and dread battle, some before Thebes of the Seven Gates in the land of Cadmus, contending for the flocks of Oedipus, and some were brought in ships across the great gulf of the sea to the land of Troy, for fair-haired Helen's sake. There in the end the cloud of death enfolded them. But Father Zeus gave them a dwelling-place and a life apart from mankind at the ends of the earth, far from the Immortals; and Cronos is king among them. And so they dwell, with hearts free from care, in the Islands of the Blest, by the deep-eddying stream of Ocean; happy Heroes, for whom the Mother of corn bears honey-sweet fruits that flourish thrice a year.

O that I lived not in after days among the fifth race of men, but either had died before or been born later! For now indeed is the race of Iron. They shall rest not by day from labour and trouble, nor from the spoiler in the night season; and the gods shall give them grievous cares. (Yet even for them shall good things be mixed with evil. And Zeus shall destroy this race also of mortal men, in the days when they shall be born with grey hairs upon their temples.) The father shall not be like to his children, nor the children to their father;

the guest shall not be true to the host that shelters
him, nor friend to friend, nor brother true to brother
as in the old days; parents shall grow quickly old and
be despised, and shall reproach their children with bitter
words. Wretches that know not the visitation of heaven!
Such as these would not repay their old parents for
their nurture. He that keeps his oath or is just or
good shall not find favour; but they shall honour rather
the doer of wrong and violence. Right shall be in might
of hand, and the spirit of ruth shall be no more. The
rogue shall do hurt to the better man with crooked words
backed by a false oath. There shall be among miserable
men a spirit of striving, a spirit ugly-voiced, rejoicing
in evil, with hateful eyes.

Then at the last, up to Olympus from the wide-wayed
earth, their beautiful faces veiled in white raiment, away
to the company of the Immortals, forsaking man, shall
depart the Spirits of ruth and of righteous indignation.

The Just shall prosper

WORKS AND DAYS 225.

Whensoever men deal right judgments to the stranger
and to their own people, and turn not aside out of the
way of justice, they flourish in their city as the flowers
upon a green tree.

In their land is peace, the nursing-mother of children;
and Zeus, whose eye is over all, never ordains for them
the sorrows of war.

Upon men of right judgment famine waits not, neither

---

[1] For Ruth (*Aidôs*) and Righteous Indignation (*Nemesis*) see
Prof. Murray, *Rise of the Greek Epic* (1907), p. 80. I have borrowed
from his translation of a part of the above passage.

ruin; but in the midst of abundance they go about the works of their hands.

For them the earth brings forth a plentiful living; and upon the hills the oak bears acorns at the top and bees in the midst;

Their sheep's fleeces are heavy with wool, and their wives bring forth children that are like unto their parents.[1]

They prosper with good things continually; neither do they go upon ship-board, but the Mother of corn bears them her harvest.

But when men are given to evil insolence and to the works of unkindliness, Zeus, the son of Cronos, whose eye is over all, ordains for them judgment.

Oftentimes a whole city reaps the recompense of an evil man, who sins and contrives the works of foolishness.

Out of heaven the son of Cronos sends a great plague upon them, even famine and pestilence together; and the people are wasted away.

Their women bring not forth, and their houses are brought low, by the will of Olympian Zeus.

Again he destroys a great host of them or overthrows a place of defence; or he takes vengeance upon their ships in the deep.

Ye also, O kings, consider this judgment!

For the Immortals are nigh at hand among men, to mark all that oppress one another with crooked judgment and heed not the visitation of heaven.

For there are upon the fruitful earth thrice ten thousand ministers of Zeus, immortal watchers of mortal men.

They keep watch over deeds of justice and unkindliness; clothed in mist and darkness, they go to and fro throughout all the earth.

---

[1] *I.e.* not monstrous births.

Justice belongs to Man only

WORKS AND DAYS 274.

O Perses, lay up these things in thy heart; give ear to justice, and utterly forget violence. For Zeus has appointed this law unto men: that fishes and beasts and fowls of the air should devour one another, since there is no justice among them; but to man he gave justice, which is far better. For if a man will speak just sentences, Zeus gives him prosperity; but whosoever of his own will swears false witness and wrongs justice, going astray beyond healing, his posterity after him grows obscure; but the posterity of a man that keeps his oath is better.

Foolish Perses, I will speak to thee with good intent. Unto wickedness men attain easily and in multitudes: smooth is the way, and her dwelling is very near at hand. But the immortal gods have ordained much sweat upon the path to virtue: long and steep is the way thither, and rough at first; but when a man has reached the height, thereafter the hard road is easy.

E

III. EARLY LYRIC, ELEGIAC, AND IAMBIC
POETS

Libation Hymn to Zeus

TERPANDER (*circ*. 675 B.C.), *frag*. 1.

ZEUS, beginning of all things, leader of all; Zeus, to thee I bring this beginning of hymns.

Seek not to scale Heaven

ALCMAN (*circ*. 650–600), *Partheneion* i. 8.

Mortal man may not go soaring to the heavens nor seek to wed the Queen of Paphos, or some silver-shining daughter of Nereus of the sea. . . .

There is a vengeance from heaven; happy is he that with cheerful mind weaves the web of one day to it end without a tear.

Solon and Croesus

HERODOTUS i. 30–34. Solon the Athenian lived *circ*. 639–559 Croesus reigned in Lydia, 560–546. This story is not historically true.

For this reason, and to see the world, Solon left Athen and visited Amasis in Egypt and Croesus at Sardis: and when he had come, Croesus entertained him in his palace Now on the third or fourth day after his coming Croesu bade his servants lead Solon round among his treasures and they showed him all that was there, the greatnes and the prosperous state of it; and when he had seen and considered all, Croesus when occasion served thus questioned him:

"Our Athenian guest, we have heard much of you, by reason of your wisdom and your wanderings, and how that you have travelled far to seek knowledge and to see the world. Now therefore I am fain to ask you, if you have ever seen a man more blest than all his fellows."

So Croesus inquired, supposing himself to be blest beyond all men. But Solon spoke the truth without flattery:

"Such a one, O king," he said, "I have seen— Tellus of Athens."

Croesus wondered at this, and sharply asked Solon, "How do you judge Tellus to be most blest?"

Solon replied: "Tellus' city was prosperous, and he was the father of noble sons, and he saw children born to all of them and their state well stablished; moreover, having then as much wealth as a man may among us, he crowned his life with a most glorious death: for in a battle between the Athenians and their neighbours at Eleusis he attacked and routed the enemy and most nobly there died; and the Athenians gave him public burial where he fell and paid him great honour."

Now when Solon had admonished Croesus by recounting the many ways in which Tellus was blest, the king further asked him whom he placed second after Tellus, thinking that assuredly the second prize at least would be his.

Solon answered: "Cleobis and Biton. These were Argives, and besides sufficient wealth they had such strength of body as I will show. Both were prize-winners; and this story too is related of them. There was a festival of Here toward among the Argives, and their mother must by all means be drawn to the temple by a yoke of oxen. But the oxen did not come in time from the fields; so the young men, being thus thwarted by lack of time, put themselves to the yoke and drew the carriage with their mother sitting thereon: for five-and-forty furlongs they drew it till they came to the temple. Having done this, and been seen by the assembly, they made a most excellent end of their lives, and the god showed by these men how that it was better for a man to die than to live. For the men of Argos came round and gave the youths joy of their strength, and so likewise did the women to their mother, for the excellence of her sons. She then in her joy at what was done and said, came before the image of the goddess and prayed that her sons Cleobis and Biton, who had done such great honour to the goddess, should be given the best boon that a man may receive. After the prayer the young men sacrificed and ate of the feast; then they lay down to sleep in the temple itself and never rose up more, but here ended their lives. Then the Argives made and set up at Delphi images of them because of their excellence."

So Solon gave to Cleobis and Biton the second prize of happiness.

But Croesus said in anger, " Guest from Athens ! is our prosperity, then, held by you so worthless that you match us not even with common men ? "

" Croesus," said Solon, " you ask me concerning the lot of man; well I know how jealous is Heaven and how it loves to trouble us. In a man's length of days he may see and suffer many things that he much mislikes. For I set the limit of man's life at seventy years; in these seventy are days twenty-five thousand and two hundred, if we count not the intercalary month. But if every second

year be lengthened by a month, . . . all the days together of the seventy years are seen to be twenty-six
thousand two hundred and fifty; and one may well
say that no one of all these days is like another in that
which it brings. Thus then, Croesus, the whole of man
is but chance.

"Now if I am to speak of you, I say that I see you
very rich and the king of many men. But I cannot yet
answer your question, before I hear that you have ended
your life well. For he who is very rich is not more blest
than he who has but enough for the day, unless fortune
so attend him that he ends his life well, having all good
things about him. Many men of great wealth are unblest,
and many that have no great substance are fortunate.
Now the very rich man who is yet unblest has but two
advantages over the fortunate man, but the fortunate
man has many advantages over the rich but unblest:
for this latter is the stronger to accomplish his desire and
to bear the stroke of great calamity; but these are the
advantages of the fortunate man, that though he be not
so strong as the other to deal with calamity and desire,
yet these are kept far from him by his good fortune, and
he is free from deformity, sickness, and all evil, and happy
in his children and his comeliness. If then such a man
besides all this shall also end his life well, then he is the
man whom you seek, and is worthy to be called blest;
but we must wait till he be dead, and call him not yet
blest, but fortunate.

"Now no one (who is but man) can have all these
good things together, just as no land is altogether self-
sufficing in what it produces: one thing it has, another
it lacks, and the best land is that which has most; so too
no single person is sufficient for himself: one thing he

has, another he lacks; but whoever continues in the possession of most things, and at last makes a gracious end of his life, such a man, O king, I deem worthy of this title.

" We must look to the conclusion of every matter, and see how it shall end, for there are many to whom heaven has given a vision of blessedness, and yet afterwards brought them to utter ruin."

So spoke Solon: Croesus therefore gave him no largess, but sent him away as a man of no account, for he thought that man to be very foolish who disregarded present prosperity and bade him look rather to the end of every matter.

But after Solon's departure, the divine anger fell heavily on Croesus: as I guess, because he supposed himself to be blest beyond all other men.

A. D. GODLEY.

Croesus and the Delphic Oracle

HERODOTUS i. 91. Croesus consulted the oracle of Apollo ("Loxias") at Delphi, whether he should make war on Persia. The answer was that, if he did so, he would "destroy a mighty empire." He was defeated and captured in his capital, Sardis, by Cyrus the Persian, who allowed him to send his fetters to Delphi and ask the god if he were not ashamed to have deceived him by the oracle.

The priestess (it is said) thus replied: " None may escape his destined lot, not even a god. Croesus has paid for the sin of his ancestor of the fifth generation: who . . . was led by the guile of a woman to slay his master, and took to himself the royal state of that master, whereto he had no right. And it was the desire of Loxias that the evil hap of Sardis should fall in the lifetime of Croesus' sons, not his own, but he could not turn the Fates from their purpose; yet did he accomplish his will and favour Croesus in so far as they would yield to him: for he delayed the taking of Sardis for three years, and this let Croesus know, that though he be now taken it is by so many years later than the destined hour. . . . But as to the oracle that was given him, Croesus doth not right to complain concerning it. For Loxias declared to him that if he should lead an army against the Persians he would destroy a great empire. Therefore it behoved him, if he would take right counsel, to send and ask whether the god spoke of Croesus' or of Cyrus' empire. But he understood not that which was spoken, nor made further inquiry: wherefore now let him blame himself. . . ."

Such was the answer of the priestess to the Lydians; they carried it to Sardis and told it to Croesus; and when he heard it, he confessed that the sin was not the god's but his own.

A. D. Godley.

The Philosophy of Solon

Solon (Stobaeus, *Eclogae* iii. 9, 23).

Muses of Pieria, glorious children of Memory and of Olympian Zeus, hear my prayer. Grant me wealth from the blessed gods, and from all men fair fame to enjoy for ever. So let me be sweet to my friends and bitter to my enemies, reverenced by the one and feared by the other.

Though I long for wealth, I would not possess it unjustly, for soon or late the punishment surely comes. Wealth that the gods give abides with a man as a tree stands firm from root to top; but wealth that men seek by presumptuous outrage comes not in due course, but follows reluctantly the lure of unjust deeds. Soon it is joined with blind folly which, like a fire kindled from a small beginning, is of little account at first, but ends in sore distress.

For the works of presumptuous men are not for long: but the eye of Zeus is upon the end of every thing. As a sudden wind in spring that scatters the clouds, and, when it has stirred the depths of the sea's waste of barren waves and made havoc of the earth's fair fields of corn, comes to the seat of the gods in the height of heaven and gives sight of the clear sky again; and now the fair sun shines in his strength over the fruitful earth and there is no more a cloud to be seen—even such as that is the vengeance of Zeus. He is not, like a man, quick to anger at each offence, but the man of sinful heart does not continue unremarked for ever; in the end he is surely brought to light. One man pays the penalty immediately, another late; and when they escape themselves and the fate of the gods overtakes them not, yet surely it comes afterwards: the innocent pay for their deeds, either their children or their posterity after them.

So each of us mortal men, good and bad alike, strains after glory for himself and thinks to possess it, until some stroke falls and immediately he is in pain; till then we are agape after the joys of Hope that ever flies before. . . .

Destiny brings to men both evil and good; there is no escape from the gifts of the immortal gods. Danger besets every work, and no one knows at the beginning which way the thing will turn. One who strives to do well, for lack of foresight falls into great and hard calamity; to another who does ill heaven grants good luck at every turn and absolves him from his folly.

In the pursuit of wealth no goal is set clearly before men's eyes: those of us who have now the greatest fortune strive twice as hard for more. What wealth could be enough for all? Certainly gain is a gift from the Immortals to men; but out of it springs ruinous blindness which, when Zeus sends it to exact vengeance, lights now upon one and now upon another.

Zeus cares for the Right

ARCHILOCHUS (*circ.* 650 B.C.), *frag.* 88.

O Zeus, Father Zeus, thine is the lordship of heaven; thou seest the violent and the lawful deeds of men; thou carest for what the beasts do rightly or amiss.

Man knows not the End

SEMONIDES of Amorgos, *frag.* 1.

My son, the end of all things is in the hand of Zeus the Thunderer, and he disposes as he will.

Wisdom is not within man's scope; for our brief day we live like beasts, knowing nothing of how heaven will bring each thing to its accomplishment.

We all feed on hope and flattering belief, striving eagerly for the unattainable. . . .

Man is like the Leaves

MIMNERMUS of Colophon (*circ.* 650–600), *frag.* 2.

We are like the leaves that shoot in the spring-time of the flowers, when they grow quickly in the sunshine.

Like the leaves, for a span of time we rejoice in the flowers of youth, taught by heaven neither good nor evil.

On either hand are the black Fates, the one holding the fullness of miserable age, the other of death.

The fruit of our prime endures but for a little while, so far as the sunlight is shed upon the earth; and when the fullness of that season is overpast, it is better to die at once than to live.

For many evils come upon the heart.

Now a man's substance is wasted, and the painful tasks of poverty are his.

Another has no children, and sorely longing for them he goes down into the darkness of Death.

Another has sickness that breaks the spirit; and there is no man to whom Zeus gives not many sorrows.

Good and Evil are the Gifts of the Gods

THEOGNIS, *Elegies* 133.   Theognis is believed to have died after 490 B.C.

No man, Kyrnus, is the cause of his own ruin or prosperity; both alike are the gift of the gods.

No man knows whether his work will come to a good end or a bad. Often good comes of it when he looks for harm, and harm when he looks for good.

A man never attains the whole of his desire; his helplessness sets bounds that hold him back.

We men know nothing, and our thoughts are vain; it is only the gods who accomplish all things to their mind.

THEOGNIS, *Elegies* 171.

Pray to the gods, for theirs is the power. Men come neither to good nor harm without the gods.

Why do the Wicked prosper ?

THEOGNIS, *Elegies* 373.

Dear Zeus, I wonder at you. For you are king of all; honour and great power are in your hand; you know well the mind and temper of every man, and your lordship is supreme over all, O king.

How is it then, son of Cronos, that your spirit can endure to keep the sinner and the righteous man in the same state, whether the heart be turned to soberness of life or to the insolence of men that are tempted to unrighteous works?

Heaven has drawn no clear line for men, not even which way a man must go to please the Immortals.

Bad men none the less enjoy prosperity, and they who refrain their spirit from foul deeds are overtaken, in their love of righteousness, by poverty that breeds helplessness and turns aside man's heart to sin, blinding his wits with overmastering necessity.

So, despite his will, a man grows bold to take upon himself foul shame; he yields to need, which teaches many an evil lesson—lies and deceits and ruinous quarrels, against his will though it be.

It is best never to be born

THEOGNIS, *Elegies* 425.

Best of all things is it, never to be born upon this earth, never to see the rays of the burning sun.

And, when a man is born, it is best that he should journey with all speed to the gates of Death, and, wrapping himself in a close covering of earth, should lie at rest.

The Gods lead Man into Sin

THEOGNIS, *Elegies* 401.

Be not too eager: a time for all things is the best rule for all man's works. Often a man makes too much haste for excellence, and he seeks gain, when a god is bent on leading him astray into great sin, and easily makes him think that bad is good and good is bad.

An Anecdote of Simonides

CICERO, *On the Nature of the Gods* i. 60. Simonides of Keos, 556–468 B.C.

Hiero the tyrant asked Simonides to explain the nature of the deity. The poet asked a day for reflection. When the question was repeated on the morrow, he asked for two days. Thus he kept on doubling the number of days, till Hiero in surprise asked the reason. "The longer I think about it," he answered, "the more obscure the question seems to me"

IV. THE IONIAN PHILOSOPHY AT MILETUS

In the sixth century B.C. the Ionian colonies on the coast of Asia Minor were the centre of Western civilisation. Science or philosophy originated at Miletus with Thales, who had travelled in Egypt and learnt from Babylon enough empirical astronomy to enable him to predict an eclipse of the sun in 585 B.C. These philosophers speculated upon the origin of the world and of life. They believed that the ultimate "nature of things" was a form of living stuff. Thales identified it with water; Anaximander called it "the Unlimited" (indefinite); Anaximenes identified it with air. They all tacitly ignore the gods of popular religion, and regard the ultimate "nature" as divine.

This Ionian tradition of physical philosophy was continued in the fifth century by Anaxagoras, Diogenes of Apollonia, and Archelaus (see Section XI.).

Thales : *All things are full of Gods*

ARISTOTLE, *de Anima* i. v. 411a 7.

THERE are some too who say that soul is interfused throughout the universe; which is perhaps why Thales supposed all things to be full of gods.

The Unlimited of Anaximander

SIMPLICIUS, *Physics* 24, 13.

Anaximander of Miletus, the successor and pupil of Thales, declared that the beginning or first element of things was the ' Unlimited '—a name which he was the first to give to the ultimate principle. He says it is not water or any of the so-called elements, but a distinct nature, which is unlimited, and out of which arise all the heavens and the worlds within them.

" And things perish into those things from which they have their birth, as it is ordained. For they pay to one another the penalty of their injustice according to the order of time."

ARISTOTLE, *Physics* iii. 4.

All the physical philosophers posit the Unlimited as a principle or beginning, with good reason, for it cannot exist for no purpose, and the only significance it can have is as a beginning: everything either *is* a beginning or *has* a beginning, and the Unlimited cannot have a beginning, for then it would have a limit. Further, as a beginning, it cannot begin to exist or perish; for whatever has a beginning of existence must also have an end, and all perishing has an end. This principle, then, as we said, has no beginning, but is held to be the beginning of other things and to " encompass and govern all things," as those philosophers say who do not recognise, besides the Unlimited, other causes such as Mind [1] or Love.[2]

And they say that this is " the divine "; for it is " immortal and imperishable," as Anaximander and most of the physical philosophers say.

The Air of Anaximenes

AETIUS i. 3, 4.

Anaximenes of Miletus declared that Air was the principle of all things; for all things arise out of air and are dissolved into it again. He says: " As our soul, which is air, holds us together, so a breath or air encompasses the whole world."

AETIUS i. 7, 13.

Anaximenes holds that Air is God.

[1] Anaxagoras.　　　　[2] Empedocles.

V. MYSTICAL RELIGION

(a) THE MYSTERIES OF ELEUSIS

The Mysteries of Demeter (the Earth- or Corn-mother) and her daughter Persephone were celebrated at Eleusis in Attica at the time of the autumn sowing. They were preceded by the "Little Mysteries," a rite of preliminary purification held in spring. The promise held out to the initiates was a "better lot" in the other world, accorded by grace of the two goddesses and not conditional upon virtuous conduct. Since the rites were secret, no contemporary description of them exists. But the Great Mysteries included a passion play representing the myth of the Rape of Persephone described in the Homeric Hymn, which is believed to date from about 600 B.C.

The Myth of Demeter and Persephone

HOMERIC HYMN TO DEMETER (abbreviated).

OF Demeter, the fair-tressed reverend goddess, I begin my song; and of her slender daughter, whom Hades ravished away. Zeus gave her to Hades when Demeter was not there. She was playing with the daughters of Ocean and gathering flowers, roses and crocuses and fair violets in the soft meadow, and hyacinths, and the narcissus which Earth, by the will of Zeus and to pleasure the Lord of many guests, brought forth to ensnare the flower-faced maiden. The flower shone marvellously, that all might worship at the sight, both immortal gods and men. From its root shot up a hundred heads, and with the sweet smell of it all the broad heaven above and all the earth laughed, and the salt wave of the sea. And the maiden, smitten with wonder, stretched out both hands to take the lovely plaything; but the earth gaped in the Nysian plain, and thereout leapt the Lord

43

of many guests with his immortal horses. Against her will he ravished her away, weeping, in his golden chariot. She uttered a shrill cry, calling upon Father Zeus, the highest and the best; but no god nor mortal man heard her voice, save Hecate, who heard the cry from her cave, and Helios, Hyperion's glorious son. . . .

Now so long as the maiden goddess saw the earth and the starry heaven and the flowing sea and the rays of the sun, and thought yet to see her dear mother and the company of the everlasting gods, so long, for all her grief, hope flattered her high heart; and the mountain peaks and the depths of the sea rang with her immortal voice. Her mother heard her, and sharp pain caught her heart, and she tore the veil from her ambrosial locks and threw a dark covering about her shoulders. Swift as a bird she went seeking over land and sea; but neither god nor man would tell her the truth, nor bird of omen give her true tidings. Then for nine days the lady Deo went to and fro over the earth, with torches in her hands. In her sorrow she tasted not of sweet nectar or ambrosia, nor washed her body. But when the light of the tenth dawn came, Hecate met her, holding a torch in her hand, and spoke a word of tidings:

"Lady Demeter, bringer of the seasons and their glorious gifts, what god of heaven or mortal man has ravished away Persephone and filled thy heart with pain? For I heard a voice, but saw not who it was. Thus I make haste to tell thee all that I know."

And the daughter of Rhea answered not, but went with her quickly, holding the torches burning in her hands. And they came to Helios, who keeps watch for gods and men, and stood before his chariot. And the goddess asked of him:

" Helios, have pity upon me, goddess though I be, if ever by word or deed I have warmed thy heart. My daughter, whom I bore, that sweet and stately plant— her voice I heard ringing through the barren fields of air, as if she suffered violence; but I saw nothing. But thou with thy rays lookest down from the height of heaven over land and sea; tell me then truly of my dear child, if anywhere thou hast seen what god or man it is that has laid violent hands upon her, when I was not there, and taken her away."

And the son of Hyperion answered:

" Daughter of fair-tressed Rhea, Queen Demeter, thou shalt know; for indeed I revere thee much and have compassion upon thy sorrow for thy daughter. Of all the gods it is none other but Zeus that has done this. He gave her to his brother Hades, to be called his bride. And Hades has ravished her away on his chariot under the misty darkness, while she cried aloud. Nevertheless, make thou an end, goddess, of thy great lamentation. It profits nothing to nurse thine anger unassuaged. Hades is thine own brother, of the same seed with thee; and when all the world was divided in three, it fell to his lot to be lord over those with whom he dwells: among the Immortals it is no shame that he should be thy son-in-law." . . .

But yet more terrible grief came upon the heart of Demeter. In anger against the son of Cronos she held apart from the assembly of the gods and high Olympus, and went away among the cities and rich fields of men, disguising her form for many days. No man nor woman that saw her knew her, until she came to the house of the wise Keleos, who then was prince in Eleusis. There, at the wayside by the Maiden Well, whence the men of

F

the city drew water, in the shade of an olive that grew
over it, she sat in grief, in the likeness of an old woman
of many years, past child-bearing and the gifts of Aphrodite, such an one as might be the nurse of a king's
children or the housekeeper in his echoing halls.

And the daughters of Keleos saw her when they came
to draw water and carry it in pitchers of bronze to their
father's house. Four were they, like goddesses, in the
flower of maidenhood, Kallidike, and Kleisidike, and
lovely Demo, and Kallithoë the eldest. They knew
not Demeter, for gods are hard for mortals to discern;
but they stood near and spoke to her winged words. . . .

(In answer to their questions Demeter says she has come
from Crete and seeks employment. The daughters of Keleos
tell their mother Metaneira, who sends word that she will take
Demeter as nurse for her son.)

And the maidens found the stately goddess at the
wayside where they had left her, and led her to their
father's house. She walked behind them in sadness with
veiled head, the dark robe floating about her delicate
feet. Soon they came to the house of Keleos, and went
through the colonnade where their lady mother sat by
the pillar of the hall, with a child of tender age in her
lap. The maidens ran to her, and when the goddess set
foot upon the threshold, her head reached to the roof-
beam and she filled the doorway with radiance of
divine light. And Metaneira was filled with awe and
reverence and pale fear, and she rose from her chair and
bade Demeter sit down. But she would not sit down upon
the shining chair, but waited silent with downcast eyes
till the wise Iambe set for her a joint-stool, and threw
over it a silvery fleece.

Then she sat down and held the veil before her face

and for a long time sat sorrowing in silence, greeting none
by word or motion, unsmiling; and she touched neither
food nor drink, wasted with longing for her daughter.
So she sat until wise Iambe, with mockeries and many
jests, turned her to smiles and laughter and kindliness
of heart; and ever thereafter Iambe pleased her mood.

Then Metaneira filled and offered her a cup of sweet
wine; but she refused it, saying that it was not lawful
for her to drink red wine; but she bade her mix meal
and water and soft leaves of pennyroyal and give it her
to drink. And Metaneira made the drink as the goddess bade and gave it to her; and the lady Deo took it,
that the rite might be observed.[1]

(Metaneira then gives her the child Demophon to nurse.)

And the goddess took the child to her fragrant breast
with her immortal hands, and the mother's heart was glad.
So, in the halls of the wise Keleos, she nursed his glorious
son, Demophon, whom Metaneira bore; and he grew
like a god, neither eating bread nor suckled with milk.

Demeter anointed him with ambrosia as if he had been
the son of a god, and breathed sweetness upon him,
holding him in her bosom. And in the night-watches
she hid him in the burning fire like a brand, and his
parents knew it not. To them it was a great wonder
how he grew and flourished, in countenance like the gods.

And she would have made him free from old age and
death, had not Metaneira, in her folly, spied upon her
by night from her fragrant chamber. She screamed and
smote her thighs in fear for her child and in the blindness
of her heart. And she cried out in lamentation:

" O my child, Demophon, the stranger is hiding thee

[1] The candidates for initiation at Eleusis partook of a draught
of this kind in remembrance of Demeter.

in the great fire, and bringing bitter sorrow and weeping upon me ! "

And the goddess heard her, and in her wrath she took out of the fire the woman's dear son whom she had borne beyond all hope in the house, and put him from her upon the floor. And in terrible anger she spoke to Metaneira:

" O blind and witless race of men, that foresee not the good or evil fate that comes upon them ! For thou, by thy folly, hast brought ruin upon thyself past remedy. By the gods' oath I swear, by the relentless water of Styx, I would have made thy son ageless and immortal for all his days and given him honour that waxes not old. But now he shall not escape death and the fates. Nevertheless honour that waxes not old shall be upon him for ever, because he has lain upon my knees and slept in my arms. For ever, as the seasons come in their yearly round, the sons of the Eleusinians shall wage war and dread battle with one another.[1]

" I am Demeter, that am held in honour and above all give gladness and good gifts to Immortals and to men. Come now, let all the people build me a great temple and an altar beneath it, below the steep wall of the citadel, above Callichorus on the jutting hill. The rites I will myself ordain, that in after days ye may perform them piously and win my grace."

Then the goddess changed her form and stature, casting off old age, and beauty breathed about her. A lovely fragrance as of incense spread from her robes, and a light shone far from her immortal face, and the hair flowed golden over her shoulders. The house was filled with radiance as of the lightning. . . .

---

[1] A yearly mock battle of stone-throwing, held at Eleusis in Demophon's honour. It may have been a fertility rite.

And all night long the women adored the stately goddess, trembling with fear [1]; and when the dawn appeared they told Keleos all that she had commanded. . . .

(The temple is built.)

But golden-haired Demeter still sat there apart from all the Blessed Ones and pined with longing for her daughter. And that year she made most terrible and pitiless for mankind upon the fruitful earth, for the land sent up no seed; it was hidden away by Demeter. In vain the oxen dragged the curved ploughshare over the fields; in vain was all the white barley cast upon the ground. Now would the race of mortal men have perished utterly by stress of famine and the gods of Olympus lost their dues of sacrifice and worship, had not Zeus taken thought in his heart. . . .

(Zeus sends Iris and then all the gods to recall Demeter to Olympus; but she will not return without her daughter. Then Zeus sends Hermes to Hades, who consents to release Persephone.)

And immediately Hades said to the wise Persephone: "Go, Persephone, to thy dark-robed mother, with a gentle spirit in thy breast, and let not thy heart be clouded with anger exceedingly. I, who am the brother of Father Zeus, shall be a fit bedfellow for thee among the Immortals; and while thou art here thou shalt be mistress of all that lives and moves, and among the Immortals the highest honour shall be thine. They who do thee wrong shall pay penalty all their days, even they who seek not thy grace with sacrifice and due offering of pious gifts."

The wise Persephone was glad at his words, and she

[1] The reference appears to be to an "all-night" ceremony (*pannychis*), part of the Eleusinian festival, perhaps originally confined to women.

sprang up for joy; but the god gave her by stealth a sweet pomegranate seed to eat, that she might not abide for ever with dark-robed Demeter.

(Persephone is taken in Hades' chariot to meet Demeter at the temple.)

And her mother said: "Child, hast thou eaten of any food in the world below? Tell me; for if not, then mayst thou dwell beside me and Father Zeus, honoured among all the Immortals; but if thou hast, thou must go back again into the secret places of the earth and dwell there a third part of every year. And whensoever the earth blossoms with all sweet flowers of spring, then from the misty darkness thou shalt arise and come again, a marvel to gods and men." . . .

(Persephone tells her story, and how Hades made her eat the pomegranate seed. Zeus sends Rhea to Demeter.)

And Rhea came swiftly down from the peaks of Olympus to the plain of Rharium, where formerly the land brought forth the food of life, but now lay idle without a blade, for Demeter had hidden away the white barley. Nevertheless in after days the land was to wave at the waxing of the spring with tall ears of corn, and at harvest the ripe swathes would lie heavy on the ground, while others were bound in sheaves. . . .

(Rhea summons Demeter to come to Olympus, telling her of Zeus' promise that Persephone shall live with the gods for two-thirds of the year, and for one-third in the underworld, and bidding Demeter relent and cause the corn to grow.)

And Demeter hearkened to the words of Rhea, and immediately she made the corn to spring up in the furrowed fields, and all the broad earth was heavy with leaves and flowers.

And Demeter went and told the matter to the kings,

Triptolemos, and Diocles the charioteer, and Eumolpos, and Keleos, leader of the people; and she taught them the performance of her rites and solemn mysteries, which none may violate, nor search into, nor publish abroad; for deep awe of heaven restrains all utterance.

Blessed among men upon the earth is he who has seen these things ; but he that is uninitiate in the rites and has no part in them has never an equal lot in the cold place of darkness.

Now when the goddess had laid down all her ordinances, she and her daughter went to Olympus to the company of the other gods.   There they dwell with Zeus, the lord of the thunderbolt, and are held in reverence and awe. Thrice happy among men upon the earth is he whom they earnestly love. They send, to dwell in his house, Wealth, who gives abundance to mortal men.

Diogenes on the Mysteries

PLUTARCH, *de aud. poet.* 21 F (Sophocles, *frag.* 837 Pearson).

Diogenes may be called in to counteract Sophocles, whose lines about the Mysteries have filled innumerable minds with discouragement:

> " O thrice-blessed they
> That ere they pass to Hades have beheld
> These Mysteries; for them only, in that world,
> Is life; the rest have utter misery."

Diogenes, when he heard a similar statement, replied, " What do you mean? Is Pataikion the thief going to have a ' better lot ' after death than Epaminondas, just because he was initiated? "

(b) Dionysus and Orphism

The religion of Dionysus is believed to have come into Greece from Thrace and Macedonia at least as early as the tenth century B.C. It was a form of worship more primitive and popular than the Olympian theology of Homer. The secret of its strength lay in the means it provided—ecstasy or sacramental communion—whereby the worshipper might become one with the god and so achieve divinity and immortality. In the sixth century, or perhaps earlier, a spiritual revival gave rise to the Orphic brotherhoods, whose chief centre was in South Italy and Sicily. It is impossible to say whether Orpheus, the patron saint of this movement, is or is not a purely legendary figure.

The Rites of Dionysus

Diodorus Siculus iv. 3.

The Boeotians and the Greeks generally and the Thracians instituted the festivals of Dionysus that are held in alternate years, believing that the god manifests himself to men at these times. Hence in many Greek states every other year the women assemble for Bacchic rites and it is the custom for virgins to bear the thyrsus in a state of inspired ecstasy, honouring the god with wild cries, while the women, in organised companies, sacrifice to the god and hold revel and celebrate the advent of Dionysus with hymns, imitating the Maenads who are said in old story to have attended on the god.

Plutarch, *Isis and Osiris* 69.

The Phrygians believe that the god sleeps in winter and is awake in summer, and they perform Bacchic rites of putting him to sleep at one season and awakening him at another.

Dionysus and Osiris

HERODOTUS ii. 48. Travelling in Egypt in the fifth century, Herodotus was impressed by the likeness between the cults of Dionysus and Osiris. Compare his views (p. 130) on the origin of the Greek gods.

To Dionysus (*i.e.* Osiris), on the evening of his festival, everyone offers a porker which he kills before his door and then gives to the swineherd himself who has sold it, for him to take away. The rest of the festival of Dionysus is ordered by the Egyptians much as it is by the Greeks, except for the dances; but in place of the phallus they have invented the use of puppets a cubit long moved by strings, which are carried about the villages by women, the male member moving and near as big as the rest of the body; a flute-player goes before, the women follow after, singing of Dionysus. There is a sacred legend which gives the reason for the appearance and motions of these puppets.

Now, this being so, it seems to me that Melampus, son of Amytheon, was not ignorant but had attained knowledge of this sacrifice. For it was Melampus who taught the Greeks the name of Dionysus, and the way of sacrificing to him, and the phallic procession; I would not in strictness say that he showed them completely the whole matter, for the later teachers added somewhat to his showing; but it was from him that the Greeks learnt to bear the phallus along in honour of Dionysus, and they got their present practice from his teaching. I think, then, that Melampus showed himself a cunning man, in that he set himself up for a prophet, and his teaching of the worship of Dionysus, besides much else, came from Egypt with but slight change; for I will not admit that it is a chance agreement between the Egyptian ritual of Dionysus and the Greek; for were that so, the Greek ritual would be of a Greek nature and not but lately introduced. Nor yet will I hold that the Egyptians took either this or any other custom from the Greeks. But I believe that Melampus learnt the worship of Dionysus chiefly from Cadmus of Tyre and those who came with Cadmus from Phoenice to the land now called Boeotia.

Indeed, wellnigh all the names of the gods came to Hellas from Egypt. For I am assured by inquiry that they have come from foreign parts, and I believe that they came chiefly from Egypt. Except the names of Poseidon and the Dioscuri . . . and Here, and Hestia, and Themis, and the Graces and the Nereids, the names of all the gods have ever existed in Egypt. I say but what the Egyptians themselves say. The gods whose names they say they do not know were, as I think, named by the Pelasgians, save only Poseidon, of whom they learnt knowledge from the Libyans.

A. D. GODLEY.

The Myth of Orpheus

APOLLODORUS, *Library* I. iii. 2.

Now Calliope (the Muse) bore to Oeagrus or, nominally, to Apollo . . . Orpheus, who practised minstrelsy and by his songs moved stones and trees. And when his wife Eurydice died, bitten by a snake, he went down to Hades, being fain to bring her up, and he persuaded Pluto to send her up. The god promised to do so, if on the way Orpheus would not turn round until he should be come to his own house. But he disobeyed and turning round beheld his wife; so she turned back. Orpheus also invented the mysteries of Dionysus, and having been torn in pieces by the Maenads he is buried in Pieria.

J. G. FRAZER.

Orphism in Attica

PAUSANIAS viii. 37, 5. Onomacritus, an Orphic teacher, reputed author of a poem "The Rites of Initiation," was at the court of Hippias, who succeeded his father Peisistratus as despot at Athens in 528–7 B.C. Orphism spread from South Italy to Attica about this time.

Onomacritus borrowed the name of the Titans from Homer, and in the rites which he composed for Dionysus he represented the Titans as the authors of Dionysus' sufferings.

Orpheus the Founder of Mysteries

ARISTOPHANES, *Frogs* 1032.

Aeschylus. See how useful the nobler poets have been from the very beginning. Orpheus revealed to us rites of initiation and abstinence from bloodshed; Musaeus, the healing of diseases and the use of oracles.

The Orphic Theogony

DAMASCIUS (head of the Neo-Platonic school at Athens about 520–530 A.D.), *On the First Principles*, 123*ff.*, preserves the outlines of the Theogony in the "Orphic Rhapsodies." This compilation contained material at least as old as the sixth century B.C.

The first principle was Unageing Time (*Chronos*). (By the early thinkers Time was indissolubly associated with motion, and by some even identified with the revolving sphere of the sky.)

Next come the pair, Aether (bright and fiery stuff) and Chaos (the yawning gulf).

In these was formed or begotten the World-Egg, with a silver shell enclosing dark mist. The Egg burst, and its upper half formed the dome of heaven, the lower contained the waters from which the earth arose.

Out of the Egg sprang Phanes (Shining One), also called
Love (*Erôs*), who was both male and female and contained the
seeds of all life. He had golden wings, bulls' heads attached
to his flanks, and on his head a serpent "resembling the forms
of all sorts of beasts." [1]

In union with Night (his own child) Phanes produced three
successive pairs of children: (1) Earth and Heaven, (2) Cronos
and Rhea, (3) Zeus and Hera.

Zeus swallowed Phanes, and, so containing the principles
of all things, created the universe anew, including the youngest
generation of the gods.

The theogony may (as some hold) have continued with the
story of Zagreus, his birth, his death at the hands of the Titans,
his resurrection or rebirth, and the punishment of the Titans,
from whose ashes sprang mankind.

This account of the origin of mankind is of great significance,
since it implies the dual nature of man, divine and earthly,
good and evil. The Titans were evil, but they had partaken
of the divine flesh, and we, their descendants, accordingly
contain a soul of heavenly origin, enclosed in a body of dark
and evil nature. The soul can escape from this prison-house
and regain its divinity (immortality).

Dionysus Zagreus

PLUTARCH, *On the E at Delphi* ix. 389 A.

As for his passage and distribution into waves and
water, and earth, and stars, and nascent plants and animals,
they hint at the actual change undergone as a rending
or dismemberment, but name the god himself Dionysus
or Zagreus or Nyctelius or Isodaites. Deaths too and
vanishings do they construct, passages out of life and new

---

[1] A representation of Phanes has been recognised by R. Eisler
(*Weltenmantel und Himmelszelt*, 1910, ii. 400) in a relief of about
the time of Hadrian in the museum at Modena. A youthful
winged figure, enwound by a snake, and having the masks of
a lion, ram, and goat at his waist, stands on the lower half
of the World-Egg, with the upper half above his head. He
holds a thunderbolt in his right hand, a sceptre in his left. The
figure is framed by an elliptical band containing the signs of the
Zodiac, and the corners of the relief are filled by the heads of
the four winds.

births, all riddles and tales to match the changes mentioned. So they sing to Dionysus dithyrambic strains, charged with sufferings and a change, wherein are wanderings and dismemberment.

"*In mingled cries*" (says Aeschylus) "*the dithyramb should ring,*
With Dionysus revelling, its king."

A. O. PRICKARD

The Myth of Dionysus Zagreus

CLEMENT OF ALEXANDRIA, *Exhortation to the Greeks* ii. p. 15 P.

The mysteries of Dionysus are the perfection of savagery. When he was still a child the Armed Youths were performing round him the dance in armour, when the Titans stealthily drew near. These Titans, we are told, beguiled the infant with childish toys and tore him to pieces. Orpheus of Thrace, the poet of the *Rite of Initiation*, speaks of "the top, the bull-roarer and jointed dolls, and golden apples from the musical-voiced Hesperides"—symbols of this rite of yours worthless enough, yet worth quoting for condemnation: knucklebone, ball, spinning-top, apples, bull-roarer, mirror, fleece! Athena abstracted the heart of Dionysus and received the name Pallas from its palpitating. The Titans who had torn Dionysus in pieces put a cauldron on a tripod and threw his limbs into it. When they had boiled them, they pierced them with spits and held them over the fire. Later Zeus appeared . . . made havoc of the Titans with a thunderbolt, and entrusted the limbs of Dionysus to his son Apollo for burial. In obedience to Zeus, Apollo carried the dismembered body to Parnassus and laid it to rest.

The Cretan Ritual of Dionysus Zagreus

FIRMICUS, *On the Error of Profane Religions* (343–350 A.D.), 6, after recounting the story in Euhemeristic terms, making Zeus a Cretan king, whose son is destroyed by the minions of his jealous stepmother, records the Cretan ritual:

The Cretans, to soothe the fierce mood of the angry tyrant (Zeus) instituted certain days as a funeral feast and coupled a yearly rite with a celebration in alternate years, performing in order due all that the boy had done or suffered at his death. They tore a live bull with their teeth, recalling the savage banquet by a yearly commemoration of it. They penetrated the solitudes of the forest uttering discordant cries and so feigning madness, that the crime might be set down to lunacy, not to guile. Before them was carried the basket in which the sister (Athena) had concealed and hidden the heart. With the music of pipes and the clash of cymbals they got up a make-belief of the rattles by which the boy had been deluded. And so a servile people paying court to a tyrant made his son a god, though a god could never have had a tomb.

A. B. COOK.

Confession of the Cretan Initiates

EURIPIDES, *Cretans*, frag. 472. The Chorus of this lost play address Minos:

Child of Tyrian Europa and of great Zeus, King of Crete with its hundred cities, I come from the holy shrines roofed by the beam of native timber, cut by the Chalyb axe and compact with bull's-hide glue binding fast the joints of the cypress wood.

Pure has been my life's course, since I was initiated in the mysteries of Zeus of Mount Ida. I have accom-

plished the thunders of night-roving Zagreus and the
Feast of the Eating of Raw Flesh; I have borne the
torches for the Mountain Mother; and, having attained
sanctification, I have received the name of Bacchus of
the Armed Youths.

And now, clothed all in white raiment, I shun contact
with human birth and with the burial of the dead, and
watchfully eschew the eating of things that have a
living soul.

Mr. A. B. Cook (*Zeus*, 1914, i. 648) comments: "The mystics
of Zeus *Idaios* here tell us how their temple was made and how
they themselves were initiated into the rites of their god. The
temple was roofed with beams of cypress, . . . a tree sacred
to Rhea rather than to Zeus. The requisite timber was grown
on the spot. Probably it formed part of a grove belonging to
the goddess and was felled with the double axe, to which even
in the iron age a certain sanctity still attached. The planks so
hewn were fitted together with no iron nails or clamps (that
would have been an impious innovation), but with glue made
of bull's hide (for the bull was an animal form of the deity
himself). The initiates evidently sought to become one with
the re-born god" (*i.e.* the Cretan Zeus, re-born as Zagreus),
"the youthful partner of their goddess. Beginning as Kouretes"
(the armed youths), "they ended as Bacchoi. Three rites are
touched upon, the making of thunder, the banquet of raw
flesh, and the roaming with torches over the mountain-side.
It seems probable that the purpose of all these ritual actions
was to identify the worshippers as far as possible with Zagreus,
and so to bring them into the most intimate relation to the
goddess. If Zagreus sat on the throne of Zeus grasping the
thunderbolt, the mystics could at least produce mock thunder
by beating drums made from the hide of the sacred bull. . . .
If he was slain in the form of a bull, they could devour a bull's
flesh raw and thereby assimilate the very life-blood of the god.
If he consorted by night with his mother, the mountain-goddess,
they too, full-charged with his sanctity, might go in quest of her
their mother and fructify her by their torches. Thenceforward
as veritable embodiments of the god they must lead a life of
ceremonial purity, being, so far as men might be, husbands
of the goddess."

Mr. Cook accepts the derivation of Zagreus from Mount
Zagros between Assyria and Media, and supposes that the
Cretan god assumed the title of his Oriental counterpart. The
Greeks understood Zagreus to mean "Mighty Hunter."

The Orphic Grave-Tablets

These tablets were found in graves in South Italy and Crete. They contain extracts from a poem of Orphic origin, which must date, at latest, from the fifth century B.C., and may be considerably earlier.   As in the Egyptian Book of the Dead, instructions are given to the soul of the dead for its guidance in the other world, formularies to be repeated, and confessions of faith and of ritual performed.   The tablets are discussed by Miss J. E. Harrison, *Prolegomena to the Study of Greek Religion,* Chap. xi., and by Professor Murray in an Appendix to that book.   I have made use of Professor Murray's translation, making a few changes to suit the text as printed by Diels in his *Fragmente der Vorsokratiker* (1912), ii. 175.

TABLET FROM PETELIA, SOUTH ITALY, fourth–third century B.C.

Thou shalt find to the left of the House of Hades a Well-spring,

And by the side thereof standing a white cypress.

To this Well-spring approach not near.

But thou shalt find another, from the Lake of Memory

Cold water flowing forth, and there are Guardians before it.

Say: " I am a child of Earth and of Starry Heaven;

" But my race is of Heaven (alone). This ye know yourselves.

" And lo, I am parched with thirst and I perish. Give me quickly

" The cold water flowing forth from the Lake of Memory."

And of themselves they will give thee to drink from the holy Well-spring,

And thereafter among the other Heroes thou shalt have lordship. . .

TABLET FROM CRETE, second century B.C.

I am parched with thirst and I perish. Nay, drink of Me, (*or* But give me to drink of)

The Well-spring flowing for ever on the right, where
the cypress is.

Who art thou ? . . .

Whence art thou ?—I am the son of Earth and of
Starry Heaven.

TABLET FROM THURII (South Italy).

But so soon as the Spirit hath left the light of the sun,
Go to the right, as far as one should go,[1] being right
wary in all things.

Hail, thou who hast suffered the Suffering.   This
thou hadst never suffered before.

Thou art become God from man.

A kid thou art fallen into milk.

Hail, hail to thee journeying on (the road to) the right
By holy meadows and groves of Persephone.

THREE GOLD TABLETS FROM THURII (fourth–third century
B.C.). Prof. Murray reconstructs the formulæ represented by the
three tablets together:

Out of the Pure I come, Pure Queen of Them Below,
And Eukles and Eubouleus, and other Gods and
Daemons:

For I also avow me that I am of your blessed race.

And I have paid the penalty for deeds unrighteous,
Whether it be that Fate laid me low or the Gods
Immortal

Or . . . with star-flung thunderbolt.

I have flown out of the sorrowful weary Wheel;

I have passed with eager feet to the Circle desired;

I have sunk beneath the bosom of Despoina, Queen
of the Underworld;

I have passed with eager feet to (or from) the Circle
desired;

------

[1] So Diels. The road to the right leads to Elysium.

G

And now I come a suppliant to holy Phersephoneia

That of her grace she receive me to the seats of the Hallowed.—

Happy and Blessed One, thou shalt be God instead of Mortal.

A kid I have fallen into milk.

TABLET OF CAECILIA SECUNDINA, Rome (third century A.D.?).

She comes from the Pure, O pure Queen of those below

And Eukles and Eubouleus.—Child of Zeus, receive here the armour

Of Memory ('tis a gift songful among men):

Thou, Caecilia Secundina, come, by Law grown to be divine.

The above is Prof. Murray's rendering. The reading and interpretation of the second and third lines are doubtful. Diels' reading gives: "Child of Zeus, glorious (feminine), and I have this gift of Memory songful among men."

Diels takes the last line as the answer of the underworld goddess.

The Judgment of the Dead

PINDAR, *Olympian* ii. 53. This ode was written for Theron, tyrant of Acragas (Sicily), in 476 B.C. Orphic influence is traceable in the doctrines of reincarnation, of a judgment of the dead and reward and punishment between incarnations, and of an escape of the soul after three virtuous lives to the Islands of the Blest.

Now wealth that is beautified by deeds of prowess brings opportunity for many things, setting the thoughts of the heart upon high endeavour; it is a clear-shining star, a true beacon to man. And if, possessing wealth, a man knows what shall be hereafter, that the lawless spirits among the dead forthwith are punished here on earth, while the sins committed in this realm of Zeus are called to account beneath the earth by One that gives judgment with harsh and binding sentence;—

And the good, where their sun shines by day, and day and night are always equal, receive their sustenance without toil, vexing not the earth with the strength of their hands, nor the waters of the sea, for a bare livelihood; but in presence of gods high in honour, whoso took delight in keeping oaths has his portion in a life free from tears; while the others endure pain that no eye can look upon.

And all they that, for three lives in either world, have been steadfast to keep their soul from all wrong-doing, travel by the highway of Zeus to the Tower of Cronos, where the Ocean airs breathe about the Islands of the Blest. There are flowers of burning gold, some on land on glorious trees and others that the water feeds, whereof they twine garlands for their hands and wreaths, by the just will of Rhadamanthys, who sits, prepared for judgment, beside the great Father, the husband of Rhea, whose throne is exalted above all. And among these are numbered Peleus and Cadmus; and thither was Achilles borne by his mother when she had moved the heart of Zeus by prayers, Achilles who cast down Hector, the invincible, the unshaken pillar of Troy, and gave to death Cycnos and Memnon, the Ethiopian son of the Dawn.

Elysium

Pindar, *Dirges, frags.* 129, 130.

For them the sun shines in his strength in the world beneath, while here it is night; and in fields of crimson roses before their city the incense-tree gives shade and golden fruits hang heavy. . . . And some take their pleasure in horses and in wrestling, some in draught-playing, others in the lyre; and among them felicity is as a tree grown to its height and full of flowers. Over all that lovely land a sweet savour is spread abroad continually, as they mix incense of all kinds with far-shining fire on the altars of the gods.

On the other side the sluggish rivers of gloomy night vomit forth their illimitable darkness.

The Final Incarnation

PINDAR, *Dirges*, *frag.* 133. The soul absolved from the primal sin is incarnate for the last time in the highest form of humanity, and then becomes divine. Compare Empedocles (p. 74).

But as for those from whom Persephone shall exact the penalty of the primal woe, in the ninth year she gives up again their souls to the sunlight in the world above.

From these come noble kings and men swift in strength and highest in wisdom, and for all time to come men call them pure Heroes.

The Divine Origin of the Soul

PINDAR, *frag.* 131 (Bergk).

The body of all men is subject to all-powerful death, but alive there yet remains an image of the living man; for that alone is from the gods.

It sleeps when the limbs are active, but to them that sleep in many a dream it revealeth an award of joy or sorrow drawing near.

JAMES ADAM.

The "image (*eidolon*) of the living man" or, literally, " or the life " means the soul. The doctrine that the soul is "from the gods" is derived from Orphism. So also is the suggestion that a day of judgment is among the visions revealed to the soul active in dreams.

VI. THE ITALIAN PHILOSOPHY

Pythagoras left Samos about 530 B.C. and (perhaps after visiting Egypt) founded the "Italian" tradition of philosophy at Croton in South Italy. His school, a fraternity modelled on the mystical cult-societies of the Orphics already established in those parts, existed until its dispersal at some date between 450 and 410. Some of his followers then migrated to Central Greece, and founded societies at Thebes and elsewhere. Like the Orphics, Pythagoras taught transmigration, the divine origin of the soul, its purification in the wheel of birth, and its final reunion with the divine. He was also a great mathematician, and taught that numbers are the realities which are represented or embodied in the visible universe. No writings of the school are preserved, earlier than the fragments of Philolaus (late fifth century).

The Imitation of God

IAMBLICHUS, *On the Pythagorean Life*, 137.

I WISH to explain the fundamental principles of religion as set forth by Pythagoras and his followers. All their injunctions with regard to conduct aim at converse with the divine. This is their starting-point; their whole life is ordered with a view to following God, and this is the governing principle of their philosophy, because it is absurd that mankind should seek their good from any other source than the gods. It is as if the citizen of a country governed by a king should pay respect to some subordinate ruler, and disregard the king himself who rules over all. They think that mankind behave in that sort of way. For since God exists and has authority over all, and it is acknowledged that good should be sought from him that has authority, and all give good things to those whom they love and take delight in, and evil to those whom they hate, it is clear that we should do those things that are pleasing to God.

65

The Divine Government

IAMBLICHUS, *On the Pythagorean Life* 174.

Further Pythagoras conceived the rule of the gods to be most efficacious for the establishment of righteousness, and he took that rule as the higher principle for the ordinance of the constitution and laws and of justice and legal rights. It may be well to add some of his particular injunctions. The Pythagoreans learnt from him to think it profitable to believe that the divine exists and looks down upon the human race and cares for it. For we have need of such government as we shall not think of withstanding in any way, and divine government is of that sort; for if the divine is such as we have described, it is worthy to rule over all things. They rightly regarded the living creature as turbulent by nature and various in its inclinations, appetites, and other passions, so that it needs the threatening of a superior power to chasten it and reduce it to order. They thought, therefore, that every man, conscious of the variety of his nature, should never forget worship and piety towards the divine, but always keep in mind the power that watches over human behaviour.

Transmigration

HERODOTUS ii. 123.

It is believed in Egypt that the rulers of the lower world are Demeter and Dionysus.[1] Moreover, the Egyptians were the first to teach that the human soul is immortal and at the death of the body enters into some other living thing then coming to birth; and after passing through all creatures of land, sea, and air (which cycle it com-

[1] Isis and Osiris.

pletes in three thousand years), it enters once more into a human body at birth. Some of the Greeks, early and late, have used this doctrine as if it were their own; I know their names, but do not here record them.

A. D. GODLEY.

From a Summary of Pythagorean Doctrine

DIOGENES LAERTIUS viii. 25, preserves a statement by Alexander Polyhistor (first century B.C.), which is believed to be taken from a Pythagorean contemporary of Plato in the fourth century B.C. (Wellmann, *Hermes* 54 (1919), 225; Diels, *Fragmente der Vorsokratiker*[4], p. xlii.)

. . . The air round the earth is motionless and unhealthy and all things in it are mortal; but the uppermost air is always in motion, pure, and healthy, and all things in it are immortal and therefore divine. The sun, moon, and other heavenly bodies are gods; for heat prevails in them, and heat is the cause of life. . . . Man also is akin to the gods, because man partakes of heat; hence also the providence of God is exercised over us. . . .

Everything lives that partakes of heat (hence plants also are living creatures), but not all living things have soul. The soul is a portion torn away from the hot and the cold ether,[1] and because it partakes also of the cold ether, soul differs from life. Soul is immortal, because that from which it is torn away is immortal. . . .

The human soul is divided into three parts: intelligence (*nous*), reason (*phrenes*), and the heart.[2] . . . The rational part is immortal; the others are mortal. . . .

---

[1] "They call the air the 'cold ether.'"
[2] The Greek *thymos* cannot be translated. This part of the soul is seated in the heart (the others being in the brain). Plato uses the term to denote that part of the soul which stands between reason and appetite, and has, as its characteristic virtue, courage.

When the soul is cast out (of the body) it wanders in the air over the earth in the likeness of the body. Hermes is warden of souls and hence is called Conductor, Keeper of the Gates, and God of the Underworld, for it is he that brings in the souls from their bodies, whether from land or sea. The pure souls are led to the highest region, while the impure do not consort with them nor with one another, but are bound by the avenging spirits (*Erinyes*) in bonds that cannot be broken. All the air is full of souls, which are called Spirits and Heroes. It is they who send to men dreams and signs of sickness or of health; and not only to men, but to cattle and other beasts. Rites of purification and expiation have reference to these beings, and so has the whole art of divination, omens, and the like.

For mankind the greatest thing is the conversion of the soul to good or to evil. Men are happy when they possess a good soul, but they are never at rest. . . . Virtue and health are harmony, and so is all goodness and God. Thus the universe is a harmonious system. . . .

Worship should be paid to gods and heroes, but not with equal honours. We should worship the gods at all times with reverent speech, wearing white garments and being in a state of purity; the heroes should be worshipped only after midday.

Purity is effected by rites of purification, lustration and aspersion; by keeping clean from contact with funeral ceremonies, childbirth, and every kind of taint and by abstaining from the flesh of animals that have been eaten or have died, from mullet and melanurus (a fish), from eggs and animals that lay eggs, and from beans and the other things forbidden also by those who perform the rites of initiation in the sanctuaries.

Eternal Recurrence

EUDEMUS (pupil of Aristotle), *Phys.* iii. fr. 51.

If one might trust the Pythagoreans, who believe in the recurrence of precisely the same series of events, you will be sitting there, and I shall be holding this staff and telling you my story, and everything will be the same.

EMPEDOCLES

Empedocles of Acragas in Sicily was born about 490 B.C. He wrote two poems, one containing a system of Nature, the other, called *Purifications*, describing the fall of mankind and of the individual soul from an original state of blessedness. Imprisoned in the wheel of birth, the soul passes through many forms of mortal body, until it escapes and is reunited with its divine source.

The Nature of God

EMPEDOCLES, *Purifications, frags.* 132–134.

Blessed is he who has gained the riches of divine wisdom; unhappy he in whose heart the imagination of the gods is veiled in darkness.

We cannot bring (the divine) near within reach of our eyes or grasp of our hands—ever the highway of persuasion that leads into the heart of man.

For he is not furnished with a human head upon his body; he has not arms, springing as two branches from his shoulders; he has no feet, nor knees to run, nor hairy parts of generation. Rather he is a Mind, holy and ineffable, and that alone, flashing with swift thoughts throughout the whole order of the world.

The Divine Law against Bloodshed

ARISTOTLE, *Rhetoric* i. 13, 2; EMPEDOCLES, *frag.* 135.

There is, as all men instinctively divine, a natural and universal law of right and wrong, apart from any mutual compact or association. . . . So Empedocles speaks of the prohibition upon killing creatures that have a living soul; this is not right for some and wrong for others;

"But the law for all extends everywhere, through the wide-ruling air and through the infinite light."

The Age of Innocence before the Fall

PORPHYRY, *On Abstinence* ii. 20; EMPEDOCLES, *frag.* 128.

Empedocles also bears testimony to this (that wine was not used in primitive libations) where in his discourse of theogony he alludes to sacrifices as follows:

"The men of that time had no god of war or of the din of battle, nor Zeus as king nor Cronos nor Poseidon, but only the Cyprian Queen" (that is to say, Love), "whom they propitiated with pure and holy offerings, with painted figures of animals and perfumes of intricate odour, and offerings of myrrh unmixed and fragrant incense, and libations of yellow honey poured upon the ground" (customs that are yet observed in some cases, as it were vestiges of the truth). "No altar was wet with blood of bulls, shed by violence, but this was the greatest abomination among men, to tear out the life and eat the strong limbs."

EMPEDOCLES, *frags.* 130, 77.

And all things were tame and gentle to man, both beasts and birds, and the flame of lovingkindness burned.

And the trees, with leaves that never fall and fruit that never fails, flourish with abundance of fruits, according as the air (is duly tempered),[1] all the year round.

[1] So Theophrastus, who understands "a certain temperature of the air, namely that of spring." Descriptions of the perpetual spring of the Golden Age are derived from Homer's Garden of Alcinous (*Od.* vii. 114) where the trees bear fruit all the year.

The Primal Sin : Bloodshed and Flesh-eating

SEXTUS EMPIRICUS, *Adversus Mathematicos* ix. 126; EM-
PEDOCLES, *frags.* 136, 137.

If justice was a consequence of the interconnection
of mankind with one another and with the gods, there
will be no justice unless there are gods—a paradoxical
conclusion. Now the followers of Pythagoras and Empedocles and the rest of the Italians say that there is a
bond of association uniting us not only to one another
and to the gods, but also to the irrational animals; for
there is a single spirit pervading the whole order of the
world like a soul, that unites us to the animals. Therefore
in killing them and feeding on their flesh we shall be
destroying our own kindred and committing wrong and
impiety.   Hence these philosophers exhorted men to
abstain from creatures that have a living soul, and they
asserted that men act impiously in " dyeing the altar of
the Immortals with hot blood."

Empedocles says:

" Will ye not cease from this ill-sounding slaughter?
See ye not that ye are devouring one another in the
unkindness of your hearts? "

And again:

" The father lifts up his own son, whose form is
changed, and sacrifices him with a prayer—infatuate
fool! The attendants hesitate to sacrifice the victim
that pleads for its life, but the father, deaf to their cries,
butchers him in his house and makes ready the evil
feast. In like manner the son lays hand upon the father,
the children upon their mother; they tear out the life
and eat the kindred flesh."

EMPEDOCLES, *frag.* 139.

Woe is me that the pitiless day of death destroyed me

not ere ever I thought of the cruel deed of devouring
with my lips!

The Banishment of the Fallen Soul

EMPEDOCLES, *frag.* 115.

There is an Oracle of Destiny, a decree of the gods
from of old, eternal, with broad oaths fast sealed: Whensoever one sinfully defiles his own hands with blood, or,
following after Strife, swears a false oath—even one
of those spirits that are heirs of everlasting life, thrice
ten thousand seasons shall he wander far from the Blessed,
being born from time to time in all manner of mortal
shapes, passing from one to another of the painful paths
of life.

For the power of the Air drives him seaward; and
Sea spews him out upon dry land; Earth casts him
into the rays of the blazing Sun, and Sun into the
eddying Air.   One from another receives him, and he
is abhorred of all.

Of these now am I also one, an exile from heaven and
a wanderer, having put my trust in raging Strife.

DIOGENES LAERTIUS viii. 77; EMPEDOCLES, *frag.* 117.

Empedocles held that the soul enters the forms of
every sort of animal and plant.   He says:
"For I have been ere now a boy and a girl, a bush,
a bird, and a dumb fish of the sea."

EMPEDOCLES, *frags.* 118, 119.

I wept and wailed when I saw the unfamiliar land.

From what honour, from what a height of bliss (was
I cast down) when I left (Olympus?) to wander here
among mortals.

PORPHYRY, *Cave of the Nymphs* 8; EMPEDOCLES, *frag.* 120.

The Pythagoreans and Plato after them called the world a cavern. In Empedocles the powers that conduct the souls say:

"We have come under this roofed-in cavern."

EMPEDOCLES, *frags.* 121, 124, 125.

. . . the joyless land, where are murder and wrath and troops of other spirits of evil, and parching plagues and putrefactions and floods roam in darkness through the meadow of Destruction.

Alack, O sorry race of mortals, race unblessed, such are the strifes and groanings wherefrom ye have been born.

From living creatures he (Strife?) made them dead, changing their forms.

PORPHYRY (STOB., *Ecl.* i. 49, 60); EMPEDOCLES, *frag.* 126.

The Fate or Nature of transmigration itself is called by Empedocles a goddess, who changes the raiment of the soul,

"Dressing (the soul) with an alien garment of flesh."

AELIAN, *On the Nature of Animals* xii. 7; EMPEDOCLES, *frag.* 127.

Empedocles says that the highest transformation for a man, if it is his lot to pass into an animal, is the lion; if into a plant, the laurel. His words are:

"Among beasts they become lions that make their lair on the mountains and couch upon the ground, and among leafy trees they become laurels."

The Purified Soul returns to God

CLEMENT OF ALEXANDRIA, *Miscellanies* iv. 150; EMPEDOCLES, *frags.* 146, 147.   Compare PINDAR, *frag.* 133 (p. 64).

Empedocles says that the souls of the wise become gods. He writes:

" And at the last they appear among men upon the earth as seers and poets and physicians and princes; and thence they spring up as gods exalted in honour, sharing the hearth of the other Immortals and the same table, free from man's woes, from destiny, and from all harm."

EMPEDOCLES, *frag.* 112. In the opening lines of the poem, addressed to his fellow-citizens of Acragas, Empedocles claims that he has himself attained the threshold of immortality described above (*frag.* 146–7). He has reached his last incarnation and has now become divine. Compare the Orphic Tablets (p. 62).

Hail! in me you see an immortal god, mortal no more.

The Body is the Tomb of the Soul

CLEMENT OF ALEXANDRIA, *Miscellanies* iii. 17; PHILOLAUS, *frag.* 14.

It is worth while to recall the expression of Philolaus, the Pythagorean, who says:

" The ancient theologians and seers bear witness that for certain purposes of punishment the soul is yoked together with the body and buried in it, as in a tomb."

PLATO, *Cratylus* 400 B.

Some say that the body (*sôma*) is the tomb (*sêma*) of the soul, as if the soul in this present life were buried; and again that it is well named *sêma* because it is the instrument by which the soul indicates (*sêmainei*) its meaning. But I think it most likely that the name was given by the followers of Orpheus, with the idea that the soul is undergoing whatever penalty it has incurred, and is enclosed in the body, as in a sort of prison-house, for safe-keeping. So the body is the place of safe-keeping (*sôma*) of the soul until the penalty it owes is discharged, and not even a letter of the name it bears need be changed.

Some Allegories of the Mystics

PLATO, *Gorgias* 492 D.

Socrates. And now tell me: you say that, if a man is to be the man he ought to be, he must not chasten his desires, but let them grow to their full strength and somehow or other provide for their satisfaction, and that this is virtue?

Callicles. Yes, I do.

Socrates. Then it is not true, as people say, that happiness consists in having no wants?

Callicles. At that rate a stone or a corpse would be happier than anybody.

Socrates. If you come to that, even on your own showing, life is a strange thing. To tell the truth I should not be surprised if Euripides were right, where he says:

" Who knows if life be death, and death be life? "

and we, perhaps, are really dead. Indeed I have heard from some wise man that in our present state we are dead and the body (*sôma*) is our tomb (*sêma*), and that that part of the soul which is the seat of the appetites is of a nature to be perpetually swayed to and fro by persuasion. Some " Sicilian wit "—or it may have been an Italian[1] —made a parable, playing on words, and called this part of the soul a jar (*pithos*), because it was so susceptible to persuasion (*pithanon*) and credulous, and the unwise (*anoëtous*) he called uninitiated (*amyetous, also meaning* " unclosed," " leaky "). In the unwise, this part of the soul where the appetites reside he compared, in respect of its intemperance and incontinence, to a jar full of holes, because it can never be filled. So, in direct opposition to your view, Callicles, he indicates that in Hades—

---

[1] The Pythagorean Philolaus.

meaning the unseen world (*aïdes*)—these uninitiate will be the most miserable of all, and will carry water into their leaky jar in a sieve equally full of holes. My friend explained that by the sieve he meant the soul. The soul of the unwise was like a sieve because it was leaky and so fickle and forgetful that it could hold nothing. These parables are certainly absurd enough; still they do illustrate my point. I want to convert you, if I can, to prefer, instead of a life of indulgence that leads to no satisfaction, an orderly life that is always content with what it has.

Man is the Chattel of the Gods

PLATO, *Phaedo* 62 A.

" Perhaps," said Socrates, " it will strike you as strange that this should be the only rule without an exception —that death should never be better than life for any man in any circumstances. It is not so in any other case. And granted that there are some for whom death is better, perhaps it seems strange to you that it should not be right for them to do this good office for themselves, but they must wait for someone else to do it for them."

Kebes laughed gently. " I should think so! " he said using an oath in his native Doric.

" Yes," said Socrates, " so stated it might seem unreasonable; but, for all that, there may be some reason in it. There is an explanation, given in a mystery, that man is as it were in a prison-house and may not set himself free nor run away from it. This saying is too high for me, it is hard to make it out. All the same, I think it is good doctrine that there are gods who look after us, and that mankind are to be counted among the chattels of the gods. Don't you agree? "

"Yes," answered Kebes.

"Well," Socrates went on, "if some creature that belonged to you were to kill itself, when you had not intimated your wish that it should die, would not you be annoyed and punish it if you could?"

"Certainly I should."

"From that point of view, then, perhaps there is reason in saying that a man must not take his own life until God sends some necessity upon him, as he has now upon me."

The Divine Justice

PLATO, *Laws* iv. 715 E.

God, as was said of old, holding the beginning and end and middle of all things that have being, in the natural course of his revolution[1] moves directly to his end. Justice ever attends him as the punisher of those who forsake the divine law; and closely following Justice, in humility and perfect orderliness, is he for whom a blessed lot is in store; whereas if any man be puffed up with boastful pride, whether of wealth or rank, or with foolish vanity of youthful beauty, and is inflamed with insolence, as one needing neither guide nor ruler, but setting up to guide others, such an one is left without God, and taking to himself others no less abandoned makes general confusion with his antics. Many will take him for a great man; but after no long time Justice exacts a full retribution, and he overturns utterly not only himself but his household and city.

[1] Apparently, the revolution of the heavens. Compare the *Phaedrus*, p. 204, below.

H

VII. HERACLEITUS AND XENOPHANES

HERACLEITUS

Heracleitus of Ephesus wrote about 500 B.C. His work, proverbial in antiquity for its obscurity, has come to us only in fragments. In some cases I have given the context in which they are quoted, but we can seldom be sure that the construction put upon them correctly represents what Heracleitus meant.

Condemnation of his Predecessors

HERACLEITUS, *frags.* 40, 57, 108.

THE learning of many things does not teach understanding; otherwise it would have taught Hesiod and Pythagoras and Xenophanes and Hecataeus.

Hesiod is the teacher of most men. They are sure he knew very many things, when he did not know day and night. For they are one.

Not one of those whose discourses I have heard has gone so far as to understand that Wisdom is apart from all

The Word (Logos)

HERACLEITUS, *frags.* 50, 1. Heracleitus claims to be the prophet of the Truth, which he calls the Word (*Logos*).

Hearkening, not to me, but to the Word, it is wisdom to confess that all things are one.

Though this Word stands for ever, men prove as unable to understand it when they first hear it as before they heard it at all. For though all things come to pass in accordance with this Word, when men have experience of words and things such as I set forth, distinguishing each thing according to its nature and explaining how it is, they seem as if they had no experience. The rest of mankind know not what they are doing when awake, just as they forget what they do in sleep.

Heracleitus' Method

HERACLEITUS, *frag.* 101. In contrast with the "learning of many things" which he condemns, Heracleitus claims to discover the Truth in himself. Our authorities explain this saying as meaning that he listened to no teacher but learnt his wisdom from himself.

I searched myself.

Wisdom is common to All

HERACLEITUS, *frags.* 113, 114, 2, 89. Though Heracleitus finds the Truth within himself, it is a Truth that is common to all.

Wisdom is common to all.

Those who speak with understanding must hold fast to (*or* strengthen themselves with) what is common to all, as a city to its law, and much more strongly. For all human laws are fed by the one divine Law. For this prevails as far as it will, and is sufficient for all, and victorious over all.

Therefore we must follow that which is common. But though the Word is common, most men live as if they had a private wisdom of their own.

The waking have one world in common; but the sleeping turn aside each into a world of his own.

The Word as Thought and Fire

HERACLEITUS, *frag.* 41. The Logos is identified with the divine Fire which passes through and governs all things.

Wisdom is one thing—to know the Thought that steers all things through all things.

Frag. 64 identifies this Thought with the eternal Fire, or "thunderbolt" of Zeus.

It is the Thunderbolt that steers the course of all things

Frag 32. Zeus or Zên is understood in the sense of *zên* = to live. Since to Heraclitus living and dying are opposite aspects of the same process, the One is willing to be called Life, and also unwilling, since Life is also Death.

The Wise is one thing only, and is willing and not willing to be called by the name of Zên.

The World is an Ever-living Fire

HERACLEITUS, *frag.* 30.

This world, the same for all, was not made by any god or man, but was always, and is, and shall be an ever living Fire, with measures of it kindling and measure being extinguished.

Birth a Misfortune ; Death a Rest

CLEMENT OF ALEXANDRIA, *Miscellanies* iii. 3; HERACLEITUS *frag.* 20.

Heracleitus at any rate seems to speak of birth as an evil, when he says:

"When they are born they wish to live and to meet with their deaths, or rather to rest; and they leave children behind them to meet their deaths."

Life is Death

CLEMENT OF ALEXANDRIA, *Miscellanies* iii. 3; HERACLEITUS *frag.* 21.

Heracleitus also, like Pythagoras and Socrates in the *Gorgias* (of Plato)[1], calls birth a death, where he says:

"All things that we see when awake are death, all things that we see in slumber are sleep."

SEXTUS EMPIRICUS, *Pyrrhon. Hyp.* iii. 230.

Heracleitus says that life and death are both in our

[1] See p. 75.

iving and in our dying; for when we are alive our souls
.re dead and buried in us, but when we die, our souls
:ome to life again and live.

Living and Dying

HERACLEITUS, *frags.* 118, 77, 36. Every birth is a death, every
death a birth. The soul, which in its purest, waking state is
fiery, sinks through the condition of sleep, in which moisture
gains upon it, to death which corresponds to the lowest ele-
mental form, earth. But even in death there is some life, which
awakens and passes up again.

The dry soul is wisest and best.

It is pleasure to souls to become moist.

It is death to souls to become water, and death to
water to become earth; but from earth comes water,
and from water soul.

Sleep is between Life and Death

CLEMENT OF ALEXANDRIA, *Miscellanies* iv. 22; HERACLEITUS,
frag. 26.

Night has been called *Euphronê*, because at that time
the soul has rest from the perceptions of sense, turns in
upon itself and has a greater share of wisdom (*phronêsis*).
Hence the mysteries are generally celebrated at night,
to indicate the withdrawal at night of the soul from the
body. . . . And what they say of sleep is to be understood
of death: both exhibit the departure of the soul, with only
a difference of degree. We find this in Heracleitus:

"Man in the night (*euphronê*) kindles a light for himself, when he has died and yet lives. In sleep, when
the vision of his eyes is quenched, he touches the dead;
when he is awake he touches the sleeping."

The River of Birth and Death

PLUTARCH, *Consolation to Apollonius* 106 e; HERACLEITUS *frag.* 88.

For when is death in us, when is it not? As Heracleitus says:

"It is the same thing in us that is alive and dead, awake and asleep, young and old. For the former shift and become the latter, and the latter shift back again and become the former."

For as out of the same clay one can mould shapes of animals and obliterate them and mould them again and so on unceasingly, so nature from the same matter formerly produced our ancestors, and then obliterated them and generated our parents, and then ourselves, and then others and yet others, round and round. The river of birth flows continually and will never stop, and so does that opposite stream of destruction which the poets call Acheron and Cocytus. So the same first cause that showed us the light of the sun, brings also the twilight of Hades. Perhaps we may see a similitude of this in the air around us, which makes alternately night and day, bringing on life and death, sleep and waking.

On the Mysteries

CLEMENT OF ALEXANDRIA, *Exhortation to the Greeks* ii. p. 18 HERACLEITUS, *frags.* 27, 14.

Indeed such rites are well-suited to night and torch-light, and worthy of . . . the Greeks, whom

"after death there await such things as they look not for."

For whom indeed does Heracleitus prophesy this?

"For night-roamers, Magians, Bacchants, Lenae initiates."

These he threatens with the things after death, for these he prophesies the fire:

"For in unholy fashion they are initiated into the mysteries practised among men."

HERACLEITUS, *frags.* 15, 5.

If it were not to Dionysus that they made procession and sang the phallic hymn, it would be a most shameless deed. But Hades is the same as Dionysus, in whose honour they rave and keep the Lenaean festival.

They purify themselves vainly by defiling themselves with blood, as if a man who had stepped into mud should wash his feet with mud. He would be thought mad, if anyone saw him doing that. And they pray to these images, as if one should talk to a house, not knowing what gods and heroes are.

There is Refreshment in Change

PLOTINUS, *Ennead* iv. 8, 1; HERACLEITUS, *frag.* 84. The context in other authors who cite the following fragments shows that "masters" means the gods. That the gods are our masters is Pythagorean doctrine (see p. 76), and the fragments can be interpreted as satire upon the ideal, implied in Pythagorean religion, of a heaven of everlasting rest and everlasting service of the gods. But the interpretation is uncertain.

Heracleitus, who urges us to this enquiry (why the soul falls at birth into a body), lays down a principle of necessary interchange between opposite conditions and speaks of a "way up and down." He says also:

"It finds refreshment in changing" and "it is weariness to labour for the same (masters) and to be ruled by them."

HERACLEITUS, *frags.* 110, 111.

It is not better for men to get all they wish for. It is sickness that makes health pleasant; evil, good; hunger, plenty; weariness, refreshment.

The Harmony of Opposites

HERACLEITUS, *frag.* 51. Heracleitus rejects the dualistic conception of the world as a battle-ground of opposite powers, one of which can be called *good*, the other *evil*, and also the conception of harmony as obtained by imposing limit upon the unmeasured conflict of extremes, *both evil*. Neither opposite is any more evil than good, for both are needed to make the "harmony" which consists in their opposite tensions; just as the bow can only be drawn by both hands pulling opposite ways. There can be no peace without strife, in which the antagonists are also perpetually doing justice upon one another.

They do not understand that what is at variance comes to terms with itself—a harmony of opposite tensions, as of the bow or the lyre.

ARISTOTLE, *Eudemian Ethics* vii. 1; HERACLEITUS, *frag.* 43 (Bywater).

Heracleitus rebuked the poet (Homer) who said: " Would that strife might pass away from among gods and men! " For there would be no harmony if there were not high and low tones, nor animals without male and female, and these are opposites.

HERACLEITUS, *frag.* 80.

We must know that War is common to all, and Strife is Justice, and that all things come into being by Strife. . . .

HERACLEITUS, *frags.* 102, 58, 67.

To God all things are fair and good and right; but men hold some things wrong and some right.

Good and evil are one.

God is day and night, summer and winter, war and peace, surfeit and hunger; but he takes various shapes, just as fire, when it is mixed with spices, is named according to the savour of each.

Man and God

HERACLEITUS, *frags.* 79, 82–83.

Man is called a baby by God, as a child is called by a man.

The most beautiful ape is ugly compared to mankind. The wisest of men, in comparison with God, will appear an ape, in wisdom, in beauty, and in all things else.

XENOPHANES

Xenophanes of Colophon (born about 565 B.C. ?) led a wandering life and was over ninety-two when he died. He wrote satires, and was regarded by the ancients as having influenced the Eleatic school of philosophy, founded by Parmenides.

Attack on Anthropomorphism

XENOPHANES, *frags.* 11, 14, 15, 16.

Homer and Hesiod have ascribed to the gods all things that among men are a shame and a reproach — theft and adultery and deceiving one another.

Mortals think that the gods are begotten, and wear clothes like their own, and have a voice and a form.

If oxen or horses or lions had hands and could draw with them and make works of art as men do, horses would draw the shapes of gods like horses, oxen like oxen; each kind would represent their bodies just like their own forms.

The Ethiopians says their gods are black and flat-nosed; the Thracians, that theirs are blue-eyed and red-haired.

[PLUTARCH] *Strom.* 4. This amounts to a denial of polytheism, since the Greeks could not conceive a multitude of gods with no degrees of rank or subordination (Zeller).

Xenophanes declares that there is no overlordship

among the gods; for it is not right to believe that a god should be subject to a master, or that any god has need of anything at all.

ARISTOTLE, *Rhetoric* ii. 23, 18. This saying implies a condemnation of all theogonies.

Xenophanes used to say: " Those who say the gods were born are just as impious as those who say they die," for in either case it follows that there is a time at which the gods do not exist.

ARISTOTLE, *Rhetoric* ii. 23, 27.

When the people of Elea asked Xenophanes whether or not they should sacrifice and make lamentation for Leucothea, he advised them, if they thought her divine, not to lament her; if human, not to sacrifice to her.

Denial of Divination

CICERO, *On Divination* i. 5.

Among the most ancient philosophers, Xenophanes was the only believer in the gods who altogether denied the existence of divination.

How to Pray

XENOPHANES, *frag.* 1.

First men, with cheerful heart, should hymn the god with reverent speech and pure words; then, after libation and prayer that we may have strength to do what is right—for that request lies nearest to hand— it is no offence to drink as much wine as a man can carry home without an attendant, supposing he be not very old. Praise for the man who, when he has drunk, sets forth famous deeds, as his memory and his voice will serve him. Let there be no tales of battles of Titans, Giants, or Centaurs, false fictions of the men of old, nor yet of civil broils—there is no profit in such things; but always to be mindful of the gods—that is good.

The One God

ARISTOTLE, *Metaphysics* i. 5. Xenophanes did not simply identify God with the visible universe, but probably meant by God a conscious animating force extended throughout the one world.

Xenophanes, the first of these adherents of the doctrine that there is only one real being (*i.e.* the Eleatic School),—for Parmenides is said to have been his disciple—made no clear statement . . . but, having regard to the whole world, he says that the One is, namely God (*or* the One is God).

XENOPHANES, *frags.* 23, 24, 25, 26.

One god, greatest among gods and men,[1] not like mortals in form, nor yet in mind.

He sees all over, thinks all over, and hears all over.

Without any trouble he sways all things by the thought of his mind.

He remains always in the same place, not moving at all; it does not befit him to move about hither and thither.

No certain Knowledge

XENOPHANES, *frag.* 34.

There never has been nor will be a man who has certain knowledge about the gods and about all the things I speak of. For even though he should happen to speak the whole truth, yet he himself does not know it; but all may have their fancy.[2]

[1] A formal and popular expression, not implying the existence of many gods.
[2] So Burnet, *Early Greek Philosophy*[3], 121, renders the last words. Others understand: "Seeming (illusion), or opinion is over all things."

VIII. THE PERSIAN WARS

The first attempt of the Persians to conquer Central Greece was made by Darius and defeated at Marathon, 490 B.C. His successor Xerxes tried again. The destruction of his fleet at Salamis (480 B.C.) was regarded by the Greeks as a judgment of heaven upon his presumption. Herodotus' narrative and Aeschylus' *Persians* are both designed to illustrate this belief.

A Warning against Presumption

HERODOTUS vii. 10. Artabanus warns his nephew Xerxes of the danger of attacking Greece.

THINK then no more of running into so great a danger when there is no necessity, but be persuaded by me to break up this meeting now, and later, when you have well considered the matter by yourself, tell us what seems to you best. I know nothing so profitable as that a man should take good counsel with himself; for then, even if his purpose be crossed, still he was none the less well advised, though he was defeated by fortune; whereas, if he is ill advised and fortune favours him, he gets a wind-fall, but he was ill advised for all that.

You see that it is always the largest animals that Heaven smites with his thunderbolt, and will not suffer them to make a show of bravery; but the small ones do not chafe his anger. You see also how his bolts fall always upon the highest houses and trees; for Heaven loves to dock the things that stand out above the rest. So also a great host is utterly destroyed by a few men, when Heaven in his jealousy sends upon them panic fear or thunder, whereby they perish unworthily. For Heaven will suffer none but himself to have high thoughts.

A deceitful Dream

HERODOTUS vii. 11ff. Xerxes at first scorns the advice of Artabanus, but then decides to take it. In a dream, however, he is threatened by a "tall and beautiful man" with ruin if he does not go to war. The dream recurs, and he asks Artabanus to put on the royal clothes, sit on the throne, and sleep in the royal bed. Then, if the dream is really sent by a god, it will come to Artabanus. Artabanus reluctantly consents. In the course of his speech, he says:

For myself I was not so much stung by your reproaches as by seeing that, when two plans were laid before the Persians, one of which would increase their pride, while the other would put an end to it by showing how harmful it is to instruct the mind to be always coveting more than one has, you chose that which was fraught with evil for yourself and for the Persians. And now that you have turned to the better course and mean to give up the expedition against Greece, you say that a dream, sent by some god, will not suffer you to lay it aside. But these things, my son, are not divine. The wandering dreams that come to men are such as I, who am older than you by many years, will tell you: whatever thoughts a man has upon his mind by day, are most likely to hover before him in the visions of his dreams; and for some days past we have had our hands full of this expedition. If, however, it be not as I suppose, but there is something divine in it, you have said all there is to say: let the dream appear to me also and give the same injunctions. But it ought not to appear any the more because I wear your clothes or sleep in your bed rather than my own, if it intends to appear at all. For this thing, whatever it may be, that visits you in your sleep, cannot surely be so far gone in simplicity as to think, when it sees me, that it is you, because I wear your clothes. What we must find out is whether it will take no account of me nor deign to appear and visit me, whether I wear your clothes or my own. For if it keeps on coming, then I too should say it was divine. . . .

(Artabanus sleeps in the king's bed and the same vision appears. It says:)

"You are the man, then, who, feigning to care for Xerxes, dissuades him from leading his armies against Greece! But neither now nor in time to come shall you attempt with impunity to turn aside what must be. As for Xerxes, he has himself been told what will happen to him if he disobeys."

In such words, Artabanus thought, the vision threatened him, and made as if to burn out his eyes with hot irons.

(Artabanus tells Xerxes of his dream and acknowledges that there is a "divine prompting," and that a "heaven-sent destruction" is overtaking Greece. The expedition is decided upon.)

The Murder of Heralds divinely punished

HERODOTUS vii. 133.

To Athens and Sparta Xerxes did not send heralds to demand earth and water. The reason was that, when Darius had formerly done so, the messengers had been thrown at Athens into the Pit, and at Sparta into a well, and bidden to take earth and water to the king from thence. What unpleasant consequence came upon the Athenians for so treating the heralds, I cannot say, except that their city and country were laid waste; but that, I believe, did not happen on this account. The Spartans, however, incurred the wrath of Talthybius, Agamemnon's herald, who has a sanctuary at Sparta, and whose descendants are the only persons privileged to act as heralds. The Spartans could obtain no good omens at their sacrifices, and this went on for a long time. In their distress, they held frequent assemblies and made proclamation inquiring whether any Spartan was willing to die for his country. Sperthias and Bulis, both men of good birth and great wealth, offered themselves to make atonement to Xerxes for his heralds who had perished; and the Spartans sent them to the Medes to die. . . . Xerxes proudly said he would not be like the Lacedaemonians, who had violated the common customs of all mankind by putting heralds to death. He would not do himself what he blamed in them, nor would he absolve the Lacedaemonians from their guilt by killing the men in return.

This conduct of the Spartans caused the wrath of Talthybius to cease for a time, though Sperthias and Bulis came home alive. But long afterwards, as the Lacedaemonians declare, it awoke once more in the war between Athens and the Peloponnese.[1] This seems to me one of the clearest cases of divine intervention. That the wrath of Talthybius should be visited upon envoys and should not cease till it had worked itself out, was no more than justice; but that it should fall upon the sons of those very men who were sent to the king on account of the wrath, namely on Nicolaus, son of Bulis, and Aneristus, son of Sperthias, seems to me plain proof of divine action.

The Delphic Oracle before Salamis

HERODOTUS vii. 140.

The Athenians sent to Delphi to consult the oracle. The envoys had hardly completed the customary rites and taken their seats in the outer chamber of the temple,

[1] In 430 B.C.

when the Pythian priestess, Aristonike by name, gave this response:

"Miserable men! why sit ye here? Flee to the ends of the earth and leave your homes and the heights of your wheel-shaped city, for there is no soundness in head or in body, neither in feet nor hands nor middle, but all is faint. Fire and the fierce War-god, in the track of a Syrian chariot, wreck your city, and many other towers besides yours shall he destroy, and give to the flames many temples of the Immortals, who even now stand streaming with sweat and shaking with fear, fore-seeing inevitable woe, while black blood flows over the high roofs.

"Begone from the shrine, and let your thoughts dwell upon misfortune!"

Hearing this, the envoys were much distressed and gave themselves up in despair at this prophecy of evil. Then Timon, a man of mark at Delphi, advised them to take an olive-branch and consult the oracle again as suppliants. The Athenians took his advice and said: "O king, have respect to these boughs of supplication and give us some better answer about our country, or we will not leave the shrine, but stay here until we die." Upon this the priestess gave them a second answer:

"Pallas has not power to appease Olympian Zeus altogether, with her many prayers and wise counsel. Yet I will speak to thee once again in words firm as adamant. When all else is taken that lies within the boundary of Cecrops and the valley of divine Cithaeron, Zeus grants to Athene that the wooden wall alone shall not be overthrown; and that shall profit thee and thy children.

"Wait not quietly for the horsemen or the great host

of footmen marching on land, but turn thy back and give place: the day shall yet come when thou shalt meet them face to face.

" O divine Salamis, thou shalt destroy the children of women, either at the scattering or at the gathering of the Corn Goddess."[1]

This answer seemed (as indeed it was) milder than the former, and the envoys wrote it down and went back to Athens. When they reported it to the Assembly, however, many different opinions arose as to its meaning. Two, in particular, were in complete conflict. Some of the older men said they thought the god meant that the acropolis would be spared, understanding the ' wooden wall' to be the palisade which had defended the acropolis in old days. Others said that the god meant the ships, and advised that these should be made ready and everything else abandoned. This latter opinion was upset by the last two lines of the oracle, which the interpreters took to mean that, if they prepared for a sea-battle, they would be defeated off Salamis.

Now there was a man who had lately come to the front at Athens, whose name was Themistocles, called the son of Neocles. He said that the interpreters had not understood the whole oracle rightly: if this line really referred to Athens, it would not have been so mildly put. It would have been ' Wretched Salamis' rather than ' Divine Salamis,' if its settlers had been destined to perish there. Rightly understood, the oracle was directed against the enemy, not against Athens. The wooden wall was the

---

[1] This phrase is generally taken to mean "at sowing or at harvest." Macan suggests, however, that it might refer to the assembling or dispersing of the worshippers at Demeter's Mysteries at Eleusis, which did coincide with the battle of Salamis.

I

ships; and he advised them to prepare for a battle at sea.

The Athenians decided that Themistocles' explanation was to be preferred to that of the interpreters.

The Story of Dicaeus and Demarêtus

HERODOTUS viii. 64.

So, after this skirmish of words, the captains made ready, according to Eurybiades' decision, to fight where they were, at Salamis. The morning broke, and at sunrise there was an earthquake felt both on land and at sea. The Greeks resolved to make prayer to the gods and to call the sons of Aeacus to their aid. And they did as they had resolved; for, after praying to all the gods, they not only invoked Ajax and Telamon from Salamis where the Greeks were, but also sent a ship to Aegina to fetch Aeacus himself and his other sons.[1]

There was a story told by Dicaeus, son of Theocydes, an Athenian who was at that time in exile and held in some esteem by the Medes. When Attica had been abandoned by the Athenians and was laid waste by the land army of Xerxes, Dicaeus chanced to be with Demarêtus the Lacedaemonian in the Thriasian Plain, and he saw, moving from Eleusis, a cloud of dust such as a host of thirty thousand men might raise. While they were wondering who the men might be who made the dust, suddenly he heard the sound of voices, and it seemed to him that they were singing the mystic hymn to Dionysus. Demarêtus, who was ignorant of the rites of Eleusis, asked him what it could be that made the sound. Dicaeus answered: " Demarêtus, it is certain that some great calamity will fall upon the king's host. For, since Attica is deserted, manifestly it is something

[1] *I.e.* images of these heroes.

more than mortal, coming from Eleusis to avenge the
Athenians and their allies. If it descends upon the
Peloponnese, there will be peril for the king himself and
his land army; but if it turns towards the ships at Salamis,
the king will be in danger of losing his fleet. This feast
is held by the Athenians every year for the Mother and
the Maid, and any Athenian or other Greek who wishes
is initiated. The sound you hear is the song of Iacchos
which they sing at this festival." And Demarêtus answered, " Hold your peace and tell no man of this matter,
for if these words should come to the king's ears, you will
lose your head, and neither I nor any man living will
be able to save you. Keep your own counsel, and the gods
will see to this army." And while Demarêtus was giving
this advice, the dust where the sound was rose aloft in a
cloud and moved towards Salamis, making for the camp
of the Greeks. So they knew that the fleet of Xerxes
would surely perish.

An Oracle of Bakis

HERODOTUS viii. 77.

I cannot dispute the truth of oracles or feel disposed
to call them in question when they are clearly expressed,
having regard to these words:

" When with mad hope, after ravaging shining Athens,
they shall bridge with ships the sacred strand of Artemis
of the Golden Weapon and sea-washed Cynosura, then
shall divine Justice quell the child of Insolence, strong
Presumption, when he raves terribly and thinks to swallow
all things up. The swords of bronze shall meet in battle,
and Ares shall empurple the sea with blood. Then shall
the son of Cronos, whose eye is over all, and Victory
bring the day of freedom for Hellas."

When Bakis speaks so clearly as this, I cannot venture to say anything against oracles, nor can I allow others to dispute them.

Non Nobis

HERODOTUS viii. 109. At a council of war after Salamis, the Peloponnesian captains refused to pursue the remnant of Xerxes' fleet and to cut the bridge across the Hellespont.

When Themistocles saw that he could not persuade the greater part of them to sail to the Hellespont, he turned to the Athenians, who, above all the rest, were grieved at the enemy's escape and were eager to take it upon themselves to sail to the Hellespont, if the others would not.   He said to them:

" I have often seen beaten men, when things were driven to desperation, renew the fight and retrieve their former mishap; and others have told me of many more cases where this has happened. Now we have had a stroke of great good fortune in driving back so great a cloud of men, and saving ourselves and Hellas. Let us not then pursue the fugitives. It is not we who have achieved this work, but gods and heroes who were jealous that one man should be king both of Asia and of Europe, and he a man of impious presumption, who holds things sacred and profane in the like esteem, who sets fire to the images of the gods and throws them down, who caused even the sea to be beaten with rods and fetters to be cast into it. For the present all is well with us, and it is better that we should stay in Greece now and look to ourselves and our households. Let every man now repair his house and sow his fields diligently, after driving away the last of the barbarians; and with the spring let us make sail for the Hellespont and Ionia."

Themistocles, in saying this, meant to make favour with the Persian, in order that he might have somewhere to turn, if any mischance should overtake him at Athens, —as indeed afterwards happened.

The Harvest of Presumption

AESCHYLUS, *Persians* 739, 799. The Ghost of Darius, evoked by his Queen Atossa and the Persian Elders, is informed of the defeat of his son Xerxes at Salamis.

Ghost. Alas, the oracles' fulfilment has come swiftly indeed, and upon my son the end foretold of heaven has fallen by the hand of Zeus. Long have I been assured that the gods would somehow bring it to pass; but when a man's own feet are hurrying to destruction, heaven also lends him speed. . . .

Not even the host that now remains in the parts of Hellas shall return in safety.

Elders. What? Does not the whole Persian army pass Helle's strait from Europe?

Ghost. Nay, but a few of all that number, if, looking to what is now accomplished, we must put faith in that which is foretold of heaven; for all is coming true.

They abide in the plain watered by Asopus' stream, that feeds the land of the Boeotians with welcome fatness. There the very height of suffering hangs over them and threatens recompense for their presumption and godless spirit; who, when they came to Hellas, spared not to despoil the images of gods and to burn their temples. Altars have been cast down, and shrines of divinities overthrown from their foundations in heaps of ruin.

Therefore, having done evil, they suffer in like measure, and yet more awaits them; they have not touched the bottom of the well of sorrows; still is it gushing forth. So thick shall the blood of their slaughter lie upon the earth of Plataea under the spear of the Dorians, that heaps of dead shall, even to the third generation, bear voiceless witness to men's eyes that no mortal may think thoughts that are too high for him.

For when the flower of pride has blossomed, death is the fruit that ripens, and all the harvest reaped is tears.

IX. THE ZEUS OF AESCHYLUS

The Gifts of Prometheus. Zeus and Destiny

AESCHYLUS, *Prometheus Bound* 436.

Prometheus. Not in disdain and not in obduracy
    Have I kept silence: nay, my thoughts devour me,
    To see myself thus made a mockery of.
    O these new gods! who was it, who but I,
    That dealt to each his own appurtenance?
    But peace to that: I speak not unto those
    From whom these things are hidden. Now consider
    The sore estate of men, how witless once
    And weak they were, until I lodged in them
    Reason, and gave them hearts to understand.
    I speak not to discover man's defect,
    But how my gifts consorted with their need.
    For first they saw and gat no good of seeing,
    They heard and heard not: all their life they seem'd
    To move as in a dream, shape mixed with shape
    Confusedly, at hazard; and they knew not
    Houses that took the sun, brick-woven or wood,
    But burrowing huddled, like to wind-borne ants,
    Far down in holes beyond all reach of day.
    And no sure sign of winter had they found,
    Neither of spring, the flowery time, nor summer,
    The time of gathering. Foot and hand they plied
    Without discernment, till the day I showed them
    The rising of the stars, and how to spell
    The vanishing thereof, hard lore. Moreover

Number, the chiefest artifice of all
And subtlest, I devised for them, and joinings
Of letters, whereby the remembrance lives
Of all things, and the craft of lovely words.
And my hand first yoked with a yoke great beasts,
That, thong-bound or bestridden, they might do
Vile service, and the seed of men to these
Transfer their travail's worst. To wheelèd frames
I fasten'd horses, patient of the rein,
The glory of affluence that flowers in pride.
And none save I it was contrived those hulls
With wings of linen, wherein sea-farers
Go to and fro in the great field of the waves.
All these devices I devised for men,
But for myself am beggar'd of conceit,
To escape the pain that now is come upon me.

Chorus. A strange thing is befallen thee! where are they,
Thy wits? thou'rt lost, and like a sorry leech
Fall'n sick, thou staggerest, impotent to hit
The medicine that shall meet thine own disease.

Prometheus. Hearken the rest, and thou wilt wonder more,
Such arts and ways my wisdom reached unto.
And this in chief: did any man fall sick,
Was no deliverance, either in things eaten,
Plaster or potion, but their sap and substance
Dwindled for lack of medicine, till I taught them
The sage commixtures of beneficent balms,
For all disorders sovereign. I defined
Ways many of divination: also dreams
I first did spell, discerning which foreshadow'd
Matter of truth. I made men understand
Inapprehensible voices: ominous
Conjunctions by the way, the curious flight

Of those crook-footed tribes of the air, all this
I bodied forth exactly, which be birds
Of nature favourable, which malign,
How each is wont to fare, and mutually
What hates they have, what leagues and fellowship.
Further of slain beasts' inward parts I taught
The perfect feature, and what hue presenting
They gain propitious gods, and how the gall
Must show a lobe diverse for fair aspect.
The shanks, uproll'd in fat, by fire I questioned,
With the long chine, and led the mind of man
To thrid the labyrinthine mysteries
Of a dim art; the oracular face of fire
Look'd with clear eyes, that heretofore were scaled.
Such my lore was: but what the earth contained
Of secret things, helpful to man, brass, iron,
Silver and gold,—can any stand to say
He did prevent me, finding them? Nay, none,
I am sure, unless he loose his tongue in folly.
Let one brief word conclude the whole in sum,—
All arts men have by the Provider [1] come.

Chorus. Yet be not prodigal of care to men,
Cold to thine own distresses. O, my hope
Bears well that thou shalt presently behold
These chains unbolted and thyself in power
No whit inferior to Zeus.

Prometheus.   Not yet
Lies in the scope of all-dispensing doom
That consummation: first with thousand throes
And aches must all be plied, ere loosing come.
Strong truly is craft, but stronger far is Fate. [2]

[1] Prometheus = the provident one.
[2] Literally "Necessity."

Chorus. And of strong Fate who has the helm, and steers?

Prometheus. The Three Weird Queens, the Avengers who forget not.[1]

Chorus. And Zeus, thou say'st, is less in might than these?

Prometheus. Whatso stands written Zeus cannot escape.

Chorus. Stands aught for him, but to reign on and on?

Prometheus. Lo, there thy quest must end.   Urge me no farther.

Chorus. Some wonderful burden sure thy heart enfolds!

Prometheus. Find thee another argument: this thing
  The time is nowise come to utter: nay,
  It must be hid full deep; for, so I hold it,
  My bonds and shame and anguish are no more.

E. R. Bevan.

The Government of the World

Aeschylus, *Suppliants* 86.

First Voice

O might we know beyond all doubt
What Zeus would—

Second Voice

        Nay, past searching out!
God's will before our human sight
Shines against blackest foil of night
Only with dull and smouldering light.

First Voice

But all effects his will intends
Fall to safe undefeated ends.

---

[1] Literally "the three Fates and the *Erinyes* (avenging spirits) who forget not."

SECOND VOICE

Tangled in gloomy thickets blind
And close beyond discerning wind
The dark ways of his secret mind.

THE WHOLE CHORUS

From towering Hope's ambitious height
    Down to Perdition's blackest pit
        He hurls the aspiring thoughts of Man,
            Yet stirs not, yet exerts no force:
Calm in his will's enabled might
    His throned imaginations sit,
        And see the World's harmonious Plan
            Move onward in its ordered course.

So let his eyes behold and see
    On earth now what intemperate sin,
        What violent heats of froward youth
            The old evil stock buds forth again!
Thus amorous and athirst for me,
    With heart's own folly spurred within
        To madness,—and the mocked heart's ruth
            Repentant in its ruinous train!

                                    WALTER HEADLAM.

The Sufferings and Reward of Io

AESCHYLUS, *Suppliants* 524. The daughters of Danaus,
descendants of Io, returning to her native land, Argos, pray
for protection from their pursuers, the sons of Aegyptus. The
ancient legend was that Io had been beloved by Zeus, trans-
formed into a cow, watched by the hundred-eyed Argos, and
driven over the world by a gad-fly. Professor Murray writes: [1]
"To a cultivated Ionian such conceptions must have belonged

[1] *The Rise of the Greek Epic*, 1907, p. 247. I quote his translation and comments. A verse translation is in Walter Headlam,
A Book of Greek Verse, 1907, p. 77.

to the very lowest regions of 'Pelasgian' folly. They had been expurgated from Homer centuries back. Yet out of that unpromising material Aeschylus extracts something which is not only genuine religious thought, but, to my feeling, even somewhat sublime thought. The love of Zeus leads its object through unearthly shame and suffering to a strange and overwhelming reward. We cannot understand. But Zeus is bound by no law but his own supreme will. He has always his own great purpose, and he moves towards it by inscrutable ways. . . ."

CHORUS

Lord of lords, blessed among the blessed, of perfection's most perfect strength, O happy Zeus, hear us, and let it be! Shield us from the pride of man, whom thou righteously abhorrest, and whelm in the dark-blue deep our black prison-house.[1] Look upon the woman's cause; look on the race born of old from the woman whom thou didst love, and make new the joyous tale. Be a rememberer of many things, O thou whose hand was laid on Io. Lo, we are beings born of thy race, though sent from this land to dwell afar.

I walk again in the print of ancient feet, where our mother was watched, moving among the flowers; the meadow of kine, whence Io fled, sea-tossed by a burning pain, knowing not her desire, to pass through many tribes of men. . . .

Her wide wanderings are then described, across the Hellespont, through Asia southwards, till she reaches at last 'the all-pasturing garden of Zeus, the snow-fed meadow visited by the whirling giant of the desert-sand, and the water of Nile untouched by sickness.' . . .

And men that had then their habitation in the land, their hearts were shaken with fear at the strange sight, a Being agonised, half-human, part of the race of kine and part of woman. They marvelled at the mystery.

[1] *I.e.* the ship of their pursuers.

Who was it that brought her peace in the end, her the far-wandering, the afflicted, the gadfly-goaded Io?

He who ruleth through ages of unresting life, Zeus [to whom years are as yesterday]. The unwounding strength of a hand, the breath of a god, gave rest to her, and her heart flowed in a sad tenderness of tears. The word of true promise became a divine seed within her, and she bore a blameless child, through ages long perfect in happiness.

Whom of gods shall I praise for works more justified? Father, planter of the garden, worker with the hand, and Lord, thinker of ancient thought, great builder of our race, Zeus, whose breath maketh all accomplishment!

He hasteth not at the command of another. Being stronger than all, he maketh great the weak. None sitteth above him, and he honoureth none. And the deed and the word are present as one thing, to despatch that end whereto the counselling mind moveth.

GILBERT MURRAY

Zeus teaches Wisdom by Suffering

AESCHYLUS, *Agamemnon* 170.

  Zeus, whosoe'er indeed he be,—
   In that name so it please him hear,—
  Zeus, for my help is none but he;—
  Conjecture through creation free
   I cast, and cannot find his peer;
  With this strange load upon my mind
  So burdening, only Zeus I find
   To lift and fling it sheer.

  One was that ruled the ring of yore,[1]—

[1] This stanza refers to the dynasties of the gods: Uranus overthrown by Cronos, Cronos by Zeus. See p. 20.

With boisterous challenge big and blown;
Him tell we not, his date is o'er;—
    Nay, the next comer is no more,—
    Found his outwrestler, and was thrown:—
But Zeus, with heart and voice acclaim
Victorious his triumphal name,
    And wisdom is thine own!

Sing praise; *'Tis he hath guided*, say,
Men's feet in wisdom's way,
Stablishing fast Instruction's rule
That Suffering be her school :—
The heart in time of sleep renews
Aching remembrance of her bruise,
And chastening wisdom enters wills that most refuse;
Stern is the grace and forcèd mercy kind
By Spirits upon their awful bench assigned.

                                WALTER HEADLAM.

Troy overthrown for the Sin of Paris

AESCHYLUS, *Agamemnon* 367.

O Zeus the King of Heaven! O Night,
With so great splendour and so bright
        Possessed, O friendly Night!
On Troy's renowned high towers was cast
Thy snare, a net so close and fast
        As neither great nor small
Should leap the immense enslaving woof:
Doom's divine drag-net, huge and proof,
        At one sweep took them all!
Be Lord Zeus of the Stranger's board
For author of this act adored:

His bolt on Alexander [1] bent
Was aimed so long as neither sent
Over the stars nor early spent
      To light with idle fall.

" *Struck by the hand of Zeus!* " ay, truth indeed,
And traceable: 'tis the act of will decreed
And purpose. Under foot when mortals tread
Fair lovely Sanctities, the gods, one said,
The easy gods are careless:—'twas profane!
Here are sin's wages manifest and plain,
The sword's work on that swelled presumptuousness,
With affluent mansions teeming in excess,
Beyond Best Measure:—best, and sorrow-free,
The wise well-dowered mind's unharmed Sufficiency!
      The Rich man hath no tower,
        Whose Pride, in Surfeit's hour,
        Kicks against high-enthroned Right
      And spurns her from his sight.

Child of designing Ate's deadly womb,
The wretch Temptation drives him to his doom.
Then cure is all in vain. The vice he wears
He cannot hide; sinister gleam declares
His mischief; as base metal at the touch
And trial of the stone, he showeth smutch
(This fond man like a child a-chase of wings),
And the awful taint on all his people brings:
To prayers is not an ear in Heaven; one frown
All conversant with such calls guilty and pulls down.
      Such Paris was, that ate
      Within the Atridae's gate,

        [1] Paris' other name.

And then disgraced the Stranger's bread
By theft of woman wed.

WALTER HEADLAM.

Not Prosperity, but Sin, breeds Misery

AESCHYLUS, *Agamemnon* 749.

There is an ancient proverb men will preach
 As framed by wisdom of old time,
That prosperous Fortune, let him only reach
 To full estate and prime,
Hath issue, dies not childless; waxen so,
Weal for his heir begets unsated Woe.

  But single in the world I hold
  A doctrine different from the old:
  Not Weal it is, but Sinful Deed
  More sinners after him doth breed
  Formed in his image; none the less
  Doth lovely offspring always bless
  The house that follows Righteousness.

Old Insolence in the evil sort of men
Young Insolence will gender, then or then,
When dawns the appointed hour, a Fiend of gloom
  For penance violent, unwithstood,
  Flushed with such reckless Hardihood
   That sin's dark ruinous Doom
   In black storm on the roof shall rage,—
The latter offspring like his parentage.

But Righteousness to the upright heart inclines;
Bright beneath smoky rafters her light shines:
Gilt-spangled halls where hands guilt-spotted are,

Swift with averted eyes forsakes,
Thence to the pure her blessing takes,
To that false lauded star,
The Power of Riches, will not bend,
But guideth all things to their proper end.

WALTER HEADLAM.

Zeus is All Things

AESCHYLUS, *Heliades, frag.* 70.

Zeus is air, Zeus is earth, Zeus is heaven;
Zeus is all things and whatsoever is higher than all things.

The Olympian Zeus of Phidias

PAUSANIAS V. xi.

The god is seated on a throne: he is made of gold and ivory: on his head is a wreath made in imitation of sprays of olive. In his right hand he carries a Victory, also of ivory and gold: she wears a ribbon, and on her head a wreath. In the left hand of the god is a sceptre, curiously wrought in all the metals: the bird perched on the sceptre is the eagle. The sandals of the god are of gold, and so is his robe. On the robe are wrought figures of animals and the lily flowers. The throne is adorned with gold and precious stones, also with ebony and ivory; and there are figures painted and images wrought on it. . . .

I know that the measurements of the height and breadth of Zeus at Olympia have been recorded, but I cannot commend the men who took the measurements. For even the measurements they mention fall far short of the impression made by the image on the spectator. Why, the god himself, they say, bore witness to the art of

K

Phidias.   For when the image was completed Phidias
prayed that the god would give a sign if the work was
to his mind, and straightway, they say, the god hurled
a thunderbolt into the ground at the spot where the bronze
urn stood down to my time.

J. G. FRAZER.

STRABO viii. p. 354.

It is related that Panaenus (Phidias' nephew, a painter
who helped to paint the image) asked Phidias after what
model he intended to make his image of Zeus.   Phidias
replied: After the image expressed by Homer in these
lines: " The son of Cronos spoke and nodded with his
dark brow; and the ambrosial locks waved from the
king's immortal head, and he shook great Olympus"
(*Iliad* i. 527).

QUINTILIAN, *Inst. Orat.* 12, 10.

Phidias' representations of gods are said to have been
superior in point of art to his representations of men:
if he had made nothing but the Athena at Athens and
the Olympian Zeus in Elis, he would still have had no
rival in ivory.   The majesty of the Zeus so rises to the
level of its subject that its beauty may be thought to have
added something to traditional religion.

X. PINDAR, BACCHYLIDES, SOPHOCLES

PINDAR

The Feast of Tantalus

PINDAR, *Olympian* i. 23. Celebrating a victory in the horse-race at Olympia, won in 476 B.C. by Hiero, tyrant of Syracuse, Pindar tells the story of Pelops, whose father Tantalus was said to have boiled him and served his flesh at a banquet to the gods on Mount Sipylus in Asia Minor. The child was restored to life by being put back into the cauldron. His shoulder, which a goddess had unwittingly eaten, was replaced with ivory. Pindar rejects this scandalous myth (he could not detect its origin in some ceremony of rebirth or initiation), substitutes the rape of the youth Pelops for the eating of the baby, and gives a different reason for the punishment of Tantalus.

Bright shines the fame of Hiero in the home of fair manhood, whither Lydian Pelops came from far to dwell.

Pelops was beloved of Poseidon who holds the Earth in his strong embrace, when Clotho had taken him out of the pure cauldron, and he was furnished with a bright shoulder of ivory.

Surely wonders are many, and peradventure mortal report goes somewhat beyond the true account. Tales inwrought with jewelled fantasy deceive us altogether. The Grace of poetry, who fashions all things flattering-sweet for mortal men, gilding them with her worth, contrives that even the unbelievable thing shall often be believed. But the days that come after are the wisest witnesses. In truth it is fitting for man to tell of gods only what is of good report; for the blame is less.

Son of Tantalus, concerning thee I will gainsay the ancient story, and tell how, when thy father called the gods to that most lawful feast upon his own Sipylus, giving them a banquet in return for theirs, then the Lord of the Shining Trident ravished thee away; for his heart was subdued by longing to carry thee upon his golden chariot to the most high house of Zeus who is worshipped in all lands; whither also Ganymede came afterwards to serve Zeus in the like manner.

And when thou hadst vanished away, and men sought long but brought thee not to thy mother, some envious neighbour presently began to say in secret that they had cut thee limb by limb with a knife into bubbling water boiling with fire, and at the last course had divided thy flesh and eaten thereof.

But for me it is impossible to call one of the Blessed Ones a cannibal. I stand aloof. Great loss falls often to evil-speakers.

If ever mortal man was honoured by the Watchers of Olympus, that man was Tantalus. But he could not brook the surfeit of his great prosperity, but incurred the punishment of blind folly, the unwieldy stone which the Father hung over him. Desiring ever to ward this from his head, he is banished from joy. And he has this helpless life of abiding pain, with the other three that suffer,[1] because he stole from the Immortals nectar and ambrosia, whereby they had made him incorruptible, and gave them to his fellows at a feast.

If a man think that he does anything unseen of heaven, he is deceived.

Therefore the Immortals thrust out his son to be once more among the generations of men who quickly die.

[1] Tityus, Sisyphus, and Ixion.

The Gods do not fight one another

PINDAR, *Olympian* ix. 28.

By inborn genius men are destined to become brave and wise. How else could Heracles have wielded his club against the trident, when Poseidon stood before Pylos and pressed him hard? Hard too was his battle with the silver bow of Phoebus, and with Hades who lifted against him the wand wherewith he leads mortal forms down the hollow way of the dead.

O my lips, cast away this word! Hateful is this poets' lore that speaks slander against the gods, and the sound of untimely boasting is a burden to the song of madness. Cease from this vain babbling; far from the Immortals leave all war and battle.

Desire not the Life of an Immortal

PINDAR, *Pythian* iii. 59. Asclepius, son of Apollo by a mortal mother, was blasted for presuming to raise a man from the dead.

It is best to seek from heaven things fitting for a spirit that is mortal, knowing what lies before us at our feet, and to what portion we are born.

O my soul, set not thy desire upon the life of an immortal; but use to the full the power that is within thy compass.

What is Man?

PINDAR, *Pythian* viii. 88.

He who wins fresh glory in his tender youth, soars high in hope. Achievement worthy of a man lends wings to uplift his thought above low cares for wealth.

In a little while the delight of man waxes to its height;

and in a little while it falls to the ground, shaken by adverse fate.

Creatures of a day, what is a man? what is he not? Man is the dream of a shadow.

Only, when a gleam of sunshine comes as a gift from heaven, a light rests upon men and life is smooth.

Seek not to become a Zeus

PINDAR, *Isthmian* v. 11.

The might of men is decided according to their inborn gifts. Two things alone there are that, where wealth blossoms, feed the sweetest flower of life: comfort and good report.

Seek not to become a Zeus. If a share of these good things fall to thy lot, thou hast everything. Men must die; things that must die befit them.

The Jealousy of Heaven

PINDAR, *Isthmian* vii. 31. This ode celebrates a victory of Strepsiades, whose uncle of the same name, son of Diodotus, had fallen in battle for Thebes, Pindar's own city. The change to good fortune in this victory at the Games of Poseidon (the "Holder of the Earth"), leads Pindar to deprecate the jealousy of heaven.

So thou, son of Diodotus, following the praise of warrior Meleager and of Hector too, by Amphiaraus' shrine in the fair flower of thine age gavest up thy spirit in the vanward press of battle, where the bravest bare up the feud of war with the hopes of despair.

The grief I suffered none can tell; but now the Holder of Earth hath granted me fair shining after storm. I will fit garlands to my hair and sing.

Only may not that jealousy of the Immortals trouble

what pleasant thing soever for a day I follow, as calmly I go toward age and on to the term of days appointed. For all alike we die; but our destiny in life is unequal; and if a man lift his eyes to that which is afar off, too weak is he to reach the bronze floor of the gods' high seat. Even so winged Pegasus flung off his lord, when he was fain to come unto the mansions of the sky and to stand, he, Bellerophon, in the conclave of Zeus. For that which is sweet beyond lawful measure there waits an ending very bitter.

But to us, O Loxias with thy wealth of golden hair, grant at Pytho too, in thine own contests, a fair crown of flowers!

With Heaven are the Ends of All Things

PINDAR, *Pythian* ii. 49.

Heaven accomplishes every end according to his expectation. He overtakes the wings of the eagle and outstrips the dolphin in the sea. He bows down the head of the proud, and gives to another glory that grows not old.

Fortune and Hope

PINDAR, *Olympian* xii. 1.

Daughter of Zeus the Deliverer, O Saviour Fortune, keep watch, I pray, over wide-ruling Himera. Thy power is upon sea and land; by thee swift ships are piloted; and thou guidest men in the assemblies of peace and in the counsels of sudden war.

To and fro toss the hopes of man, cleaving the waste foam-drift of a perfidious sea. No man upon earth has found a sure token from heaven of how it shall fare with him. Warnings of what will come are wrapt in blind darkness.

Gods and Men are of One Kindred

PINDAR, *Nemean* vi. 1.

Of one kindred, one only, are men and gods, and of one mother do we both draw our breath; but by difference of power we are utterly divided: man is a thing of nought, but for the gods the bronze floor of heaven stands as a seat unshaken for ever.

Nevertheless we bear some likeness to the Immortals, either in greatness of spirit or in bodily form; although we know not where, from day to day or in the night watches, it is written by fate that we should end our course.

The Destiny of Man

PINDAR, *Nemean* xi. 37.

The ancient virtue of a race yields its crop of strong men in alternate generations. The dark plough-lands give not their harvests continuously; and not in every circling year will the trees bear equal wealth of fruit in their fragrant blossom, but only in alternation.

Even so is the race of mortal men driven by the wind of Destiny, and from Zeus no clear sign comes to attend their course. Yet, none the less, we embark on the proud ship of manhood, straining after great achievements; for importunate Hope has chained our limbs,[1] while the flowing tides of foreknowledge are far away.

The hunter after gain should seek it in due measure. Too sharp are the onsets of madness that come of unattainable desires.

---

[1] As a galley-slave, chained to the oar (Fennell).

BACCHYLIDES

The Perils of Hope

BACCHYLIDES, *Odes of Victory* iii. 63. For a victory of Hiero, tyrant of Syracuse, 468 B.C. Bacchylides has told the story of Croesus, rescued by the gods from the pyre where he meant to burn himself after the fall of Sardis, and translated by Apollo to the land of the Hyperboreans on account of his rich gifts to Delphi.

But of all that now live in Hellas, there is none shall say that he has sent to Apollo more gold than thou, illustrious Hiero.

A man whose heart feeds not on envious thoughts may well praise the favourite of heaven, the warrior who delights in horses, who holds the sceptre of Zeus the god of Justice and has fellowship with the Muses of the violet locks. . . .

But treacherous is the Hope that creeps into the hearts of men who live but for a day. The lord Apollo said to Admetus:

" Thou art mortal, and there are two thoughts that thou must cherish together: that to-morrow's sunlight will be the last that thou shalt see; or that for fifty years thou wilt live out thy life in abundance of wealth. So long as thy acts are righteous, be of a cheerful spirit: that is the chiefest gain."

I speak words of meaning for the wise. The heights of the air no rank mist taints; the waters of the sea are incorrupt; gold is a delight; but man cannot pass by hoary age and win back the strength of his youth.

Yet the light of prowess wanes not with the mortal body; it is cherished by the Muse.

SOPHOCLES

The Laws of Heaven

SOPHOCLES, *Antigone* 446.

Creon. Now, tell me thou: didst thou know an edict had forbidden this? Thy answer in few words!

Antigone. I knew it. How should I not? It was for all men's ears.

Creon. And thy daring overstepped this law?

Antigone. Even so; it came not as proclaimed by Zeus; nor yet does the Justice who dwells with the gods beneath set among mankind such laws as this. And I found not such strength in thy decrees, as that a mortal should override the unwritten statutes of heaven, that cannot fail. Their life is not of to-day or yesterday, but from all time, and no man knows the date when first it dawned.

SOPHOCLES, *Oedipus the King* 863. In *Athens, an Ode,* Swinburne incorporates a rendering of lines sung by the Chorus in this play. He refers to Antigone.

Yea in her was all the prayer fulfilled, the saying
   All accomplished: *Would that fate would let me wear*
Hallowed innocence of words and all deeds, weighing
  Well the laws thereof, begot on holier air,
Far on high sublimely stablished, whereof only
  Heaven is father; nor did birth of mortal mould
Bring them forth, nor shall oblivion lull to lonely
  Slumber. Great in these is God, and grows not old.

A. C. SWINBURNE.

Never to be born is best

SOPHOCLES, *Oedipus at Colonus* 1225.

Never to be born is, past all reckoning, best; next best, by far, when a man has come into the world, that, as soon as may be, he should return thither whence he came.

For when the days of his youth are gone, and the foolish delights thereof are fled away, the stroke of affliction smites him and spares not; he is weary and has no rest from envy and strife, faction and warfare, and the shedding of blood.

And at the last his portion is old age, abhorred of all men, for that it is weak and has no friend or comrade, but dwells alone with all things evil.

The Curse on the House of Oedipus

SOPHOCLES, *Antigone* 582. The word translated "doom" is *atê*, which has also the sense of the infatuate blindness of a person under a curse. In line 604 I understand *konis* to mean a storm of dust. Compare the story of Dicaeus, p. 94.

Blest is their portion whose life has not tasted of evil. For when a house is shaken from heaven, for them their doom fails not evermore, creeping down the long line of their race; as when, blown by the ocean blasts of tempest from the north, a surge o'erruns the dark depth under the sea; up from the abyss it rolls black ooze, and the shores that front its breaking blow boom, moaning in the storm.

From of old, in the house of the sons of Labdacus, I see sorrow upon sorrow of the dead falling ever; generation frees not generation; but some god wrecks them, and they have no release. For now when above the last root of the house of Oedipus the light had been spread abroad, down, in its turn, is it swept and smothered by dust of a murderous storm from the nether gods, blindness of reason and avenging madness.

Thy power, O Zeus, what human trespass can restrain? The power which neither Sleep, that ensnares all else, can take, nor the untiring months of heaven; but thou, supreme in lordship that ages not with time, holdest the dazzling splendour of Olympus. And for the future, near and far, as through the past, this law shall have strength to prevail: Nothing that is exceeding great moves in the life of mortals save under a doom.

For that far-roving Hope, though many men have comfort of her, to many is a delusion of light-thoughted desires; and he whom she haunts knows nought till he burn his foot against hot fire. For with wisdom hath one [1] given forth the famous saying, that, soon or late, evil seems good to him whose mind heaven draws to his doom; and from the blindness of that doom his act is clear only for a moment's span.

The State of Man

SOPHOCLES, *Ajax* 118. The mad Ajax has just left the stage, boasting of the vengeance he will wreak on his enemies.

Athena. Seest thou, Odysseus, how great is the strength of heaven? Was not this Ajax wary and brave in the hour of action as any thou couldst have found?

Odysseus. I know none more so; and, though he be my enemy, I pity his miserable case, bound as he is beneath the yoke of calamity. I think of my own state no less than of his; for I see that all we who live are nothing but phantoms, or a fleeting shadow.

Athena. With this before thine eyes, then, never speak boastfully thyself against heaven, nor be puffed up if thy arm be stronger than another's, or thy heap of riches higher. A day brings low all human things, and again lifts them up. Heaven, that abhors the evil, loves the wise of heart.

[1] Theognis, see above, p. 40.

Heaven contrives Human Fate

SOPHOCLES, *Ajax* 1028. Teucer speaks over the dead body of Ajax.

Pray you, consider this fortune that has befallen two men. Hector, with the very girdle that Ajax had given him, was made fast to the chariot rail, and mangled till the breath of life had left him. And Ajax had as a gift from Hector this sword whereon he fell, and is slain thereby. Was it not a fiend that forged this blade? Was not that girdle wrought by the cruel fingers of Death?

It is heaven that contrives this, and all things else for men. So I maintain; and if there be any whom that saying likes not, let him hold to his own thoughts, as I to mine.

Piety is immortal

SOPHOCLES, *Philoctetes* 1440. Heracles warns Philoctetes and Neoptolemus against impious acts when they shall have taken Troy.

But, when ye lay waste the land, bethink you of piety towards heaven. To Father Zeus piety is of more account than all things else; for it dies not with men, but, whether they die or live, it cannot perish.

The Power of Love

SOPHOCLES, *frag.* 941 (Pearson).

The Cyprian Queen, my children, is not only the Cyprian; there are many other names she bears. She is Death; she is imperishable force; she is raving madness; she is untempered longing; she is lamentation. Nothing that works or is quiet, nothing that drives to violence, but as she wills. Her impress sinks into the mould of all things whose life is in their breath. Who must not yield to this goddess? She enters into every fish that swims; she is in every four-footed breed upon the land; among the birds everywhere is the beating of her wing; in beasts, in mortal men, and in the gods above. No god with whom she wrestles, but is thrice thrown.

If it be lawful to say it—and lawful it is to speak the truth—in the breast of Zeus she reigns, a tyrant that needs no armed guard. There is no design of mortal or of god that is not cut short by Love.

Why do the Wicked prosper?

SOPHOCLES, *Aletes, frag.* 107.

Strange, that impious men, sprung from wicked parents, should prosper, while good men of generous breed should be unfortunate! It is not right that heaven should deal so with men. The gods should manifestly reward the pious, and the unrighteous should suffer some manifest punishment for their wickedness. Then the wicked man would not flourish.

Nothing to which Heaven prompts is shameful

SOPHOCLES, *frag.* 247. Professor Pearson comments: "It is natural to compare the passage with Euripides' famous line (*frag.* 292), 'If gods do anything base, they are no gods,' and the contrast is significant of the attitude of the two poets towards morality and religion. Sophocles is serenely confident that no reconciliation of the claims is necessary; if morality seems to conflict with the will of the gods, so much the worse for it. But for Euripides, if the gods seem to enjoin an immoral action, they become untrue to their nature and are no longer trustworthy."

No man is wise save he that is esteemed by heaven. Fixing thine eyes upon the gods, thou must tread the path they bid thee tread, though it should carry thee beyond the bound of customary right. For nothing to which heaven prompts is shameful.

XI. THE IONIAN PHILOSOPHY AT ATHENS

ANAXAGORAS

The Ionian philosophy which originated at Miletus was transplanted to Athens by Anaxagoras, who is said to have lived there for thirty years (480–450 B.C.?). After his prosecution for impiety, he retired to Lampsacus in Asia Minor and continued to teach. He is chiefly famous for his doctrine that motion in the universe is caused by Mind (*Nous*), a supersensible substance, unmixed with any bodily qualities. This Mind, however, merely initiates the rotatory motion which leads to the evolution of a world. It is not represented as either good or benevolent.

Science and Superstition

PLUTARCH, *Life of Pericles* iv.

The philosopher with whom Pericles was most intimately acquainted; who gave him that force and sublimity of sentiment superior to all the demagogues; who, in short, formed him to that admirable dignity of manners, was Anaxagoras the Clazomenian. . . .

These were not the only advantages which Pericles gained by conversing with Anaxagoras. From him he learned to overcome those terrors which the various phenomena of the heavens raise in those who know not their causes, and who entertain a tormenting fear of the gods by reason of that ignorance. Nor is there any cure for it but the study of nature, which, instead of the frightful extravagances of superstition, implants in us a sober piety, supported by a rational hope.

We are told, there was brought to Pericles, from one of his farms, a ram's head with only one horn; and Lampo the soothsayer, observing that the horn grew strong and firm out of the middle of the forehead, declared that the two parties in the state, namely, those of Thucydides and Pericles, would unite, and invest the whole power in him with whom the prodigy was found; but Anaxagoras having dissected the head, showed that the brain did not fill the whole cavity, but had contracted itself into an oval form, and pointed directly to that part of the skull whence the horn took its rise. This procured Anaxagoras great honour with the spectators; and Lampo was not less honoured for his prediction, when, soon after, upon the fall of Thucydides, the administration was put entirely into the hands of Pericles.

But, in my opinion, the philosopher and the diviner may well enough be reconciled, and both be right; the one discovering the cause and the other the end. It was the business of the former to account for the appearance, and to consider how it came about; and of the latter to show why it was so formed, and what it portended. Those who say that, when the cause is found out, the prodigy ceases, do not consider that if they reject such signs as are preternatural, they must also deny that artificial signs are of any use: the clattering of brass quoits,[1] the light of beacons, and the shadow of a sundial, have all of them their proper natural causes, and yet each has another signification.   J. AND W. LANGHORNE.

The Nature of Mind

ANAXAGORAS, *frag.* 12.

Whereas all other things have in them a portion of everything, Mind is unlimited and self-ruled, and is not mixed with anything, but is just alone by itself.

For if it were not by itself but were mixed with anything else, it would partake of all things, if it were mixed

[1] A military signal.

with any (for in everything there is a portion of everything, as I said before), and the things mixed with it would prevent it from having power over anything in the same way that it has being alone by itself. For it is the thinnest of all things and the purest, and it has all knowledge about everything and the greatest strength.

And Mind has power over all things, greater and smaller, that have life.

Also Mind exercised power over the whole revolution, so that it began to revolve originally. At first it began to revolve from a small beginning, and the revolution is spreading further and will spread further still. And the things that are being mingled together and separated off and distinguished—all these Mind knew. And Mind set in order all things as they were to be, and as they were (before) but now have ceased to be, and as they are, and this revolution wherein now revolve the stars and the sun and moon and the air and fire that are separated off. And this revolution (*or* "the revolution itself") caused them to be separated off; and from the rare is separated off the dense, from the cold the hot, from the dark the bright, and from the wet the dry. And there are many parts of many things; but nothing is completely separated or distinguished from anything else, except Mind.

And Mind is all alike, both the greater and the smaller; whereas nothing other than Mind is like any other thing; but each single thing was and is most manifestly those things of which it has most in it.

Mind initiates the Evolution of the World

SIMPLICIUS, *Physics* 300, 27; ANAXAGORAS, *frag.* 13.

It is clear that Anaxagoras did make use of Mind to explain becoming; for he identified becoming with a

L

process of separation caused by motion, and the motion is caused by Mind. He says:

"And when Mind began to cause motion, separating off took place from all that was moved, and all that part which Mind moved became distinct. And as things were set in motion and distinguished, the revolution kept making them become much more distinct."

ANAXAGORAS, *frags.* 14, 15, 16.

And Mind, which is for ever, certainly is also now where everything else is—in the surrounding mass and in the things that are united with it and in the things that have been separated off.

The dense, moist, cold, and dark came together where (the earth) is now, while the rare, the hot, and the dry moved outwards to the further part of the fire.

From these (? the opposite qualities above mentioned), as they are separated off, the earth is solidified; for from clouds water is separated off, and from water earth; and from the earth stones are solidified by the cold, and stones move outwards more than water.

(These stones, flung off by the movement of the earth, and heated by their own motion, form the heavenly bodies.)

HIPPOLYTUS, *Refutation of all the Heresies* i. 8, 6.

Anaxagoras said that the sun and moon and all the stars are fiery stones carried round by the rotation of the aether. . . . The sun surpasses the Peloponnesus in size. The moon has not a light of her own, but gets it from the sun. . . . The moon is eclipsed by the earth screening the sun's light from it, and sometimes, too, by the bodies below the moon coming before it. The sun is eclipsed at the new moon, when the moon screens it from us. . . . Anaxagoras was the first to determine what concerns the eclipses and the illumination of the sun and moon.   J. BURNET.

The Trial of Anaxagoras

DIOGENES LAERTIUS ii. 12.

Accounts of Anaxagoras' trial differ. Sotion in the *Succession of Philosophers* says that he was . . . condemned for saying that the sun was an incandescent mass of rock, and that he was defended by his pupil Pericles and exiled with a fine of five talents. Satyrus in his *Lives* says the trial was instituted by Thucydides, the political rival of Pericles, that Anaxagoras was accused not only of impiety but also of being a pro-Persian, and that he was condemned to death in his absence.

DIOGENES OF APOLLONIA

This philosopher was not an original thinker, but taught the system of Anaximenes with some additions. He is chiefly important as being one of the philosophers satirised in the *Clouds* of Aristophanes (see p. 158 *ff*.)—a fact which shows that his doctrines were known to the ordinary public in Athens.

Air as Intelligence and Deity

SIMPLICIUS, *Physics* 152; DIOGENES, *frags*. 3, 4.

Diogenes proceeds to show that his first principle (Air) contains abundance of intelligence.

"For," he says, "it could not without intelligence be so distributed as to keep the measures of all things, of winter and summer, of night and day, of rains and winds and fair weather. And anyone who cares to reflect will find that everything else is disposed in the best possible way."

He then adduces the argument that men and all other animals live by this principle, which is the Air, and derive from it the soul and intelligence they possess. His words are:

"There are further these strong proofs: men and all other animals live by air which they breathe; and this is their soul and intelligence, as this treatise will clearly show; and if this is taken away, they die and their intelligence fails."

DIOGENES, *frag.* 5.

And my belief is that the thing that has intelligence is what men call the Air, and that this is what governs all and has power over all. Just this, I hold, is God; and it reaches everywhere, disposes all things, and is in everything, and there is nothing that does not partake of it. Nothing, however, partakes of it in the same way as anything else, but there are many modes both of air itself and of intelligence; for air is very various—hotter or colder, wetter or drier, more stationary or moving more swiftly, and there are many other differences in it, and infinite varieties of taste and colour.

Also, the soul of all living creatures is the same thing —air, that is warmer than the air outside us, in which we are, but much colder than the air near the sun. The warmth, however, is not alike in any two living things (nor, for that matter, in any two men), but the difference is slight, so that they are similar. But none of the things that are differentiated can be exactly like one another without becoming identical.

So, because of the variety of differentiation, living things are many and various, unlike one another in form, in manner of life, and in intelligence, owing to the multitude of differentiations. Nevertheless it is one and the same thing whereby they all live and see and hear, and from it they have their other powers of understanding.

DIOGENES, *frags.* 7, 8.

And this thing itself is an eternal and immortal body, while other things come into being or pass away.

It seems to me clear that it is great and powerful, eternal and immortal, and of great knowledge.

PHILEMON, *frag. incert.* 2. Air, as Deity, speaks the prologue to a comedy.

I am he whose eye no god or man can escape in anything he does, or shall do, or has ever done. I am Air, and you may also call me Zeus. Only a god could be, as I am, everywhere—here in Athens, at Patrae, in Sicily, in every city and every house, and in all of you. There is no place where Air is not; and one who is everywhere present must of course know everything.

ARCHELAUS

God is Air

DIOGENES LAERTIUS ii. 16.

Archelaus of Athens . . . pupil of Anaxagoras and teacher of Socrates, was the first to transplant the philosophy of nature from Ionia to Athens.[1] . . . He also seems to have dealt with ethics. . . . He said that right and wrong exist, not in nature, but by convention (law)

AETIUS i. 7, 15.

Archelaus held that God is air and intelligence, but that it was not God that made the world.

[1] Rather he was the first native Athenian to teach the Ionian philosophy introduced by Anaxagoras.

XII RATIONALISM. THE AGE OF THE SOPHISTS

PROTAGORAS

Agnosticism

PROTAGORAS of Abdera (born about 500 B.C.?), *frag.* 4. Our authorities have not preserved the context of this statement, but they connect it with a story that Protagoras was prosecuted for impiety.

Concerning the gods I cannot know for certain whether they exist or not, nor what they are like in form. There are many things that hinder certainty—the obscurity of the matter and the shortness of man's life.

PRODICUS

Deification of useful things

SEXTUS EMPIRICUS, *adv. math.* ix. 18.

Prodicus of Ceos says that the men of old regarded as gods the sun and moon, rivers and fountains, and in general everything serviceable to human life, because of its serviceableness, just as the Egyptians deify the Nile. Hence bread was regarded as Demeter, wine as Dionysus, water as Poseidon, fire as Hephaestus, and so on with every useful thing.

HERODOTUS

On the Origin of the Gods

HERODOTUS ii. 52.

Formerly, in their sacrifices, the Pelasgians called upon gods (this I know, for I was told at Dodona) without giving name or appellation to any; for they had not as yet heard of such. They called them gods (*theoi*) because all things and the due assignment thereof were by them set in order (*thentes*). Then, after a long while, they learnt the names first of the rest of the gods, which came to them from Egypt, and, much later, the name of Dionysus; and presently they inquired of the oracle at Dodona concerning the names; for this place of divination is held to be the most ancient in Hellas, and at that time it was the only one. When the Pelasgians, then, inquired at Dodona if they should adopt the names that had come from foreign parts, the oracle bade them use the names. From that time onwards they used the names of the gods in their sacrifices; and the Greeks received these later from the Pelasgians.

But whence each of the gods came into being, or whether they had all for ever existed, and what outward forms they had, the Greeks knew not till (so to say) a very little while ago; for I suppose that the time of Hesiod and Homer was not more than four hundred years before my own; and these are they who taught the Greeks of the descent of the gods, and gave to all their several names, and honours, and arts, and declared their outward forms. But those poets who are said to be older than Hesiod and Homer were, to my thinking, of later birth.

The earlier part of all this is what the priestesses of Dodona tell; the later, that which concerns Hesiod and Homer, is what I myself say. A. D. GODLEY.

The Evidences of Design

HERODOTUS iii. 108. This is said to be the first mention of a "divine providence" ordering the detailed arrangements of Nature to an end. Protagoras expresses a similar idea in Plato's *Protagoras*, 320 E.

The Arabians also say that the whole country would be full of these snakes were it not with them as I have

heard that it is with vipers. It would seem that the
wisdom of divine providence (as is but reasonable) has
made all creatures prolific that are cowardly and fit to
eat, that they be not minished from off the earth by
devouring, whereas but few young are born to creatures
cruel and baneful.   A. D. GODLEY

THRASYMACHUS

The Gods do not regard Man

THRASYMACHUS of Chalcedon, *frag.* 8.

The gods do not regard human things; otherwise
they would not have overlooked the most important
of human goods, righteousness; for we see that men do
not practise righteousness.

METRODORUS

The allegorical Interpretation of the Gods

TATIAN, c. 21.   Metrodorus was a friend of Anaxagoras.

Metrodorus of Lampsacus in his book on Homer
turns everything into allegory in a very simple-minded
way.   Hera, Athena, and Zeus are not, according to him,
what they are supposed to be by those who consecrate
precincts for them, but natural substances and arrangements of elements.

ANTIPHON

On Divination

GNOMOL. VINDOB. 50, p. 14 W (Diels, *Vors.*³ ii. 291, 34).

Antiphon was asked to define the art of the seer
or diviner. He replied: " It is the conjecture of a
sagacious man."

KRITIAS

The Invention of the Gods

KRITIAS (one of the "Thirty Tyrants" at Athens, 404–3 B.C.), *Sisyphus*, a Satyric drama.

Sisyphus. There was a time when human life was orderless, like the beasts', and subject to violence, and there was no reward for the good nor punishment for the bad. Next, as I think, men made for themselves laws of punishment, that Justice might be lord over all alike and hold insolence in servitude; and any who offended was punished.

But, although the laws kept them from open deeds of violence, men went on doing them in secret; and then it was, I believe, that some clever and sagacious man first invented for mortals the fear of the gods, so that there might be something to frighten the wicked, even though their acts or words and thoughts were secret. For that reason then he introduced the doctrine that the divine is a spirit endowed with the vigour of immortal life, hearing and seeing by means of his thought and with excess of wisdom noting these deeds, and wearing a divine form. " He will hear whatever mortals say, and be able to see whatever they do. Though you plot some wickedness in silence, the gods will know of it, for their thoughts are not as ours." With such words he introduced the pleasantest of doctrines, veiling the truth with a false tale.

And for the dwelling of the gods he chose the place that would have the most startling effect on men, the place he knew to be the source of human terrors as well as of the things that succour this miserable life—the round sky above us, where he saw the lightnings with the dreadful crash of thunder, and the form of heaven with starry eyes inwrought with cunning beauty by the craftsman, Time; where moves the bright molten mass of the star of day, and whence the rain-shower sets out on its journey to the earth.

Such were the bugbears with which he scared mankind; and for that purpose imagined this admirable story and established the deity in a suitable habitation, and so extinguished lawlessness by law.

DIAGORAS

The Atheist

SEXTUS EMPIRICUS, adv. math. ix. 53.

Diagoras of Melos, the dithyrambic poet, is said to have been at first extremely superstitious . . . but when he had been wronged by a man who committed perjury and no harm came to the perjurer, he changed over and said there was no God.

CICERO, On the Nature of the Gods iii. 89.

When Diagoras, called the godless (atheos), visited Samothrace, a friend said to him: " You think the gods have no regard to the affairs of mankind. Look at all these votive pictures; don't you see how many have been rescued by their vows from the storm and reached harbour safely? " Diagoras replied: " That is how it works out : those who are shipwrecked and drowned don't get painted."

On another occasion, during a storm at sea, the frightened sailors said they were only getting what they deserved for taking him into the same ship with them. Diagoras pointed to a number of other ships labouring in the same distress, and asked them whether they thought each of them had a Diagoras on board.

Hippocrates

The Protest of Science

Hippocrates, *On the Sacred Disease* (Epilepsy) i.

With regard to the Sacred Disease, as it is called, the matter stands thus: it seems to me to be in no way more divine or sacred than any other disease; but it has a natural origin like the rest. Men have supposed its nature and cause to be something divine because of their inexperience and its marvellous character; for it is quite unlike other diseases. But while its divine character is supported by the difficulty of understanding it, it is done away with by the facile mode of treatment by which they cure it, namely purifications and charms. And if its marvellous character is to be a reason for thinking it divine, there will be many more than one sacred disease; for I shall show that there are others equally marvellous and portentous, which no one regards as sacred. On the one hand, quotidian, tertian, and quartan fevers seem to me no less sacred and divinely caused, though they are not marvelled at; and on the other hand I see men raving and out of their minds for no manifest cause, and doing many extravagant things. I know many who in their sleep groan and cry out, or choke with suffocation, or start up and escape out of doors and are beside themselves until they are waked, when they become as sane and sensible as before, though pale and weak; and this not once, but many times. There are many other cases of every description; but it would take too long to give an account of them all.

In my judgment the men who first consecrated this disease were the sort of men who to this day are mages and purifiers, mendicant quacks and impostors—all those professors of exceptional piety and superior knowledge. Having no remedy that would do any good, they took the divine character as a cloak to cover their incompetence, and pronounced this malady to be sacred, in order to conceal the fact that they knew nothing. With suitable explanations they arranged a treatment that would secure them from all risk. They prescribed purifications and charms, and enjoined abstinence from baths and from many kinds of food that are unsuitable to the sick . . forbade the patient to wear black (black being a deadly colour), or to wear goatskin or sleep on it, or to put one foot or hand over the other, all these being hindrances.

The divine nature of the disease was the ground for all these observances, which they imposed with an air of superior wisdom, giving other colourable reasons, so that, if the patient were cured, the glory might redound to their own skill, while if he should die, they might be secure of their defence and be able to cast the blame on the gods, not on themselves; for they avoided giving any food or drug or administering hot baths, that might be thought to have caused the death.

Now I suppose the inhabitants of the interior of Libya must all be in bad health, because they eat goat's meat and sleep on goatskin, having nothing else to use for bedclothes, dress, or shoes: their only herds consist of goats and cows. If the use of goatskin and goat's meat engenders and increases this disease, and abstinence from both cures it, then divinity has nothing to do with it, and the purificatory ceremonies are useless. The harm done, and the cure effected, are due to the food eaten, and the divine power disappears. Thus, so far as I can see, those who undertake to cure these disorders by such means, do not really consider them sacred or divine; for, if they can be removed by purifications and the treatment described, what is there to prevent an attack being induced by other means of the same kind? But then the cause turns out to be human action, not the divine. If a man can drive away an affection like this by performing magical rites of purification, he can also induce it by another set of practices,—an argument which disposes of divine intervention.

With these discourses and artifices they affect a superior knowledge, deceiving mankind by prescribing ceremonial abstinence and purity, and their talk is all of gods and spirits. They believe themselves to be using the language of piety, but they seem to me rather to be irreligious and to deny the existence of the gods; their piety and religion are impious and irreligious, as I will show.

They claim to know how to draw down the moon and to eclipse the sun, to cause storm and fair weather, rains and drought, to make the sea calm and the land fertile,[1] and to perform all other such marvels. Whatever the means by which they say these things can be done— whether by rites or by some other device or practice— they seem to me impiously to deny that gods exist or have any power or can prevent any of these supreme wonders. By performing them, are they not formidable to the gods themselves? If a man, by magic arts and sacrifices, is going to draw down the moon and eclipse the sun and make storm and calm, I shall not hold any of these things to be divine, but rather human, since the divine power is overmastered and enslaved by human intelligence.

But perhaps it is not so. Rather men are driven by need of a livelihood to imagine and contrive all manner of ingenuities in the matter of this disease as in all other

---

[1] θάλασσαν εὔπλοον καὶ γῆν εὔφορον, Wilamowitz, *Herakles* ii. 262.

matters, attributing to heaven the explanation for every phase of it. At every circumstance they invoke the divine. If the patients behave like goats, or bellow, or have spasms on the right side, they say the Mother of the Gods is the cause. If they scream on a high note, they say they are like horses and make Poseidon responsible. If they pass excrement, as frequently happens in the stress of an attack, they bring in the title of the divinity of the Highways (Demeter ?); or if the excrement is small and hard, like that of birds, it is Apollo Nomios. Ares is responsible for foaming at the mouth and drumming with the feet. Nightly terrors, panics, raving, leaping out of bed, bugbears, flight out of doors—these they call assaults of Hecate and onslaughts of Heroes. In using purifications and charms they treat the divine, as I think, in the most irreligious and godless manner; for they purify the victims of this disease with blood and other such things, just as if they were tainted with some impurity, or under a curse, or bewitched, or had done some impious deed; whereas they ought, on the contrary, to offer sacrifice and prayer and take them to the temples to supplicate the gods. But, instead of doing that, they purify them. The objects used in the rite they either bury, or cast into the sea, or carry away to the mountains where no one shall touch or tread on them. They ought to take them to the temples and duly offer them to the god, if a god is really the cause.

For my part, I do not think that man's body is tainted by divinity—the most perishable of things by the purest; but if it should chance to be tainted or affected by something else, it would need to be purified and cleansed, rather than defiled, by divinity. At any rate the greatest and most unholy offences are purified by the divine, which cleanses and serves to wash them away. We ourselves trace boundaries about the temples and precincts of the gods, which no impure person is to pass over; and when we enter we sprinkle lustral water, not as if we were receiving a taint, but rather cleansing ourselves of any impurity we may have. Such is my opinion about ceremonies of purification.

LEUCIPPUS

Nothing happens without a Cause

LEUCIPPUS (founder of the Atomic philosophy, also taught by Democritus), *frag.* 2.

Nothing happens at random, but all things upon some ground and by force of necessity.

DEMOCRITUS

The Atomists' Doctrine of the Soul

ARISTOTLE, *On the Soul* I. ii. 3.

There are some who maintain that soul is pre-eminently and primarily the cause of movement. But they imagined that that which is not itself in motion cannot move anything else, and thus they regarded the soul as a thing which in motion. Hence Democritus affirms the soul to be a sort of fire or heat. For the "shapes" or atoms are infinite and those which are spherical he declares to be fire and soul. . . . The aggregate of such seeds, he tells us, forms the constituent elements of the whole of nature (and herein he agrees with Leucippus), while those of them which are spherical form the soul, because such figures most easily find their way through everything and, being themselves in motion, set other things in motion. The atomists assume that it is the soul which imparts motion to animals. It is for this reason that they make life depend upon respiration. For, when the surrounding air presses upon bodies and tends to extrude those atomic shapes which, because they are never at rest themselves, impart motion to animals, then they are reinforced from outside by the entry of other like atoms in respiration, which in fact, by helping to check compression and solidification, prevent the escape of the atoms already contained in the animals; and life, so they hold, continues so long as there is strength to do this.

R. D. HICKS

On the Gods

SEXTUS EMPIRICUS adv. math. ix. 24.

Democritus says that the men of old, when they saw what happens in the sky, such as thunder, lightning, thunderbolts, conjunctions of the stars, and eclipses of the sun and moon, were terrified and thought that these things were caused by gods.

SEXTUS EMPIRICUS adv. math. ix. 19; DEMOCRITUS, frag. 166.

Democritus says that "certain images approach men," some of them being beneficent, others maleficent. Hence he used to pray that he might "meet with propitious images." These images, he said, are of superhuman size and nearly, though not quite, indestructible, and by their appearance and speech they foreshew the future to men. The men of old, receiving the impression of these images, supposed that there was a God; for apart from these no god possessing an imperishable nature exists.

DEMOCRITUS, frags. 30, 175, 217, 297.

A few learned men [1] lift up their hands toward

[1] Diogenes of Apollonia (see p. 127 ff.) is specially meant (Diels). Clement quotes this saying with approval.

the place of what we Greeks now call the Air, and say, "Zeus considers all things, and he knows all; he gives and takes away, and is king of all."

The gods, now as from of old, give all good things to mankind. But evil, harmful, and useless things are not, and never have been, gifts of the gods. Men bring these things upon themselves by their own blindness and folly.

The gods love only those who hate wrong-doing.

Some men who know nothing of the dissolution of the mortal nature, but are conscious of their own bad manner of life, trouble themselves while life lasts with anxieties and fears, inventing fables about the time after death.

THUCYDIDES

On Oracles

THUCYDIDES v. 26.

Altogether the war lasted twenty-seven years. . . . He who reckons up the actual periods of time will find that I have rightly given the exact number of years with the difference only of a few days. He will also find that this was the solitary instance in which those who put their faith in oracles were justified by the event. For I well remember how, from the beginning to the end of the war, there was a common and often repeated saying that it was to last thrice nine years.

B. JOWETT.

The Speech of Diodotus

THUCYDIDES iii. 45. Part of a speech delivered at Athens in a debate on the revolt of Mitylene (427 B.C.). Cleon had demanded a savage punishment, on the ground that mercy was inconsistent with the maintenance of the Athenian empire. I have included this passage (though it can scarcely be said

M

to be about religion) as a preface to the next, the Melian Dialogue, where the claims of mercy and of empire are again confronted. The Melian incident itself immediately precedes the disastrous expedition to Sicily—an illustration of the temper of mind described here by Diodotus.

In the cities of Greece the death penalty has been affixed to many offences actually less than this; yet still, intoxicated by their hopes, men take the risk. No man ever, before embarking on a dangerous course, passed sentence on himself that he would not succeed in his design; and no city entering on revolt ever set about doing so with the conviction that her resources—whether her own or obtained from her allies—were insufficient. All men are born to error in public, as in private, conduct; and there is no law that will hinder them; for mankind has exhausted the whole catalogue of penalties, continually adding fresh ones, to find some means of lessening the wrongs they suffer from evil-doers. Probably in early ages the punishments affixed to the worst offences were milder; but as transgression went on, in time they seldom stopped short of death; yet still, even so, there are transgressors.

Either then some greater terror than death must be discovered, or at any rate death is no deterrent. No; poverty inspires daring by the stress of necessity; the licence of prosperity inspires covetous ambition by insolence and pride; and the other conditions of human life, as each is possessed by some irremediable and mastering power, by passion lead men on to perilous issues.

Desire and Hope are never wanting—the one leading the way, the other busy in attendance. Desire devising the attempt, and Hope flattering with suggestions of the riches in Fortune's store, very often lead to ruin, and, invisible as they are, prevail over the dangers that are seen.

And besides these, Fortune contributes no less to intoxication; for sometimes she presents herself unex-
pectedly at a man's side and leads him forward to face
danger at a disadvantage; and cities even more than
individuals, in proportion as their stake is the greatest
of all—freedom or empire—and each, when all are with
him, unthinkingly rates himself the higher.

In a word, it is impossible—and only a simpleton would
suppose the contrary—that human nature, when it is
passionately bent upon some act, should be averted from
its purpose by force of laws or any other terror.

The Melian Dialogue

THUCYDIDES v. 84 (abridged).

The Athenians next made an expedition against the
island of Melos. The Melians are colonists of the Lacedaemonians who would not submit to Athens like the
other islanders. At first they were neutral and took no
part. But when the Athenians tried to coerce them by
ravaging their lands, they were driven into open hostilities.
The generals encamped with the Athenian forces on the
island. But before they did the country any harm they
sent envoys to negotiate with the Melians. Instead of
bringing these envoys before the people, the Melians
desired them to explain their errand to the magistrates
and to the chief men. They spoke as follows:

Athenians. We Athenians will use no fine words;
we will not go out of our way to prove at length that we
have a right to rule, because we overthrew the Persians;
or that we attack you now because we are suffering any
injury at your hands. We should not convince you if
we did; nor must you expect to convince us by arguing
that, although a colony of the Lacedaemonians, you have

taken no part in their expeditions, or that you have never
done us any wrong. But you and we should say what we
really think, and aim only at what is possible, for we
both alike know that into the discussion of human affairs
the question of justice only enters where the pressure of
necessity is equal, and that the powerful exact what they
can, and the weak grant what they must.

Melians. Well, then, since you set aside justice and
invite us to speak of expediency, in our judgment it is
certainly expedient that you should respect a principle
which is for the common good; and that to every man
when in peril a reasonable claim should be accounted a
claim of right, and any plea which he is disposed to urge,
even if failing of the point a little, should help his cause.
Your interest in this principle is quite as great as ours,
insomuch as you, if you fall, will incur the heaviest
vengeance, and will be the most terrible example to
mankind.

Athenians. The fall of our empire, if it should fall, is
not an event to which we look forward with dismay,
for ruling states such as Lacedaemon are not cruel to
their vanquished enemies. And we are fighting not so
much against the Lacedaemonians, as against our own
subjects who may some day rise up and overcome their
former masters. But this is a danger which you may leave
to us. And we will now endeavour to show that we have
come in the interests of our empire, and that in what we
are about to say we are only seeking the preservation of
your city. For we want to make you ours with the least
trouble to ourselves, and it is for the interests of us both
that you should not be destroyed. . . .

Melians. But we know that the fortune of war is sometimes impartial, and not always on the side of numbers.

If we yield now, all is over; but if we fight, there is yet a hope that we may stand upright.

Athenians. Hope is a good comforter in the hour of danger, and when men have something else to depend upon, although hurtful, she is not ruinous. But when her spendthrift nature has induced them to stake their all, they see her as she is in the moment of their fall, and not till then. While the knowledge of her might enable them to be ware of her, she never fails. You are weak, and a single turn of the scale might be your ruin. Do not you be thus deluded; avoid the error of which so many are guilty, who, although they might still be saved if they would take the natural means, when visible grounds of confidence forsake them, have recourse to the invisible, to prophecies and oracles and the like, which ruin men by the hopes which they inspire in them.

Melians. We know only too well how hard the struggle must be against your power, and against fortune, if she does not mean to be impartial. Nevertheless we do not despair of fortune; for we hope to stand as high as you in the favour of heaven, because we are righteous, and you against whom we contend are unrighteous; and we are satisfied that our deficiency in power will be compensated by the aid of our allies the Lacedaemonians; they cannot refuse to help us, if only because we are their kinsmen, and for the sake of their own honour. And therefore our confidence is not so utterly blind as you suppose.

Athenians. As for the gods, we expect to have quite as much of their favour as you: for we are not doing or claiming anything which goes beyond common opinion about divine or men's desires about human things. For of the gods we believe, and of men we know, that by a law of their nature wherever they can rule they will. This law was not made by us, and we are not the first who have acted upon it; we did but inherit it, and shall bequeath it to all time, and we know that you and all mankind, if you were as strong as we are, would do as we do. So much for the gods; we have told you why we expect to stand as high in their good opinion as you. And then as to the Lacedaemonians—when you imagine that out of very shame they will assist you, we admire the simplicity of your idea, but we do not envy you the folly of it. The Lacedaemonians are exceedingly virtuous among themselves, and according to their national standard of morality. But, in respect of their dealings with others, although many things might be said, a word is enough to describe them,—of all men whom we know they are the most notorious for identifying what is pleasant with what is honourable, and what is expedient with what is just. . . .

The Melians, after consulting among themselves, resolved to persevere in their refusal, and made answer as follows:

"Men of Athens, our resolution is unchanged; and we will not in a moment surrender that liberty which our city, founded seven hundred years ago, still enjoys; we will trust to the good-fortune which, by the favour of the gods, has hitherto preserved us, and for human help to the Lacedaemonians, and endeavour to save ourselves. We are ready however to be your friends, and the enemies neither of you nor of the Lacedaemonians, and we ask you to leave our country when you have made such a peace as may appear to be in the interests of both parties.

Such was the answer of the Melians; the Athenians, as they quitted the conference, spoke as follows:

"Well, we must say, judging from the decision at which you have arrived, that you are the only men who deem the future to be more certain than the present, and regard things unseen as already realised in your fond anticipation, and that the more you cast yourselves upon the Lacedaemonians and fortune and hope, and trust them, the more complete will be your ruin." . . .

The place was now closely invested, and there was treachery among the citizens themselves. So the Melians were induced to surrender at discretion. The Athenians thereupon put to death all who were of military age, and made slaves of the women and children. Then they colonised the island, sending thither five hundred settlers of their own.

During the same winter the Athenians conceived a desire of sending another expedition to Sicily, larger than that commanded by Laches and Eurymedon. They hoped to conquer the island. Of its great size and numerous population, barbarian as well as Hellenic, most of them knew nothing, and they never reflected that they were entering on a struggle almost as arduous as the Peloponnesian War.   B. JOWETT.

The End of the Athenian Expedition against Sicily
THUCYDIDES vii. 50 (413 B.C.).

The Athenian generals, seeing that their enemy had been reinforced by a new army, and that their own affairs, instead of improving, were daily growing worse in every respect, and being especially troubled by the sickness of their troops, repented that they had not gone before. Even Nicias now no longer objected. . . . The preparations were made and they were on the point of sailing, when the moon, being just then at the full, was eclipsed. The mass of the army was greatly moved, and called upon the generals to remain. Nicias himself, who was too much under the influence of divination and omens, refused even to discuss the question of their removal until they had remained thrice nine days, as the soothsayers prescribed. This was the reason why the departure of the Athenians was finally delayed.[1]   B. JOWETT.

THUCYDIDES vii. 76.

Nicias, seeing the army disheartened at their terrible fall, went along the ranks and encouraged and consoled them as well as he could. In his fervour he raised his voice as he passed from one to another, and spoke louder and louder, desiring that the benefit of his words might reach as far as possible.

"Even now, Athenians and allies, we must hope: men have been delivered out of worse straits than these, and I would not have you judge yourselves too severely on account of the reverses which you have sustained or of your present undeserved miseries. I too am as weak as any of you; for I am quite prostrated by my disease, as you see. And although there was a time when I might have been thought equal to the best of you in the happiness of my private and public life, I am now in as great danger, and as much at the mercy of fortune, as the meanest. Yet my days have been passed in the performance of many a religious duty, and of many a just and blameless action. Therefore my hope of the future remains unshaken, and our calamities do not appal me as they might. Who knows that they may not be lightened? For our enemies have had their full share of success, and if our expedition

---

[1] The true cause of lunar eclipses had been discovered by Anaxagoras a generation before this time. See p. 126.

provoked the jealousy of any god, by this time we have
been punished enough. Others ere now have attacked
their neighbours; they have done as men will do, and
suffered what men can bear. We may therefore begin
to hope that the gods will be more merciful to us; for
we now invite their pity rather than their jealousy."

B. JOWETT.

THUCYDIDES vii. 86. The Athenians having been utterly
defeated, Nicias surrendered. He was put to death by the
victorious Syracusans.

No one of the Hellenes in my time was less deserving
of so miserable an end; for he lived in the practice of
every virtue. . . .

Of all the Hellenic actions which took place in this
war, or indeed of all Hellenic actions which are on record,
this was the greatest — the most glorious to the victors,
the most ruinous to the vanquished; for they were utterly
and at all points defeated, and their sufferings were pro-
digious. Fleet and army perished from the face of the
earth; nothing was saved, and of the many who went
forth few returned home.

Thus ended the Sicilian expedition.

The news was brought to Athens, but the Athenians
could not believe that the armament had been so completely annihilated, although they had the positive assur-
ances of the very soldiers who had escaped from the scene
of action. At last they knew the truth; and then they
were furious with the orators who had joined in pro-
moting the expedition,—as if they had not voted it themselves—and with the soothsayers, and prophets, and all
who by the influence of religion had at the time inspired
them with the belief that they would conquer Sicily.

B. JOWETT.

XIII. EURIPIDES

If the Gods sin

EURIPIDES, *Ion* 429. Creusa, daughter to the King of Athens, bore a son, Ion, to Apollo. The infant, conveyed by Hermes to Delphi, is reared there in the service of the temple, ignorant of his parentage. Creusa, not knowing what has become of her child, is married to Xuthus. She comes with her husband to Delphi to consult the oracle about their childlessness. Meeting Ion, now a youth, she tells her own story as having happened to a friend. Ion is troubled. She goes into the temple.

Ion. Why does this stranger heap reproaches upon the god in dark and riddling words? . . . But what have I to do with Erechtheus' daughter? She is nothing to me. I will take my golden ewer and fill the basins with lustral water.

Yet I must admonish Phoebus. What ails him? He ravishes maidens and forsakes them, begets children by stealth and cares not, though they die. O, do not so! Since thou art powerful, follow after goodness! When a man has an evil nature, the gods punish him. How is it right that you gods should prescribe the law for man, and then be guilty of lawlessness yourselves? If—it cannot be, yet I will put it so—if you were to pay to men the fine for lustful violence,[1] thou, and Poseidon, and Zeus the lord of heaven would beggar your temples of their treasure in paying for your wrongs. For wrong it is, to seek your pleasures with no regard to consequence.

No more can men justly be called wicked, if we only imitate what the gods call good. Wicked rather are those who so instruct us!

[1] A law of Solon fixed a fine for violence to a virgin.

EURIPIDES, *Bellerophon, frag. 292.*

If gods do anything base, they are no gods.

Men charge their own Sins upon the Gods

EURIPIDES, *Iphigeneia among the Taurians,* 380. Iphigeneia was constrained by her savage captors to act as priestess to a goddess called Artemis, to whom all Greek castaways were sacrificed.

Iphigeneia. I cast reproach upon the false subtleties of this goddess, who, if a man stain himself with blood-shed or touch a corpse or a woman fresh from child-birth, bars him from her altars and holds him to be defiled, and yet herself takes pleasure in human sacrifice. It cannot be that Leto, the bride of Zeus, gave birth to such folly. No, I hold incredible Tantalus' banquet to the gods—that gods should taste the flesh of a child! I think it is this people, themselves manslayers, who charge their own wickedness on the goddess; for I do not believe that any divinity is evil.

EURIPIDES, *Trojan Women* 969. After the capture of Troy, Menelaus confronts Helen with Hecuba. Helen pleads the traditional story of the Judgment of Paris, and lays the responsibility for her sin on Aphrodite, whom even Zeus cannot resist. Hecuba replies:

Hecuba. First I will champion the goddesses, and prove that there is no justice in this woman's plea. I do not believe that Hera and Virgin Pallas could fall so low in folly that Hera would sell Argos to barbarians, or Pallas Athens to be the Phrygians' slave, coming to Ida in childish vanity to win a prize for beauty. Why should a goddess have such a lust for beauty? Did Hera seek to win a better husband than Zeus himself? Or was Athena bent on marriage with some god — she who, for hatred of marriage, chose virginity above all gifts?

Do not make goddesses fools, to gloss the evil that is in yourself: the wise will hardly be convinced!

Aphrodite, you say, came with my son to Menelaus' house. How laughable! Could she not have stayed quiet in heaven and wafted you, and all Amyclae with you, to Ilium?

My son shone out in beauty above all. When you saw him, it was your own thought that became ' Aphrodite.' ' Aphrodite ' is the name for every human folly.

We know nothing

EURIPIDES, *Hippolytus* 1102.

Chorus. Surely the thought of the gods, when it comes over my mind, lifts the burden of sorrow; but, while I hope in the darkness for some understanding, I faint and fail, when I compare the deeds of men with their fortunes. All is change, to and fro; the life of man shifts in endless wandering.

EURIPIDES, *Hippolytus* 189.

Nurse. The life of man is all suffering, and there is no rest from pain and trouble. There may be something better than this life; but whatever it be, it is hidden in mists of darkness. So we are sick of love for this life on earth and any gleam it shows, because we know nothing of another. What lies beyond is not revealed, and we drift on a sea of idle tales.

EURIPIDES, *Helen* 1137. The plot of the *Helen* turns on the story that the real Helen never went to Troy, but was spirited away by the gods to Egypt. The ten years' war and sack of Troy and all the sufferings of Greeks and Trojans were for the sake of a phantom Helen, who finally vanished into air.

Chorus. What mortal who has pushed his search to the furthest bound dares say that he has found what

God is, or what is not God, or what lies between, when he sees the purposes of heaven sway this way and that and back again in a turmoil of unforeseen and contradictory chances?

Thou, O Helen, wast born the daughter of Zeus, in Leda's womb begotten by the swan whose plumes thy father wore. Then the cry rang through Hellas: *False traitress, godless and unrighteous woman!*

I know nothing clear or certain, of all that men believe. Only the word of heaven I find true.

Birth, not Death, should be lamented

EURIPIDES, *Cresphontes, frag.* 449. Herodotus v. 4 records that this custom was actually practised by a Thracian tribe, as it was also by the heathen Prussians in the fifteenth century (Chadwick, *The Heroic Age,* 1912, 411).

It were better that we should call our friends together to lament over the newly-born, that he has come to such a world of sorrows.

And when a man is dead and has found rest from trouble, we should rejoice and carry him from the house with songs of gladness.

There are no Gods

EURIPIDES, *Bellerophon, frag.* 286.

Does any say that there are gods in heaven? No! there are none, if a man will not be fool enough to credit the old tale. Let not my words guide your judgment; see for yourselves. I say that tyranny slays its thousands and despoils their goods, and men who break their oath cause cities to be sacked; and, doing so, they are happier than men who walk quietly in the ways of piety from day to day. And I know of small states, where the gods are honoured, that are overmastered in battle by numbers and become subject to greater states that are far less god-fearing.

The Justice of Heaven

EURIPIDES, *Melanippe, frag.* 506.

Do you think that deeds of wrong fly up on wings to heaven, and then someone writes them on the tablets of Zeus, who looks upon the record and gives judgment upon men? Why, the whole heaven would not suffice for Zeus to write man's sins thereon, nor Zeus himself to consider them and send a punishment for each. No; Justice is here, close at hand, if you will but see it.

EURIPIDES, *Trojan Women* 884.

Hecuba. O thou that upholdest the earth, and above the earth art throned, whosoever thou art, by surmise hardly to be known, whether natural necessity or man's intelligence, Zeus, on thee I call; for along the noiseless path thou treadest, all mortal things are guided in the way of Justice.[1]

Menelaus. What's this? A new fashion of praying to the gods!

Zeus, the Air of Heaven

EURIPIDES, *frag.* 941.

Seest thou yonder infinite Air on high, that clasps the earth in the dew's soft embrace? Hold this for Zeus, count this to be God.

EURIPIDES, *frag.* 911.

Golden wings are upon my shoulders; on my feet the Siren's winged sandals. I shall go soaring to the firmament of heaven, to be made one with Zeus.

[1] Compare Plato, above, p. 77.

Life and Death

EURIPIDES, *Polyidos, frag.* 638.

Who knows if this life be not death, and death be not
accounted life in the world below?

Chorus of Bacchanals

EURIPIDES, *Bacchanals* 64.

From the Asian land, from the holy hill of Tmolus,
I come swiftly.

To Bacchus I cry; for him all travail is joy, all weariness
is ease.

Who stands in the way? Who spies upon us from
the house?

Let him avoid the place! Let him not profane his lips
with unhallowed speech!

For I will praise Dionysus with the hymn ordained
from of old.

Happy is he who is blessed with the knowledge of
heavenly mysteries, and whose life is pure;

Whose soul is made one with the company of them that
worship on the mountains; who is made clean
and sanctified;

Who keeps the rites of the Great Mother, Cybele; who
waves on high his thyrsus, and, with ivy crowned,
follows in Dionysus' train.

Come, ye Bacchanals, come! Bring home the Child
of the Thunder, the god who is son of a god.

From the Phrygian hills to the wide ways of the cities
of Hellas, bring home the Thunder-Child, Dionysus!

With bitter travail was he conceived, by force of the
winged thunder-bolt of Zeus.

He was cast forth from his mother's womb, when the
lightning smote her and she died.

But immediately Zeus received him in a chamber of
second birth;

In his own thigh he enfolded him, shut fast with golden
clasps, and hid him from the eyes of Hera.

And, when the destined time was fulfilled, he brought
him forth, a bull-horned god, and wreathed him
with wreaths of serpents.

Wherefore even now the Maenads make prey of the
wild serpents, and twine them in the tresses of
their hair.

O nurse of Semele, O Thebes, crown thyself with the
crown of ivy.

Break forth, break forth with blossoming of briony,
bright berries and green leaves.

With branches of pine-tree and of oak, come, let the
spirit of the god be upon thee.

Put upon thyself the dappled fawn-skin with tufted
fringe of silvery fleece; where the light wand
tosses, be made pure.

Soon the whole earth shall dance, and the leader of every
company be made one with the god.

To the mountain, to the mountain, where waits the
throng of women, from loom and shuttle driven
by the frenzy of Dionysus!

O holy cavern of Crete, birth-chamber of Zeus, where
the Armed Priests kept watch,

Where helmeted Corybants first filled the vault with
the throbbing of the timbrel, blending in wild tune
therewith the low-breathed music of the Phrygian
flutes.

The timbrel they gave into the hand of Rhea, the Mother; the sound of its beat was mixed with the Bacchanals' cry.

And from the Mother the wild Satyrs took it, to wed with the dances of the feast that makes glad the heart of Dionysus.

O joy upon the mountains, when from the company of racing feet there is one that sinks to the ground,

One that is clad in the holy fawn-skin, a hunter in chase of the wild goat's blood and the glory of torn flesh,

In the eager chase to the Phrygian, Lydian, mountains, when the Child of the Thunder leads the cry!

Then flows the earth with wine and milk; it flows with nectar of the honey-bee.

With smoke as of Syrian frankincense, the wand of Bacchus shoots up a beacon flame;

With the speed of his running, dancing, feet he challenges all who stray, and with cries he makes them to leap.

He casts loose his delicate locks to the wind; and above the cries is the thunder of his calling: Come, ye Bacchanals, come!

Come, ye Bacchanals, with the glory of Tmolus and his golden streams;

Sing to Dionysus with the deep thundering of the drum; with clamour of Phrygian voices make joyful outcry to the God of Joy.

With musical throbbing of the pipe and with beat of revelling feet, as ye troop to the mountain, to the mountain!

Then with joy, as a foal that leaps beside his mother in the grass, even so leap and run the swift feet of the Bacchanal.

N

XIV. SOCRATES

Socrates in Comedy

In the *Clouds* (423 B.C.), Aristophanes made a comprehensiv
attack upon the new-fashioned education which, as he thought
was demoralising the youth of Athens. He chose Socrates, a
a well-known and providentially grotesque figure, to represen
all the rationalist tendencies that he disliked. Most scholars, i
accordance with Socrates' disclaimer in the *Apology* of Plato
agree that Socrates did not teach the Ionian philosophy or th
rhetoric of the Sophists, and that Aristophanes' picture is
libellous caricature.

Strepsiades, an elderly peasant, has married an aristocrati
lady from the city. Their son Pheidippides has brought hi
father into debt by horse-racing. Strepsiades, who has hear
that the new professors can teach how to make "the wors
appear the better reason," has the brilliant idea of putting hi
son, whose wits are brighter than his own, to school with Socrates
Pheidippides refuses with disgust, and Strepsiades has to g
himself. A student admits him to the house. Socrates i
discovered suspended in a basket.

ARISTOPHANES, *Clouds* 218.

Streps. Hallo! who's that? that fellow in the basket
Student. That's HE.
Streps.   Who's HE?
Student.   Socrates.
Streps.   Socrates!

    You sir, call out to him as loud as you can.

Student. Call him yourself: I have not leisure now.
Streps. Socrates! Socrates!

    Sweet Socrates!

Socr.   Mortal! why call'st thou me?
Streps. O, first of all, please tell me what you are doing
Socr. I walk on air, and contem-plate the Sun.
Streps. O then from a basket you contemn the Gods,
    And not from the earth, at any rate?
Socr.   Most true.

158

I could not have searched out celestial matters
Without suspending judgment, and infusing
My subtle spirit with the kindred air.
If from the ground I were to seek these things,
I could not find: so surely does the earth
Draw to herself the essence of our thought.
The same too is the case with water-cress.

Streps. Hillo! what's that?
Thought draws the essence into water-cress?
Come down, sweet Socrates, more near my level,
And teach the lessons which I come to learn.

Socr. And wherefore art thou come?

Streps. To learn to speak.
For, owing to my horrid debts and duns,
My goods are seized, I'm robbed, and mobbed, and
   plundered.

Socr. How did you get involved with your eyes open?

Streps. A galloping consumption seized my money.
Come now; do let me learn the unjust Logic
That can shirk debts: now do just let me learn it.
Name your own price, by all the Gods I'll pay it.

Socr. The Gods! why, you must know the Gods with us
Don't pass for current coin.

Streps. Eh? what do you use then?
Have you got iron, as the Byzantines have?

(Strepsiades is now initiated by a ceremony parodied from
the Corybantic or Orphic mysteries.)

Socr. Come, would you like to learn celestial matters,
How their truth stands?

Streps. Yes, if there's any truth.

Socr. And to hold intercourse with yon bright Clouds,
Our virgin Goddesses?

Streps. Yes, that I should.

Socr. [*Pointing to a pallet-bed.*] Then sit you down upon
  that sacred bed.

Streps. Well, I am sitting.

Socr.   Here then, take this chaplet.

Streps. [*Remembering a scene in a play of Sophocles where
  Athamas is brought in with a chaplet on his
  head to be sacrificed.*] Chaplet? why? why?
  now, never, Socrates:

 Don't sacrifice poor me, like Athamas.

Socr. Fear not: our entrance-services require
 All to do this.

Streps.   But what am I to gain?

Socr. You'll be the flower of talkers, prattlers, gossips:
  [*Dancing round Strepsiades and deluging him with
  a shower of white powder.*]

 Only keep quiet.

Streps.   Zeus! your words come true!
 I shall be flour indeed with all this peppering.

(Socrates solemnly invokes the Clouds, his patronesses, to
appear. They come and greet the neophyte.)

Streps. O Earth! what sound, how august and profound!
  it fills me with wonder and awe.

Socr. These, these then alone, for true Deities own,
  the rest are all God-ships of straw.

Streps. Let Zeus be left out: He's a God beyond doubt:
  come, that you can scarcely deny.

Socr. Zeus, indeed! there's no Zeus: don't you be so
  obtuse.

Streps.   No Zeus up aloft in the sky!
 Then you first must explain, who it is sends the rain;
  or I really must think you are wrong.

Socr. Well then, be it known, these send it alone; I can
  prove it by arguments strong.

Was there ever a shower seen to fall in an hour when
the sky was all cloudless and blue?

Yet on a fine day, when the Clouds were away, he
might send one, according to you.

Streps. Well, it must be confessed, that chimes in with
the rest: your words I am forced to believe.

Yet before, I had dreamed that the rain-water streamed
from Zeus and his chamber-pot sieve.

But whence then, my friend, does the thunder descend?
that does make me quake with affright!

Socr. Why 'tis they, I declare, as they roll through
the air.

Streps.　　　　What! the Clouds? did I hear you aright?

Socr. Ay: for when to the brim filled with water they
swim, by Necessity carried along,

They are hung up on high in the vault of the sky, and
so by Necessity strong

In the midst of their course they clash with great force,
and thunder away without end.

Streps. But is it not He who compels this to be? does
not Zeus this Necessity send?

Socr. No Zeus have we there, but a Vortex of air.

Streps.　　　　What! Vortex? that's something, I own.

I knew not before, that Zeus was no more, but Vortex
was placed on his throne!

But I have not yet heard to what cause you referred
the thunder's majestical roar.

Socr. Yes, 'tis they, when on high full of water they fly,
and then, as I told you before,

By Compression impelled, as they clash, are compelled
a terrible clatter to make.

Streps. Come, how can that be? I really don't see.

Socr.　　　　　　　　Yourself as my proof I will take.

Have you never then eat the broth-puddings you get
  when the Panathenaea comes round,
And felt with what might your bowels all night in
  turbulent tumult resound?

Streps. By Apollo, 'tis true, there's a mighty to-do, and
  my belly keeps rumbling about;
Quite gently at first, papapax, papapax, but soon pappa-
  pappax away,
Till at last, I'll be bound, I can thunder as loud,
  papapappappappappax, as They.

Socr. Shalt thou then a sound so loud and profound from
  thy belly diminutive send,
And shall not the high and infinite Sky go thundering
  on without end?
For both, you will find, on an impulse of wind and
  similar causes depend.

Streps. Well, but tell me from Whom comes the bolt
  through the gloom, with its awful and terrible
  flashes;
And wherever it turns, some it singes and burns, and
  some it reduces to ashes!
For this 'tis quite plain, let who will send the rain,
  that Zeus against perjurers dashes.

Socr. And how, you old fool of a dark-ages school, and
  an antediluvian wit,
If the perjured they strike, and not all men alike, have
  they never Cleonymus hit?
Then of Simon again, and Theorus explain: known
  perjurers, yet they escape.
But he smites his own shrine with his arrows divine,
  and " Sunium, Attica's cape,"
And the ancient gnarled oaks: now what prompted
  these strokes? *They* never forswore, I should say

SOCRATES

Streps. Can't say that they do: your words appear true.
Whence comes then the thunderbolt, pray?

Socr. When a wind that is dry, being lifted on high,
is suddenly pent into these,

It swells up their skin, like a bladder, within, by
Necessity's changeless decrees:

Till, compressed very tight, it bursts them outright,
and away with an impulse so strong,

That at last by the force and swing of its course, it
takes fire as it whizzes along.

Streps. That's exactly the thing that I suffered one spring,
at the great feast of Zeus, I admit:

I'd a paunch in the pot, but I wholly forgot about
making the safety-valve slit.

So it spluttered and swelled, while the sauce-pan I held,
till at last with a vengeance it flew:

Took me quite by surprise, dung-bespattered my eyes,
and scalded my face black and blue! . . .

Socr. Now then you agree in rejecting with me the Gods
you believed in when young,

And *my* creed you'll embrace: " *I believe in wide Space,
in the Clouds, in the eloquent Tongue.*"

Streps. If I happened to meet other God in the street,
I'd show the cold shoulder, I vow.

No libation I'll pour: not one victim more on their
altars I'll sacrifice now.

(Strepsiades is admitted as a pupil, but when he reappears
and receives some instruction on the stage, he is dismissed as
incurably stupid. He induces Pheidippides to take his place.
The following scene illustrates the disastrous results. Strepsiades
comes out of his house screaming, pursued by his son.)

Streps. Oh! Oh!

Help! Murder! Help! O neighbours, kinsfolk,
townsmen,

Help, one and all, against this base assault,
Ah! Ah! my cheek! my head! O luckless me!
Wretch! do you strike your father?

Pheid.   Yes, Papa.

Streps. See! See! he owns he struck me.

Pheid.   To be sure.

Streps. Scoundrel! and parricide! and house-breaker!

Pheid. Thank you: go on, go on: do please go on.
I am quite delighted to be called such names!

Streps. Strike your own father?

Pheid.   O dear yes: what's more,
I'll prove I struck you justly.

Streps.   Struck me justly!
Villain! how can you strike a father justly?

Pheid. Yes, and I'll demonstrate it, if you please.

Streps. Demonstrate this?

Pheid.   O yes, quite easily.
Come, take your choice, which Logic do you choose?

Streps. Which what?

Pheid.   Logic: the Better or the Worse?

Streps. Ah, then, in very truth I've had you taught
To reason down all Justice, if you think
You can prove this, that it is just and right
That fathers should be beaten by their sons!

Pheid. Well, well, I think I'll prove it, if you'll listen,
So that even you won't have one word to answer.

Streps. Come, I should like to hear what you've to say.

Chorus. 'Tis yours, old man, some method to contrive
                    This fight to win:
He would not without arms wherewith to strive
                    So bold have been;
            He knows, be sure, whereon to trust.
            His eager bearing proves he must.

So come and tell us from what cause this sad dispute
    began;
Come, tell us how it first arose: do tell us if you can.
Streps. Well, from the very first I will the whole con-
    tention show:
'Twas when I went into the house to feast him, as
    you know,
I bade him bring his lyre and sing, the supper to
    adorn,
Some lay of old Simonides, as, how the Ram was shorn:
But he replied, to sing at meals was coarse and obsolete;
Like some old beldame humming airs the while she
    grinds her wheat.
Pheid. And should you not be thrashed who told your
    son, from food abstaining
To SING! as tho' you were, forsooth, cicalas enter-
    taining.
Streps. You hear him! so he said just now or e'er high
    words began:
And next he called Simonides a very sorry man.
And when I heard him, I could scarce my rising
    wrath command:
Yet so I did, and him I bid take myrtle in his hand
And chant some lines from Aeschylus, but he replied
    with ire,
" Believe me, I'm not one of those who Aeschylus
    admire,
That rough, unpolished, turgid bard, that mouther
    of bombast! "
When he said this, my heart began to heave extremely
    fast;
Yet still I kept my passion down and said, " Then
    prithee you,

Sing one of those new-fangled songs which modern
    striplings do."
And he began the shameful tale Euripides has told
How a brother and a sister lived incestuous lives of old.
Then, then I could no more restrain, but first I
    must confess
With strong abuse I loaded him, and so, as you may
    guess
We stormed and bandied threat for threat: till out
    at last he flew,
And smashed and thrashed and thumped and bumped
    and bruised me black and blue.

Pheid. And rightly too, who coolly dared Euripides to
    blame,
  Most sapient bard.

Streps.   Most sapient bard! you, what's your
    fitting name?
  Ah! but he'll pummel me again.

Pheid.   He will; and justly too.

Streps. What! justly, heartless villain! when 'twas I
    who nurtured you.
I knew your little lisping ways, how soon, you'd hardly
    think,
If you cried "bree!" I guessed your wants, and used
    to give you drink:
If you said "mamm!" I fetched you bread with
    fond discernment true,
And you would hardly say "cacca!" when through
    the door I flew
And held you out a full arm's length your little needs
    to do:
      But now when I was crying
      That I with pain was dying,

You brute! you would not tarry
Me out of doors to carry,
But choking with despair
I've been and done it there.

Chorus. Sure all young hearts are palpitating now
To hear him plead,
Since if those lips with artful words avow
The daring deed,
And once a favouring verdict win,
A fig for every old man's skin.

O thou! who rakest up new thoughts with daring
hand profane,
Try all you can, ingenious man, that verdict to obtain.

Pheid. How sweet it is these novel arts, these clever
words to know,
And have the power established rules and laws to
overthrow.
Why in old times, when horses were my sole delight,
'twas wonder
If I could say a dozen words without some awful
blunder!
But now that he has made me quit that reckless mode
of living,
And I have been to subtle thoughts my whole attention
giving,
I hope to prove by logic strict 'tis right to beat my father.

Streps. O! buy your horses back, by Zeus, since I would
ten times rather
Have to support a four-in-hand, so I be struck no more.

Pheid. Peace. I will now resume the thread where I
broke off before.
And first I ask: when I was young, did you not
strike me then?

Streps. Yea: for I loved and cherished you.

Pheid.   Well, solve me this again,

Is it not just that I your son should cherish you alike,

And strike you, since, as you observe, to cherish means
to strike?

What! must my body needs be scourged and pounded
black and blue

And yours be scathless? was I not as much freeborn
as you?

"Children are whipped, and shall not sires be
whipped?"[1]

Perhaps you'll urge that children's minds alone are
taught by blows:—

Well: Age is Second Childhood then: that everybody
knows.

And as by old experience Age should guide its steps
more clearly,

So when they err, they surely should be punished
more severely.

Streps. But Law goes everywhere for me: deny it, if
you can.

Pheid. Well, was not he who made the law, a man, a
mortal man,

As you or I, who in old times talked over all the
crowd?

And think you that to you or me the same is not
allowed,

To change it, so that sons by blows should keep their
fathers steady?

Still, we'll be liberal, and blows which we've received
already

We will forget, we'll have no *ex-post-facto* legislation

[1] Parodied from a line in tragedy.

—Look at the game-cocks, look at all the animal
　　creation,

Do not *they* beat their parents? Aye: I say then,
　　that in fact

They are as we, except that they no special laws enact.

Streps. Why don't you then, if always where the game-
　　cock leads you follow,

Ascend your perch to roost at night, and dirt and
　　ordure swallow?

Pheid. The case is different there, old man, as Socrates
　　would see.

Streps. Well then, you'll blame yourself at last, if you
　　keep striking me.

Pheid. How so?

Streps. 　　　　Why, if it's right for me to punish you
　　my son,

You can, if you have got one, yours.

Pheid. 　　　　　　Aye, but suppose I've none.

Then having gulled me you will die, while I've been
　　flogged in vain.

Streps. Good friends! I really think he has some reason
　　to complain.

I must concede he has put the case in quite a novel light:

I really think we should be flogged unless we act aright.

Pheid. Look to a fresh idea then.

Streps. 　　　　　　He'll be my death, I vow

Pheid. Yet then perhaps you will not grudge ev'n what
　　you suffer now.

Streps. How! will you make me like the blows which
　　I've received to-day?

Pheid. Yes, for I'll beat my mother too.

Streps. 　　　　　What! What is that you say?

Why, this is worse than all.

Pheid.   But what if, as I proved the other,
  By the same Logic I can prove 'tis right to beat my
        mother?

Streps.   Aye! what indeed! if this you plead,
        If this you think to win,
        Why then, for all I care, you may
        To the Accursed Pit convey
        Yourself with all your learning new,
        Your master and your Logic too
        And tumble headlong in.

O Clouds! O Clouds! I owe all this to you!
Why did I let you manage my affairs!

Chorus. Nay, nay, old man, you owe it to yourself.
  Why didst thou turn to wicked practices?

Streps. Ah, but ye should have asked me that before,
  And not have spurred a poor old fool to evil.

Chorus.   Such is our plan. We find a man
        On evil thoughts intent,
      Guide him along to shame and wrong,
        Then leave him to repent.

Streps. Hard words, alas! yet not more hard than just.
  It was not right unfairly to keep back
  The money that I borrowed.

                  Come, my darling,
  Come and destroy that filthy Chaerephon
  And Socrates; for they've deceived us both!

Pheid. No. I will lift no hand against my Tutors.

Streps. Yes do, come, reverence Paternal Zeus.

Pheid. Look there! Paternal Zeus! what an old fool!
  Is there a Zeus?

Streps.   There is.

Pheid.   There is *no* Zeus.
  Young Vortex reigns, and he has turned out Zeus.

Streps. No Vortex reigns: that was my foolish thought
   All through this vortex here. Fool that I was . . .
Pheid. Well, rave away, talk nonsense to yourself.
Streps. O! fool, fool, fool, how mad I must have been
   To cast away the Gods, for Socrates.

(The play ends with an assault, led by Strepsiades, upon the
house of Socrates, which he burns down.)

B. B. ROGERS.

Socrates' early Experiences in Philosophy

PLATO, *Phaedo* 95 E. Part of a conversation represented by
Plato as having occurred on the day of Socrates' death.

Socrates, after a long pause of silent reflection, said:
" It is no small matter that you require, Kebes. It
involves a general discussion of the cause of things coming
into existence and passing away. If you like, I will enter
on this discussion—at least of my own experiences; and
then if you find anything I say useful, you shall use it
to produce conviction on the points you mentioned."

" I should like nothing better," said Kebes.

" Very well," continued Socrates, " I will tell you.
When I was young, Kebes, I conceived an extraordinary
passion for the wisdom they call the science of nature.
A grand science I thought it—to know the causes of
everything: why it comes to be, why it perishes, why it
exists. I was always turning over in my mind questions
of this sort: 'Are living things compacted, as some hold,
by a sort of putrefaction arising in the hot and the cold?
Is the blood the organ of consciousness, or is it air, or
fire? Or is it none of these, but the brain which gives
us the sensations of hearing, sight, and smell, and from
these arise memory and judgment, while from memory
and judgment, when they reach a state of quiescence,

comes knowledge?' I considered also the way in which these things cease to exist, and the phenomena of the sky and earth; and I ended by deciding that for this sort of speculation I had as little of a natural turn as could be conceived. . . .

"One day, however, I heard someone [1] reading from a book (as he said) of Anaxagoras, to the effect that it is Mind that orders and is the cause of all things. With this cause I was overjoyed. I found something satisfactory in Mind being responsible for everything; and I thought that, if this be so, surely Mind would order and dispose each and all things in the best possible way. So if anyone wanted to find out the explanation of any given thing— how it comes to be, or exists, or ceases to be—he had better discover how it was best for that thing to be or to act or be acted upon in whatsoever way. On this showing a man had only to consider, with respect to himself or anything else, what was best; it would follow that he would also know what was worse, since one who knows what is good must also know what is bad.

"Reflecting in this way, I thought with joy that I had found in Anaxagoras a teacher of the reason of things after my own heart. I thought he would explain to me, first, whether the earth is flat or round, and then would go on to set forth the reason and the necessity, speaking of what was better, and how it was better that it should be of such a shape; and supposing he said it was in the centre, I expected him to go on and explain how it was better it should be in that position. If he made that clear to me, I had made up my mind not to hanker any more after

[1] Possibly Archelaus, the first Athenian man of science, whose pupil Socrates is said to have been. In ancient, as in mediæval times, reading was a difficult art, and a man reading "to himself" would read aloud. For Anaxagoras see above, p. 123.

any different kind of reason. I was prepared, too, to learn in the same way about the sun and moon and the other stars, about their relative speeds, their turnings, and the other things that happen to them, how it was better for each to act and be acted upon as it is. I never dreamed that one who asserted that they were ordered by Mind would bring in any other reason besides its being best that they should be as they are. I supposed that he would assign, as the cause, to each what is best for each, and would go on to explain the common good for all. I would not have parted with my hopes for a great price; but with much eagerness I sought out the books and read them as fast as I could, in order to know as soon as possible about the best and the worse.

"So exalted were my hopes, and heavy was my fall, when, as I read on, I found that the man made no use of this Mind and did not make it in any way responsible for the ordering of the world, but accounted for things by means of air and fire and water and a host of other absurd causes. It seemed to me that his case was very like that of one who should say that Socrates, in all he does, acts with intelligence, and then, when he tried to give the reasons of any particular action of mine, should begin by saying that the reason why I am sitting here now is that my body is composed of bones and sinews; and while my bones are hard and have joints which separate them, my sinews, which, together with the flesh and the skin which contains them, enfold the bones, can be contracted and relaxed; and so when my bones swing in their sockets, my limbs, relaxing and contracting the sinews, make me able to bend myself at this moment, and that is the reason of my sitting here in a bent posture; and should next go on to account for my talking to you by

o

other causes of the same sort, attributing it to sound and
air and hearing and a hundred other things of that kind,
neglecting to give the real reasons, which are that, when
the Athenians had judged it better to condemn me, for
that very reason I too have decided that it is better to
sit here, and more just to stay and abide whatever penalty
they ordain; for, by the Dog, I fancy these sinews and
bones of mine would have been in Megara or Boeotia long
ago, taken there by a belief about what is best, if I had
not thought it more just and honourable to abide whatever penalty Athens might ordain, rather than leave the
country and run away.

"No; to speak of such things as reasons is too absurd;
though it would be true to say that without having these
things—bones and sinews and the rest—I should not be
able to do what I thought fit; but to say that I act as I
do *because* of them and not because of my choice of the
best, and yet all the time I am acting with intelligence,
would be an uncommonly loose way of talking. Fancy not
being able to see that the cause of something is one thing,
and that without which the cause would not be a cause
is another! which latter I think that people in general
feel, as it were with fingers groping in the dark, and give
it a wrong name, calling it a cause. So it comes about
that one makes the earth stay still under the sky by putting
a whirling motion round it; while another puts the air
under it as a support, like a stand under a broad lid; but
the power which enables the things to be situated at this
moment as it is best for them to be placed, these people
do not investigate, and they do not think of it as having
a supernatural force. No, they believe they could discover some Atlas stronger than this, more immortal
and more world-sustaining; and they think of nothing

as held together by the good, and, in fact, by the bonds of constraining ' obligation ' in the literal sense."

A Defence of Socrates' Piety

XENOPHON, *Recollections of Socrates* i. 1.

I have often wondered by what arguments those who indicted Socrates could have persuaded the Athenians that his life was justly forfeit to the state. The indictment was to this effect: " Socrates is guilty of crime in refusing to recognise the gods acknowledged by the state, and importing strange divinities of his own; he is further guilty of corrupting the young."

In the first place, what evidence did they produce that Socrates refused to recognise the gods acknowledged by the state? Was it that he did not sacrifice? or that he dispensed with divination? On the contrary, he was often to be seen engaged in sacrifice, at home or at the common altars of the state. Nor was his dependence on divination less manifest. Indeed that saying of his, " A divinity gives me a sign," was on everybody's lips. So much so that, if I am not mistaken, it lay at the root of the imputation that he imported novel divinities; though there was no greater novelty in his case than in that of other believers in oracular help, who commonly rely on omens of all sorts: the flight or cry of birds, the utterances of man, chance meetings, or a victim's entrails. Even according to the popular conception, it is not the mere fowl, it is not the chance individual one meets, who knows what things are profitable for a man, but it is the gods who vouchsafe by such instruments to signify the same. This also was the tenet of Socrates. Only whereas men ordinarily speak of being turned aside, or urged onwards by birds, or other creatures encountered on the path, Socrates suited his language to his conviction. "The divinity," said he, "gives me a sign." Further, he would constantly advise his associates to do this, or beware of doing that, upon the authority of this same divine voice; and, as a matter of fact, those who listened to his warnings prospered, whilst he who turned a deaf ear to them repented afterwards. Yet, it will be readily conceded, he would hardly desire to present himself to his everyday companions in the character of either knave or fool. Whereas he would have appeared to be both, supposing the God-given revelations had but revealed his own proneness to deception. It is plain he would not have ventured on forecast at all, but for his belief that the words he spoke would in fact be verified. Then on whom, or what, was the assurance rooted, if not upon God? And if he had faith in the gods, how could he fail to recognise them?

But his mode of dealing with his intimates has another aspect. As regards the ordinary necessities of life, his advice was, "Act as you believe these things may best be done." But in the case of those darker problems, the issues of which are incalculable, he directed his friends to consult the oracle, whether the business should be undertaken or not. "No one," he would say, "who wishes to manage a house or city with success: no one aspiring to guide the helm of state aright, can afford to dispense with aid from above. Doubtless skill in carpentering, building, smithying, farming, or the art of governing men, together with the theory of these processes, and the sciences of arithmetic, economy, strategy are affairs of study, and within the grasp of human intelligence. Yet there is a side even of these, which the gods reserve to themselves, the bearing of which is hidden from mortal vision. Thus, let a man sow field or plant farm never so well, yet he cannot foretell who will gather in the fruits: another may build him a house of fairest proportion, yet he knows not who will inhabit it. . . . To suppose that all these matters lay within the scope of human judgment, to the exclusion of the preternatural, was preternatural folly. Nor was it less extravagant to go and consult the will of Heaven on questions which it is given us to decide by dint of learning. . . .

No one ever heard him say, or saw him do, anything impious or irreverent. Indeed, in contrast to others he set his face against all discussion of such high matters as the nature of the universe; how the " kosmos," as the *savants* [1] phrase it, came into being; or by what forces the celestial phenomena arise. To trouble one's brain about such matters was, he argued, to play the fool. He would ask first: Did these investigators feel their knowledge of things human so complete that they betook themselves to these lofty speculations? Or did they maintain that they were playing their proper parts in thus neglecting the affairs of man to speculate on the concerns of God? He was astonished they did not see how far these problems lay beyond mortal ken; since even those who pride themselves most on their discussion of these points differ from each other, as madmen do. For just as some madmen, he said, have no apprehension of what is truly terrible, others fear where no fear is; . . . some honour neither temple, nor altar, nor aught else sacred to the name of God; others bow down to stocks and stones and worship the very beasts:—so is it with those thinkers whose minds are cumbered with cares

[1] Literally "the sophists."

concerning the Universal Nature.   One sect[1] has discovered that Being is one and indivisible.   Another[2] that it is infinite in number.   If one[3] proclaims that all things are in a continual flux, another[4] replies that nothing can possibly be moved at any time. . . . The theory of the universe as a process of birth and death is met by the counter-theory, that nothing ever could be born or ever will die.

But the questioning of Socrates on the merits of these speculators sometimes took another form.   The student of human learning expects, he said, to make something of his studies for the benefit of himself or others, as he likes.   Do these explorers into the divine operations hope that when they have discovered by what forces the various phenomena occur, they will create winds and waters at will, and fruitful seasons?   Will they manipulate these and the like to suit their needs?   or has no such notion perhaps ever entered their heads, and will they be content simply to know how such things come into existence?   But if this was his mode of describing those who meddle with such matters as these, he himself never wearied of discussing human topics: What is piety?   what is impiety?   What is the beautiful?   what the ugly?   What the noble?   what the base?   What are meant by just and unjust?   what by sobriety and madness?   what by courage and cowardice?   What is a state?   what is a statesman?   what is a ruler over men?   what is a ruling character?   and other like problems, the knowledge of which, as he put it, conferred a patent of nobility on the possessor, whereas those who lacked the knowledge might deservedly be stigmatised as slaves.   H. G. DAKYNS.

[1] The Eleatics.   [2] E.g. the Atomists.
[3] Heracleitus.   [4] Zeno.

Socrates' religious Practice

XENOPHON, *Recollections of Socrates* i. 3.

His formula of prayer was simple : ' Give me that which is best for me,' for, said he, the gods know best what good things are—to pray for gold or silver or despotic power were no better than to make some particular throw at dice or stake in battle or any such thing the subject of prayer, of which the future consequences are manifestly uncertain.

If with scant means he offered but small sacrifices he believed that he was in no wise inferior to others who make frequent and large sacrifices from an ampler store. It were ill surely for the very gods themselves, could they take delight in large sacrifices rather than in small, else oftentimes must the offerings of bad men be found acceptable rather than of good; nor from the point of view of men themselves would life be worth living if the offerings of a villain rather than of a righteous man found favour in the sight of Heaven. His belief was that the joy of the gods is greater in proportion to the holiness of the giver, and he was ever an admirer of that line of Hesiod which says:

' According to thine ability do sacrifice to the immortal gods.'

" Yes," he would say, " in our dealings with friends and strangers alike, and in reference to the demands of life in general, there is no better motto for a man than that: '*Let a man do according to his ability*.' "

H. G. DAKYNS.

A Conversation on Piety

PLATO, *Euthyphro* 12 D–end (abridged). Socrates on the eve of his trial meets Euthyphro, a pompous formalist who prides himself on his piety, and is about to prosecute his father for manslaughter on the highest religious grounds. Socrates challenges him to define piety and impiety. The definition: "Piety is what all the gods love, impiety is what they all hate," is rejected on the ground that to be beloved of the gods is only an accident of piety, not its essence. Euthyphro confesses that he is bewildered, and Socrates then puts forward a suggestion: that piety is "a part of justice," a species of right conduct. The word for piety (*hosiotēs*), commonly translated "holiness," means a quality, often ranked with the cardinal virtues, Justice, Temperance, etc. It carries a suggestion of sanctity, ceremonial purity, the formal and scrupulous side of religiousness. The word translated by "care" has no suitable English equivalent. It means "tending," but it is not natural to us to think of tending our gods as a groom tends horses.

Socr. Now see what follows. If piety is a part of right conduct, we must find out, I suppose, which part it is. . . .

Euth. Well, Socrates, I should say that piety and religion are that part of right conduct which has to do with the care we bestow on the service of the gods; the rest would be the part that has to do with mankind.

Socr. That strikes me as a good answer, Euthyphro; but I am still not satisfied upon one small point. I do not yet understand what kind of care you mean. You surely do not mean that the gods are the object of the same sort of care as that we bestow on other things. For instance, we should say that only a groom understands the care of horses, shouldn't we?

Euth. Certainly.

Socr. Because the groom's art consists in the care of horses, as the huntsman's consists in the care of dogs, and the herdsman's in the care of cattle?

Euth. Yes.

Socr. And holiness and piety are care for the gods. Is that what you mean, Euthyphro?

Euth. It is.

Socr. Then is not the object effected by any kind of care always the same? Is it not the good or benefit of the thing cared for? The groom's skill benefits and improves the horses under his care, the huntsman improves his dogs, the herdsman his cattle, and so in all cases. Does then care for the gods, which is piety, benefit and improve the gods? Would you agree that, every time you perform a pious action, you are making one of the gods better?

Euth. Of course not.

Socr. No; I am quite sure you don't mean that, Euthyphro; that was why I asked what you meant by care for the gods. I thought you didn't mean care of that sort.

Euth. You were right, Socrates; I do not.

Socr. Good. But then what sort of care for the gods will piety be?

Euth. Such care as slaves bestow on their masters.

Socr. I understand: a kind of service paid to the gods

Euth. Precisely.

Socr. Well then, can you tell me what result the service of a doctor produces? Is it not health?

Euth. Yes.

Socr. And the service of a shipwright—what does that produce?

Euth. A ship, of course.

Socr. Tell me, then, what result the service of the gods will produce. You must know, since you claim to know more about religion than anyone else.

Euth. A true claim, Socrates.

Socr. Then tell me, in heaven's name, what is that

grand result which the gods use our services to
produce?

Euth. Many admirable results, Socrates.

Socr. So does a general, my friend; but you can easily
sum them up as the achievement of victory in war. A
farmer, too, produces many admirable results, but they
all amount to making the earth bear food. What do
the many admirable results produced by the gods
amount to?

Euth. I told you just now, Socrates, that it is no easy
matter to arrive at an exact understanding of all these
things. However, in general terms, I can say this: when
a man knows that, in his prayers and sacrifices, he is
saying and doing what is acceptable to the gods, that is
true piety, such as preserves household and state. What
is unacceptable is impiety, and that brings universal ruin
and destruction.

Socr. I am sure you could have answered my question
in sum much more briefly, if you had chosen. Evidently
you are not eager to instruct me. . . . However, I am
asking you questions and I must follow wherever you lead
me. So, once again, what do you mean by piety? A sort
of art of prayer and sacrifice, isn't it?

Euth. Yes.

Socr. And sacrifice is giving to the gods, while prayer
is asking of them?

Euth. Certainly.

Socr. On that showing, then, piety is an art of asking
of the gods and giving to them.

Euth. You understand my meaning perfectly, Socrates.

Socr. That is because I am hungry for your wisdom,
my friend, and so I am all attention, and not a word you
say will fall to the ground. But tell me, what is this

service of the gods? You say it is asking of them and giving to them.

Euth. I do.

Socr. Then to ask rightly will be to ask for those things we need to obtain from them.

Euth. Naturally.

Socr. And to give rightly will be to give them in return the things they need to obtain from us. There would be little skill in making presents to a person who had no need of them.

Euth. True.

Socr. Then piety will be a kind of traffic between gods and men.

Euth. Yes, a kind of traffic, if you prefer to call it so.

Socr. I have no preference for the name, if it is not true. But explain. What good to the gods are the gifts they receive from us? What they give, anyone can see: every good thing we have is a gift from them. But how are they profited by what they receive from us? Or do we get the better of them in this traffic to the extent of getting all good things from them while they get nothing from us?

Euth. But do you imagine, Socrates, that the gods are benefited by what they receive from us?

Socr. Well, what are these gifts of ours to the gods?

Euth. What else do you suppose but honour and homage and, as I said just now, what is acceptable?

Socr. So piety is acceptable to the gods, Euthyphro, but not profitable nor dear to them?

Euth. I think it is dearer to them than anything else.

Socr. Oh, then once more that is what piety means—what is dear to the gods?

Euth. Most certainly.

Socr. Don't you see that our argument has gone round

in a circle to the point where it was before? You must remember that at an earlier stage we found that piety and what is dear to the gods were not the same, but two different things.

Euth. Yes, I do.

Socr. And now don't you perceive that you are saying they are the same? Either our former conclusion was wrong, or, if that was right, we are wrong now.

Euth. So it seems.

Socr. Then we must begin our inquiry into the nature of piety all over again, for I have no intention of giving in until I have understood. Do not disdain me, but give your whole mind to the question and tell me the truth this time. If anyone knows, it is you; and, like Proteus, you must not be let go until you have told me. You could never have undertaken to prosecute your father in his old age for murdering a labourer, if you had not a clear knowledge of what piety and impiety are. You would have feared to risk the anger of heaven, in case you were doing wrong, and you would have been afraid of what men would say. But now I am convinced you think you know perfectly what is pious and what is not. So tell me without concealment, what you think about it.

Euth. Another time, then, Socrates. I am in a hurry now, and it is time for me to be going.

Socr. My dear friend, what are you doing! By going away you are destroying all my hopes of clearing myself of Meletus' accusation by learning from you what piety and impiety are. I had meant to explain to him that now Euthyphro had made me wise about religion, and that I had given up making rash statements about, and introducing novelties, and was going to lead a better life in the future.

Socrates refuses to renounce his Vocation

PLATO, *Socrates' Speech in his Own Defence* 28 D. This speech
is not a literal report of what Socrates said in court, but Plato
no doubt is faithful in spirit and substance.

The truth is, Athenians, that, wherever a man's post
may be, whether he has chosen it himself as the best place
for him or been set there by a superior, there it is his duty
to remain at all risks, without thinking of death or anything else except dishonour. When the officers whom
you elected to be my superiors at Potidaea, at Amphipolis,
and at Delium stationed me at my post, I stayed there,
like anyone else, at the risk of death; and it would be
strange if fear of death or of anything whatever should make
me a deserter now, when heaven, as I believe, has laid
upon me the duty to spend my life in seeking wisdom and
in examining myself and others. Such conduct would
be strange indeed; and I should really deserve to be put
on my trial for not believing in gods; for I should be
disobeying the oracle, fearing death, and thinking myself
wise when I was not. To fear death is, in fact, to think
you are wise when you are not; for it is to think you
know what you do not know. No one knows whether
death may not be the greatest good a man can have; yet
men fear it as if they were certain it was the worst of
evils. What is this but folly—that shameful folly of
thinking we know what we do not know? Here again
I am, perhaps, superior to the ordinary man; if I
were to make any claim to be wiser than others, it would
be because I do not think I have any sufficient knowledge
of the other world, when in fact I have none. What I
do know is that it is bad and dishonourable to do wrong
and to disobey a superior, be he man or god. Accordingly,
when I am confronted by evils which I know to be evils,

I will never take fright and run away from a thing which, for anything I know, may be a good.

Accordingly, even supposing that you now acquit me, and are not convinced by Anytus' argument that either I ought never to have been brought to trial or, now that I am here, you are bound to condemn me to death, because, if I should escape, all your sons would be hopelessly corrupted by practising what Socrates teaches— supposing you were to say to me: " Socrates, this time we will not listen to Anytus; we will let you go, on this condition, that you shall spend no more time upon this search after wisdom: only, if you are caught at it again, you shall be put to death "—if, I say, you would offer to acquit me on these terms, my answer would be: " Athenians, I hold you in much affection and esteem; but I will obey heaven rather than you, and, so long as breath and strength are in me, I will never cease from seeking wisdom or from exhorting you and pointing out the truth to any of you whom I may chance to meet, in my accustomed words : ' My good friend, you are a citizen of Athens, a great city famous for wisdom and strength; are you not ashamed to spend so much trouble upon heaping up riches and honour and reputation, while you care nothing for wisdom and truth and the perfection of your soul ? ' And if he protests that he does care for these things, I shall not immediately release him and go my way; I shall question and cross-examine and test him, and if I think he does not possess the virtue he affects, I shall reproach him for holding the most precious things cheap, and worthless things dear. This I shall do to everyone whom I meet, young or old, citizen or stranger, but especially to you, my fellow-citizens, inasmuch as you are of my own people. For be assured that such is heaven's command; and I believe that no better piece of fortune has ever befallen you in Athens than my enlistment in the service of heaven.

"For I have no other business but to go about persuading you all, both young and old, to care less for your bodies and your wealth than for the perfection of your souls, and to make that your first concern, and telling you that goodness does not come from wealth, but wealth and every other good thing, public or private, comes to mankind from goodness. If, by saying that, I am corrupting the young men, so much the worse; but if it is asserted that I have anything else to say, then that is not true. Therefore, Athenians," I should conclude, ' you may listen to Anytus or not; you may acquit me or not; for I shall not change my ways though I were to die a thousand deaths."

XV. PLATO

Plato (427–347 B.C.) wrote imaginary conversations, the earliest of which were intended to defend the memory of Socrates and to illustrate his method. Plato continued to use this literary form for the development of his own philosophy. That he, and he alone, understood the profound spirit of his master is beyond doubt; but we cannot say with certainty where the thought of the historic Socrates ends and the thought of Plato begins.

Socrates restates his Defence for his Friends

PLATO, *Phaedo* 63 B.

"Let me try," said Socrates, "to make before you a more convincing defence than I made in court. I should be wrong, Simmias and Cebes," he went on, "not to be distressed at death, did I not believe that I shall go to the presence of gods who are wise and good, and of dead men who are better than the men now in this world. Let me assure you that I hope to find myself in the company of good men, though of that I am not altogether certain; but I am as certain as I can be in such a matter that I shall come into the presence of gods who are the best of masters. That is why I am not so much distressed: I have good hope that the dead have some sort of existence, and indeed, according to the old doctrine, an existence much better for the good than for the wicked. . . .

"I wish now to render an account to you, my judges, of my belief that a man who has really spent his life in philosophy has reason to meet death with a good courage and to be confident that after death all will be well with him in that other world. How this may be, I will try to explain.

"The world, perhaps, does not see that dying and death are the only study of men who rightly engage in philosophy. If that is true, surely it would be absurd that a man who had all his life desired nothing else than death should be distressed when that which had so long been his study and desire actually came."

Here Simmias laughed. "Really, Socrates," he said, "you make me laugh, though I am at this moment hardly in a laughing mood. The world, if it could hear what you have said, would think it a very apt description of the philosopher. My own countrymen would entirely agree that philosophers are ripe for death; and they would add that it is no news to them that philosophers deserve to get it."

"And they would be right, Simmias, except in saying that it was no news to them; for they have never understood in what sense the true philosopher is ripe for death, or what sort of death he deserves, or how he deserves it. We will let them alone and talk among ourselves. We think that death is a thing that can be defined?"

"Certainly," answered Simmias.

"As nothing else than the separation of the soul from the body?—that to be dead means that body and soul are separated and each has come to exist apart by itself? Is death anything but that?"

"No, it is that," he replied.

"Now consider whether you agree with me on another point that will help us, I think, to a better understanding of our subject. Do you think it is like a philosopher to take very seriously what are called pleasures, such as eating and drinking?"

"Certainly not, Socrates," said Simmias.

"Or sex?"

P

" No."

" Or the whole business of looking after the body?
Will the philosopher rate that highly? Will he think
much of getting superior clothes and shoes and all the
other fine things to ornament his person, or will he think
nothing of them except when he is positively obliged
to attend to them? "

" I should say the true philosopher would think nothing
of such things."

" In short you think his concern is not with the body;
he keeps clear of the body, so far as he can, and turns
towards the soul."

" Yes."

" In this respect, then, we see the philosopher as one
who, above all men, sets free his soul from its association
with the body."

Simmias agreed.

" And in the world's opinion, to find no pleasure in
bodily things and take no part in them makes life not
worth living. If a man cares nothing for the pleasures
of the body, he is as good as dead."

" That is perfectly true."

" And when we come to positive progress in wisdom,
does the body stand in the way, if you take it for an
associate in that pursuit, or does it not? Take, for example, sight and hearing. Is there any real truth to be
found by man in them? The very poets are never tired
of telling us that we never see or hear anything exactly
as it is. And if those senses are not clear and accurate,
the rest can hardly be so, because they are all inferior to
sight and hearing. Don't you agree? "

" I do."

" When is it, then, that the soul lays hold of truth?

For, obviously, whenever it takes the body with it in the search, its companion leads it astray."

" True."

" If any truth ever becomes clear to the soul, is it not when it is reasoning ? "

" Yes."

" And it reasons best when it is not harassed by any of these sensations, hearing or sight, pain or pleasure; when it lets the body go its own way, withdrawing as far as it can from all association and contact with it, and then reaches out after truth by itself."

Simmias assented.

" Is not this another way in which the philosopher's soul above all despises the body and escapes from it, trying to get away by itself ? "

" Evidently."

" Now, what do you say to this, Simmias ? Do we recognise any such thing as absolute justice ? "

" Certainly we do."

" And absolute beauty, and goodness ? "

" Of course."

" Have you ever seen such a thing with your eyes ? "

" Never," replied Simmias.

" Or apprehended them with any other bodily sense? I include all the things in which the real being of anything consists—absolute magnitude, absolute health or strength—in a word, all such things. Are they perceived in their true reality by means of the body ? Do we not rather come nearest to the knowledge of any such thing, when we set ourselves very carefully to think about any one of them we may be considering, just as it is in itself ? "

" Undoubtedly."

" And is not this purity of thought to be attained

most perfectly by approaching every such term just with
the intellect alone, without dragging in sight or any other
sense to take part in the reasoning process? When we
attempt to track out any real thing as it is by itself in its
purity, the intellect by itself in its purity must be employed. A man must do his best to set himself free from
eyes and ears—one might almost say, from the body altogether; because, as soon as the body comes in, it troubles
the soul and will not allow it to gain truth and wisdom.
Is not that the only way to succeed in laying hold upon
reality, Simmias?"

"Nothing could be truer, Socrates."

"Must not all this," continued Socrates, "suggest
to genuine philosophers a thought which one of them
might express by saying to another: 'It seems that we
can reach home only by a sort of by-path; because, so long
as we have this body and our soul is clouded and confused with such an evil associate, we shall never be satisfied
or gain what we desire, namely, the truth. The body
takes up all our time with the endless trouble of providing
the food it needs; and every attack of illness hinders us
in our search for reality. It fills us with desires and
appetites and fears and every sort of nonsensical phantasy,
so that, in literal truth, it makes it impossible for us ever
to think about anything. Wars, factions, fighting, have
no other origin than the body and its desires. All wars
are made for the sake of getting money, and we are obliged
to get money for the sake of the body, to whose service
we are enslaved. It is all this that leaves us no leisure to
seek wisdom. Worst of all, if it does leave us a moment
in which we can turn to think about something, once
more it breaks in upon our thoughts at every step and
troubles them with such confusion and dismay that we

cannot see the truth plain—all because of the body. Certainly our case is clear, that, if ever we are to have any pure knowledge, we must get free from the body and contemplate things as they are with the soul alone; only then, it seems, shall our desire be satisfied with that wisdom which we profess to love. All we have said goes to show that wisdom may be ours when we are dead, but never while we are alive. For if we cannot have any pure knowledge while the body is with us, then either we shall never win it or only after death; for not till then will the soul be separate from the body and alone with itself. And, while life lasts, we shall, it seems, come nearest to having knowledge, if we have as little to do with the body as possible, and no more association with it than is absolutely necessary; if we keep ourselves pure from the infection of its nature, until God himself shall set us free; and when we are thus purified and released from the folly of the flesh, we shall, in all likelihood, be with others in the same condition, and know, of ourselves, whatsoever is pure; and surely that is truth; for the impure is not permitted to apprehend the pure.'

"Such I think, Simmias, must be the thoughts of all who rightly love knowledge; and that is what they would say to one another. . . .

"It is a fact, then, that the occupation of the true philosopher is a rehearsal of death, and to him of all men death is least terrible. Consider: he is at variance with his body at every point and longing to possess his soul alone. When the moment comes, what could be more unreasonable than to be frightened and distressed, instead of setting out with joy to the place where he may hope to find the thing that he has, all his life, passionately desired—wisdom, and to be free from the company of the thing

with which he was at enmity? Many a man, when
human love or wife or son has died, has of his own wil
chosen to make his journey to the world of death, drawn
by the hope of seeing there those whom he longed for and
of being with them. Shall one who is truly in love with
wisdom and has conceived the same passionate hope tha
in the other world he will meet with her as he will fine
her nowhere else—shall he be distressed at dying and no
set out upon his way thither rejoicing? Dear Simmias
there can be no doubt, if he is really a lover of wisdom
so intense will be his conviction that he will never mee
with wisdom in her purity anywhere but there. If thi
be so, what could be more unreasonable, as I said, tha
that such a man should be afraid of death?"

The Case against Popular Religion

PLATO, *Republic* ii. 362 D. The *Republic* is a dialogue o
"Justice" or righteousness. After an inconclusive argumen
in which Socrates defends morality against Thrasymachus, th
sophist, his opponent retires unconvinced. The young brother
Glaucon and Adeimantus then challenge Socrates to prove tha
morality, social and individual, is worth having for its ow
sake, apart from any consequences or rewards and penaltie
in this life or in the next. Glaucon states the "common opinion
that morality is a mere matter of convention, originating in
social compact; and that men behave morally only because the
cannot, or dare not, do otherwise. Adeimantus then interven
to complete the case which Socrates has to answer.

When Glaucon had ended and I was meditating
reply, his brother Adeimantus exclaimed: "Surel
Socrates, you cannot suppose that that is all there is t
be said."

"Why, isn't it?" said I.

"The most essential part of the case has been left out,
he replied.

"Well," I answered, "there is a proverb about th

value of a brother's aid. If Glaucon has failed, it is for you to make good his deficiencies. Though, so far as I am concerned, he has said quite enough to put me out of the running and make me incapable of rescuing the cause of Justice."

"Nonsense," said Adeimantus; "there is more to be said, and you must listen to it. If we want a clear view of what I take to be Glaucon's meaning, we must study the opposite side of the case, the arguments used when justice is praised and injustice blamed. When children are told by their fathers and all their other relatives that it is a duty to be just, what is commended is not justice in itself but the respectability it brings. We are to make people think we are just, in order to gain high positions and marry well and obtain all the other advantages which Glaucon mentioned as accruing to the just man from his good reputation.

"In this matter of having a good name, they go further still: they throw in the favourable opinion of heaven, and can tell us of no end of good things which they say the gods give to the pious. There is the good old Hesiod [1] who says the gods make the just man's oak-trees 'bear acorns at the top and bees in the middle; and their sheep's fleeces are heavy with wool,' and a great many other good things of that sort. And Homer speaks in the same strain:

"Like a blameless king who fears the gods and upholds right judgment; and then the dark earth yields wheat and barley, and the trees are laden with fruit; the young of his flocks are strong, and the sea gives abundance of fish."

"Musaeus and his son Eumolpus [2] endow the just with gifts from heaven of an even more spirited sort. They

---

[1] See above, p. 28.   [2] Supposed authors of Orphic writings.

take the righteous to the other world and provide them with a banquet of the Saints, where they sit for all time drinking with garlands on their heads, as if virtue could not be more nobly rewarded than by an eternity of intoxication. Others, again, give a yet greater extension to the wages of heaven: the pious man who keeps his oaths is to have children's children and to leave a posterity after him. When they have sung the praises of justice in that strain, with more to the same effect, they proceed to plunge the sinners and unrighteous men into a sort of mud-pool in the other world, and set them to carry water in a sieve. Even in this life, too, they give them a bad name, and make out that the unjust suffer all those penalties which Glaucon described as falling upon the good man who has a bad reputation: they can think of no others. That is how justice is recommended, and injustice decried.

" Besides all this, think of the way in which justice and injustice are spoken of, not only in ordinary life, but in the poets. All with one voice din into our ears that self-control and justice, admirable as they may be, are difficult and troublesome, whereas vice and injustice are pleasant and very easily to be had; it is mere convention to regard them as dishonourable. They tell us that dishonesty is generally more profitable than honesty. They will cheerfully speak of a bad man as happy and load him with honours and social esteem, provided he be rich and otherwise powerful; while they despise and disregard one who has neither power nor wealth, though all the while they acknowledge that he is the better man of the two.

" Most surprising of all is what they say about the gods and virtue : that heaven itself often allots misfortune and a hard life to the good man, and gives prosperity to the wicked. Strolling soothsayers come to the rich man's doors with a story of a power which they possess by the gift of heaven, to atone for any offence that he or his ancestors have committed, by sacrifice and incantations agreeably accompanied by feasting. If he wishes to injure an enemy, he can, at a trifling expense, do him a hurt with equal ease, whether he be an honest man or not, by means of certain invocations and spells which, as they profess, prevail upon the gods to do their bidding. In support of all these claims they call the poets to witness. Some, by way of advertising the easiness of vice, quote the words: 'Unto wickedness men attain easily and in multitudes; smooth is the way and her dwelling is very near at hand. But the gods have ordained much sweat upon the path to virtue' and a long road that is rough and steep.[1]

"Others, to show that men can turn the gods from their purpose, cite Homer: 'Even the gods themselves listen to entreaty. Their hearts are turned by the entreaties of men, with sacrifice and meek prayers and libation and burnt offering, whensoever anyone transgresses and does amiss.'[2] They produce a whole arsenal of books in which Musaeus and Orpheus, described as descendants of the Muses and the Moon, prescribe their ritual; and they persuade whole cities, as well as individuals, that, both in this life and after death, wrong-doing may be absolved and purged away by means of sacrifices and agreeable performances which they are pleased to call rites of initiation. These deliver us from punishment in the other world, where awful things are in store for us if we do not perform the sacrifices.

[1] Hesiod, see above, p. 29.
[2] *Iliad* ix. 497. See above, p. 10.

"When all this stuff is talked about the estimation in which virtue and vice are held by heaven and by mankind, what effect can we suppose it has upon the mind of a young man hearing it, if he is quick-witted enough to gather honey from all these flowers of popular wisdom and to draw his own conclusions as to the sort of person he should be and the way he should go, in order to lead the best possible life? In all likelihood he would say to himself, in Pindar's words: ' Shall I mount by the way of right or the by-paths of deceit to a higher fortress,' where I may entrench myself for the rest of my life? For, according to what they tell me, I have nothing to gain but trouble and manifest loss from being honest, unless I also get a name for being so; whereas, if I am dishonest and provide myself with a reputation for honesty, they promise me a marvellous career. Very well, then; since ' outward seeming,' as wise men inform me, ' over- powers the truth ' and decides the question of happiness, I had better give myself up to it. I must ensconce myself behind an imposing façade designed to look like virtue, and trail the fox behind me, ' the cunning shifty fox ' [1] — Archilochus knew the world as well as any man. You may say it is not so easy to be wicked without ever being found out. Perhaps not; but great things are never easy. Anyhow, if we are to reach happiness, everything we have been told points to this as the road to be followed. We will form secret societies to save us from exposure; besides, there are men who teach the art of winning over popular assemblies and courts of law; so that, one way or another, by persuasion or violence, we shall get the better of our neighbours without being punished. You might object that the gods are not to be deceived

[1] An allusion to a fable by Archilochus.

and are beyond the reach of violence. But suppose that there are no gods, or that they do not concern themselves with the doings of men; why should we concern ourselves to deceive them ? Or, if the gods do exist and care for mankind, all we know or have ever heard about them comes from current tradition and from the poets who recount their family history; and these same authorities also assure us that they can be won over and turned from their purpose ' by sacrifices and meek prayers ' and votive offerings. We must either accept both these statements or neither. If we are to accept both, we had better do wrong and use part of the proceeds to offer sacrifice. By keeping straight we may escape the punishment of heaven, but we shall be renouncing the profits of wrong-doing; whereas by doing wrong we shall make our profit and escape punishment as well by means of the entreaties which win over the gods when we 'transgress and do amiss.' But then, you will say, in the other world the penalty for our misdeeds on earth will fall either upon us or upon our children's children. We can counter that objection by reckoning on the great efficacy that lies in mystic rites and the divinities of absolution, vouched for by the authority of the greatest cities and by the sons of the gods who have appeared as poets and spokesmen of heavenly inspiration. . . .

"What lies at the bottom of all this is nothing but the fact from which Glaucon, as well as I, started upon this long discourse. We put it to you, Socrates, with all respect, in this way. All you who profess to sing the praises of right conduct, from the ancient heroes whose discourses have survived, down to the men of the present day, have never denounced injustice or praised justice apart from the reputation, honours, and rewards they bring; but what effect either of them in itself has upon its possessor when it dwells in his soul unseen of gods or men, no one has ever yet explained either in prose or poetry. No one has proved that a soul can harbour no worse evil than injustice, no greater good than justice. Had all of you said that from the first and tried to convince us from our youth up, we should not be keeping watch upon our neighbours to prevent them from doing wrong to us, but everyone would keep a far more effectual watch over himself, for fear lest, by wronging others, he should open his doors to the worst evil of all."

Theology in the Ideal State

PLATO, *Republic* 378 E (abridged). Socrates has objected to the use, in elementary education, of myths representing gods and heroes as behaving immorally. Adeimantus asks what myths are to be used in the ideal state.

I replied: "You and I, Adeimantus, are not, for the moment, poets, but founders of a state. As such, it is not our business to make up myths; all that belongs to us is to know the types to which our poets must conform when they compose their stories, and from which they must not be suffered to deviate."

"True," answered Adeimantus; "but what are these types, as you call them, in the case of theology?"

"Of this sort," said I. "The poet, whether he is writing epic, lyric, or drama, surely ought always to represent God as he really is."

"Yes, he ought."

"And God is good, and to be described as such?"

"Of course."

"And what is good is never harmful, is it?"

"No, I don't think it is."

"Can the harmless do any hurt?"

"No."

"Or what does no hurt, do any evil?"

"Once more, no."

"And what does no evil, cannot be the cause of any evil?"

"How should it be?"

"Again, the good is beneficent."

"Yes."

"And therefore the cause of well-being."

"Yes."

"Then the good is not the cause of everything, but only of what is as it should be. It is not responsible for evil."

"Certainly," he replied.

"If so, God, since he is good, cannot be the cause of all things, as people say, but only of a few things that happen to men. He is not responsible for the greater part, for the good things in human life are far fewer than the evil, and whereas the good must be ascribed to God only, for the evils we must look for some causes other than God."

"I think that is perfectly true," said Adeimantus.

(Socrates then condemns the poets for attributing both good and evil to the gods, and for asserting that they instigate men to sin in order to punish them. The only purpose of punishment must be to improve the sinner.)

"Now, what do you think of this second principle? Do you think that God is a sort of magician who might appear in various shapes at different times, now actually changing his own form into a number of other forms, now tricking us into believing that he has done so; or do you think that his nature is simple, and that he would be the last to pass out of his own proper form?"

" I cannot say offhand," he replied.

(Socrates argues that the best things are least liable to be changed by outward agencies, and that a perfect being cannot desire to change himself. Stories which tell of transformations of the gods are rejected.)

" But perhaps," I went on, "though the gods are not of a nature to change in themselves, they may deceive us by their magic into thinking that they appear in a variety of forms."

" Perhaps."

"Why," said I, "would a god tell a lie or act one by putting before us an unreal appearance?"

" I do not know."

" Do you not know that the true lie—if that is a possible expression—is a thing that all gods and men hate?"

"What do you mean?"

" I mean this, that no one willingly lies with the highest part of himself and about the highest things; there is nothing he fears so much as to entertain falsity there."

" I do not even yet understand."

" Because you think I mean something out of the ordinary; whereas all I mean is: lying with the soul about the truth. To lie or to be deceived and ignorant about the truth and to harbour falsity in the soul, is a thing no one would consent to. A lie in that quarter is hated above everything."

" It is indeed."

"Well then, as I was saying, this ignorance in the soul of one who is deceived has the best title to be called the true lie; for the spoken lie is only a representation or image of a previous condition of the soul, not pure unadulterated falsity. Is it not so?"

" It is."

(It is then argued that God can have no occasion for lying in any of its legitimate uses, *e.g.* to an enemy or a madman.)

"God, then, is a being of perfect simplicity and truth in action and in speech. He does not really depart from his own nature, nor does he impose upon others, whether by apparitions or by words or by sending signs to men waking or asleep."

"I am convinced by your argument," he replied.

(Stories of deceptive dreams sent by the gods and misleading oracles are then denounced, and Adeimantus agrees that the above principles of theology should be adopted as laws.)

The Nature of the Soul and the Vision of Truth

PLATO, *Phaedrus* 245 C. After a formal proof that soul, being self-moving and the source of all motion, must be without beginning of existence and imperishable, Socrates describes the triple nature of the soul and its vision of truth before incarnation. The only knowledge we can attain in this world is a recollection or "reminiscence" of truth apprehended before birth, when the soul had immediate acquaintance with the "forms" (or "Ideas") which are the true realities only imperfectly represented in the sense-world. The imagery in this passage is borrowed from the Eleusinian mysteries and the Orphic and Pythagorean doctrines.

Enough, then, of the immortality of the soul: we must now speak of its form, acknowledging that only a god could set forth its true nature at length; as men we must be content to speak more briefly and in a figure. Let us then liken the soul to a thing of composite nature—a chariot with two winged horses and a charioteer. Now, in the gods, horses and charioteer are all noble and of noble origin; in other beings there is a mixture. In us the master has to drive a pair of horses, one of whom is a fine horse of noble character and birth, whereas the other is the reverse; so that in our case the management is difficult and harassing.

Let me try to explain the meaning of 'mortal' and

'immortal creature.' Soul in general takes charge of all that is lifeless, traversing the whole circuit of heaven and passing into a diversity of forms. When perfect and fully winged, it moves aloft and governs the whole order of the world; but a soul that moults its feathers falls until it lays hold upon some solid thing, where it makes its dwelling, taking an earthen body, which, because of the soul's power, seems to move itself. The whole, compact of soul and body, is called a living thing, with the addition 'mortal.' 'Immortal' it cannot be called on any reasonable ground; though, never having seen a god or adequately conceived one, we mould in our imagination a kind of immortal living thing, having both soul and body, joined in one nature for all time. Be that, however, and what we say concerning it, as heaven wills.

Let us next take account of the loss of the soul's feathers. The reason why they fall off is this. The nature of wings consists in their power to raise heavy things aloft to the region where the gods dwell; there is no bodily part more closely kin to the divine; and the divine is beauty, wisdom, goodness, and the like. By these, then, the plumage of the soul is nourished and increased; while their opposites, foulness and evil, cause it to waste and die.

Now Zeus, the great captain in heaven, driving a winged chariot, moves first upon his way, disposing and ordering all things under his care. After him comes a host of gods and spirits, arrayed in eleven bands; for only Hestia stays behind in the house of the gods, but the rest that are of the number of the Twelve lead and govern their array, each in his appointed rank. Within the heaven there are many sights to bless their eyes, and many courses wherein they move, each happily performing his proper work, followed by whoso can and will; for jealousy has no place in the choir of heaven. But when they go to banquet and high festival, they journey to the height of the vault under the heaven by a steep way, where the gods' chariots, obedient to the rein, move easily in even balance, but it goes hard with the rest; for the horse who has evil in him labours heavily, and drags down towards the earth any charioteer who has not thoroughly broken him in. This is the appointed hour of trial and extreme anguish for the soul.

The souls which are called immortal, when they reach the height, pass outside and take their stand upon the back of heaven; and there its revolution carries them round and they behold the things that are outside the heaven.

Of this region above the heaven no earthly poet has sung, or ever shall sing, worthily. It is like this (for we must make bold to speak the truth, especially when truth itself is our theme): here is the dwelling-place of that colourless, shapeless, intangible reality which is visible only to reason, the guide of the soul, and is the object of all true knowledge. So the intelligence of a god, being nourished by pure reason and knowledge, and the intelligence of every soul that is concerned to accept its proper nourishment, is glad to see after a long time that which truly is, and feeds upon this comfortable vision of truth until the revolving heaven brings it round again to the same point. In the journey round, the soul plainly beholds Justice itself, and Temperance, and Knowledge —not that knowledge which is subject to change and varies with the different objects that we in this world speak of as having existence, but the knowledge which lies in that which really and truly is; and when the soul has feasted upon the vision of these and of all the other

Q

things that truly are, it enters again the inside of the heaven and goes home. Then the charioteer brings his horses to the manger, and gives them ambrosia to eat and nectar to drink. This is the life of the gods.

The other souls fare differently. The soul which best follows the divine and takes the impress of its likeness lifts up the head of its charioteer into the region outside and is carried round with the revolving heaven; but, troubled by the horses, it has difficulty in seeing clearly the true realities. Another keeps the head uplifted for a while, and at other times sinks down, seeing only a part because of the turbulence of the horses. The rest of the souls that follow, though they all long for the upper world, have not the power, but are carried round submerged, jostling and trampling on one another, each trying to be in front. So they strive and sweat in a noisy struggle, in which many are lamed and have their wings broken by the bad driving of the charioteers; and all of them depart with fruitless labour, uninitiate into the revelation of truth, and, having failed of knowledge, feed upon the husks of belief.

The reason of their great eagerness to see the Plain of Truth is that the pasture proper to the noblest part of the soul grows in that meadow, and the growth of the wings which bear the soul aloft is nourished thereby. And the Law of Destiny is this. Any soul that has clearly seen some truth when it was in the company of a god, shall be free from harm until the next revolution; and if it can always so continue, it shall always be unhurt. But if a soul has not been able to keep up and has failed to see, and through some misfortune, weighed down by a burden of forgetfulness and wickedness, has moulted its wings and fallen to earth, then the law is that this soul shall not be planted in any bestial form at the first birth; but the soul which has seen most shall pass into the seed of a man who shall become a lover of truth and of beauty, inspired by the Muses and by Love; the next into the seed of a constitutional king, or a man of war and a ruler; the third into a statesman, ruler of a household, or trader; the fourth into one who gives health to the body by laborious exercise or by medicine; the fifth shall have the life of a soothsayer or initiating priest; to the sixth shall belong the life of a poet or other imitator; the seventh shall be a craftsman or a farmer; the eighth a sophist or demagogue; the ninth a tyrant.[1]

In all these lives, according as a man lives righteously or unrighteously, he receives a better portion or a worse. For each soul cannot return to the place whence it came until after ten thousand years—it takes all that time for its wings to grow—save only the soul of one who has sought wisdom without deceit or loved his youthful associates in that pursuit: the souls of such as these, in the third period of a thousand years, if they have chosen this life three times successively, thereby become full-fledged and fly away.

The other souls, when they have finished their first life, come to judgment; and after judgment some go to punishment in prison-houses under the earth, others are borne aloft by Justice to some region of the heaven where they spend their time as they have deserved in the life they led in human form. Then, after a thousand years, the souls of both kinds come to cast lots and choose their second life, and each chooses according to its will. Henceforward a human soul may pass into the life of a

[1] Contrast this Platonic list with Empedocles' highest class p. 74). The doctrine of reincarnation in the next paragraphs follows the same lines as Pindar (p. 62).

beast, and from a beast he who has once been man may become man again; for the soul which has never seen the truth can never come into human form.

For man must have understanding by way of what is called the ' form '—a unity collected by reflection from many acts of perception; and this is recollection of the things formerly seen by our soul when it travelled in the divine company, despising the things we now call real and looking upwards to true reality. Hence it is just that only the mind of the philosopher should get wings; for he is always, so far as he can, dwelling in memory on those things, the contemplation of which makes divinity divine. So the man who makes a right use of these means of recollection is always being initiated into the perfect mystery and he alone becomes truly perfect; and being exalted above human interests to converse with the divine, he is rebuked by the world as a madman; for the world cannot see that he is possessed by divine inspiration.

Likeness to God

PLATO, *Theaetetus* 176 A. Socrates has drawn a contrast between the man of the world and the philosopher, whom the world regards as unpractical.

Theodorus. If you could convince everyone, Socrates, as you convince me, there would be more peace, and fewer evils, in the world.

Socrates. Evil can never cease to exist, Theodorus; good must always have its contrary. Evil has no place in the divine world, but this region of our mortal nature must of necessity be haunted by it. That is why we should make all haste to escape from this world to the other. The way of escape lies in becoming as like God as possible

and that means becoming righteous and holy with the
help of wisdom. But it is no very easy matter to persuade
men that the right motive for eschewing wickedness
and following after goodness is not, as the world supposes, the hope of acquiring a good reputation instead
of a bad. That is the current doctrine,—no better, in
my judgment, than an old wives' tale; but the truth
may be put in this way. In God there is no sort or kind
of unrighteousness. He is perfectly righteous; and there
is nothing more like him than a man who becomes as
righteous as he can. Herein lies the test of manhood and
ability in the true sense, or, on the other hand, of nothing-
ness and unmanliness. To learn this is to be wise and
truly good; to be ignorant of it is manifest unwisdom and
wickedness. Every other form of reputed ability or skill
that is displayed in political ambition or in the arts, is vul-
gar in the one case, and in the other base and mechanical.

The best that can be done for the unrighteous and
unholy in word and deed is not to admit that his being
a scoundrel makes him a clever man; for they glory in
his reproach, taking it to mean that they are no fools,
no useless burdens to the earth, but such as a man must
be who is to hold his own in the dangerous chances of
public life. The truth, then, must be told: they are
what they think they are not, all the more for thinking
so; for they mistake the penalty of unrighteousness—
the worst mistake that can be made.

The Creation of the World

PLATO, *Timaeus* 27 D. Timaeus, a Pythagorean, describes
creation in mythical terms.

First, then, in my judgment we must distinguish two
things: that which eternally is, but has no becoming,

and that which is always becoming, but never is. The
one, being always the same, is comprehensible by though
with the aid of reasoning; the other, which is alway
becoming and perishing but never really is, is the objec
of belief formed by the aid of unreasoning perception.

Now anything that becomes must of necessity aris
by the agency of some cause; for without a cause nothin;
can be generated. Moreover, whenever an artificer work
with constant reference to an immutable pattern whos
fashion and function he reproduces, his work, so accomplished, must be good; whereas, if he has taken for hi
model some created thing, his work will not be good.
So of the whole heaven, or cosmos—let us call it by what
ever name may be acceptable to it—we must first as
the question that must always be asked at the outset
whether it always was, without ever beginning to exis
or has come into existence from some beginning. It ha
come into existence; for it can be seen and touched an
has a body, and all such things are sensible; and sensibl
things, apprehended by belief with the aid of percep
tion, are, as we have seen, things that become and ar
generated. And that which becomes must, we say, b
brought into being by some cause.

No doubt it is a hard task to find the maker and fathe
of this universe; and, if we had found him, it would b
impossible to declare him to all men. But once more w
must ask this question concerning the universe: whe
its architect fashioned it, to which of the two kinds
pattern did he look—to that which abides unchangeabl

---

[1] In the *Republic*, Book x, God who creates things aft
immutable patterns existing eternally in the nature of thin;
is similarly contrasted with the human artist who merely copi
the appearance of some transient sensible object.

or to that which has come into being? If the order of
this world is beautiful and its maker is good, it is plain
that he looked to the eternal; but if—I dare not even
name the alternative, from which it would follow that
his pattern was the created thing. Indeed it must be clear
to anyone that he looked to the eternal; for the world is
the fairest of creatures, and of all causes he is the best.

Having, then, come into being in this way, the world
has been fashioned after the image of the immutable
that is comprehended by reason and thought; and, that
being so, it follows that this world is a likeness of something. Now in speaking of a likeness and its original,
according to the great principle that, in beginning any
subject, we should be guided by the nature of the matter,
we must lay it down that our discourse will be of the same
character as the objects which it explains. Where the
object is permanent and stable and discoverable by the
aid of reason, our discourse will be permanent and unchangeable; it ought not to fall short of being as incon-
trovertible and certain as it is possible for any words to
be. But where the object is only an image made after
the likeness of that permanent object, our discourse will
have only a corresponding degree of likelihood. As real
being is to becoming, so is truth to belief.[1] If then,
after so many accounts have been given of the gods and
of the generation of the universe, we should not prove
able to give any account that is perfectly exact and

---

[1] "Belief" (*pistis*, the word adopted by the Christians for
faith) is, to Plato, inferior to knowledge. Its object is the
transient or mutable things in the sensible world; whereas
knowledge is of eternal objects and truths in the intelligible
world. Physical science, in so far as it depends on sense observation, cannot be more than "belief" in a "probable story";
but abstract mathematical truth belongs to the intelligible world.

consistent with itself, let no one be surprised. We must be content to produce one that is at least as likely as any other, remembering that I who speak and you my judges are but men, so that in these matters it befits us to accept a story ('myth') that has some likelihood, and to seek for nothing further.

Let us declare, then, for what reason this universe of becoming was framed by its author. He was good; and in the good no jealousy of anything can ever arise. Therefore, being without jealousy, he desired that all things should be made as like to himself as possible. This is that sovereign principle of creation and of the cosmos that we shall be most surely right to accept from men of understanding. For God, desiring that all things should be good, and that, so far as possible, no evil should exist, taking all that was visible as it came to him, not in a state of rest, but moving without order or harmony, brought it from disorderliness to order, thinking that such a state was in every way better than the other.

Now it may never be that the work of the best should be anything but the best and fairest work. Taking thought, therefore, he perceived that, among things whose nature it is to be visible, no irrational creature can be fairer than the rational, when each is taken as a whole, and again that reason cannot dwell in anything that has not a living soul. So, because he argued thus, in fashioning the universe, he put reason in soul, and soul in body, in order that his work might be, according to nature, fairest and best. In this way, then, following the probable account, we ought to say that, by the providence of God, this world came into being, a living creature containing in very truth a reasonable soul.

The Confutation of Atheism

PLATO, *Laws* x. 885 B (abridged). The *Laws* is Plato's latest work. The chief speaker, the Athenian, represents Plato. The other speakers are the Cretan Cleinias, and the Lacedaemonian Megillus.

Athenian. No one who believes in the existence of gods such as the law acknowledges ever voluntarily does an impious deed or utters a lawless word. If he does so, it is for one of three reasons. Either he does not believe in the gods, as I said; or, secondly, he believes that they exist but have no care for mankind; or, thirdly, that they are easy to be entreated and turned aside by sacrifice and prayer.

Cleinias. What, then, are we to say or do to them?

Athenian. Let us first hear how our scornful opponents would state their case. I can imagine them bantering us. " True," they might say, " some of us do not believe in gods at all; others accept your second and third alternatives. We claim, then, on your own principle that laws should be prefaced by a persuasive preamble, that before you begin to threaten us severely, you should try to convince us, on sufficient evidence, that the gods do exist and are too good to listen to the voice of the charmer who would turn them aside, by means of gifts, from the course of justice. As things are, we hear that they can be so influenced and much else to the like effect from poets and orators of acknowledged excellence and from prophets and priests and others without number; with the result that most of us, instead of feeling any inducement to refrain from wrong-doing, do wrong and then look for some means of atonement. From lawgivers like yourselves, who profess to be exceptionally humane, we expect that you should try to persuade us of the existence of the gods, more convincingly, if not more eloquently, than other advocates."

Cleinias. Surely it is easy to be convinced of truth when we assert the existence of gods.

Athenian. How would you put it?

Cleinias. To begin with, there are the earth and the sun, the stars and the universe, and this perfect order of the seasons with the division of months and years. Besides, all men, Greeks or barbarians, believe in gods.

Athenian. I will not say I have too much respect for the wicked; but I am afraid they would despise such an answer. You Cretans and Lacedaemonians do not understand the ground of their objection. You imagine that the only thing that drives them into an impious life is that they cannot control their desires for pleasure. You live so far out of the world that you overlook another cause, a dangerous form of folly which masquerades as the highest wisdom. At Athens we have accounts of the gods, in verse and in prose, such as, I understand, do not exist under your admirable constitution. The oldest of these describe the origin of the heavens and of the whole world, and proceed at once to the birth of the gods and their behaviour to one another. The stories are ancient, and I do not like to find fault with their influence, good or bad, upon the reader; but, so far as the duties of children to parents are concerned, I cannot commend them as profitable or as containing a single word of truth.

But let us leave the old legends and turn to the evils for which the wisdom of these later days must be held responsible. When you and I, as evidence for the existence of gods, point to sun and moon, stars and earth, and call them divine, we shall find that people who have listened to these modern philosophers will reply that these things are nothing but so much earth and stones, which cannot have any regard for the doings of mankind. . . .

How can one argue for the existence of the gods and not be angry? It is impossible not to feel indignation and abhorrence for the men who have made such argument necessary and still do so—men who will not believe the stories they heard at their nurse's breast and at their mother's knee, murmured over them like charms in playful or serious mood, and repeated again in prayers at the moment of sacrifice with all the accompaniment of sights and sounds that must delight a child, when his parents, at the altar, address the gods in prayer and supplication, on their own and their children's behalf, with the deepest earnestness, as if the existence of the gods were beyond all doubt;—men who see and hear all men, both Greeks and barbarians, in prosperity or in times of trouble, bowing themselves in worship at the rising of the sun and moon and at their going down, as if there could be no suspicion that the existence of the gods were not as certain as anything in the world. When we are constrained to argue with men like this, who despise all these things upon no ground whatever that anyone with the least spark of reason would call sufficient, how is it possible to find gentle words of admonition, when we must begin by proving to them that the gods exist?

Yet the attempt must be made; it would never do that half the world should be mad with lust for pleasure, and the other half with indignation at them. No anger, then, shall trouble the course of the preamble we address to these perverted minds. Our indignation shall be quenched, and we will suppose that we are gently reasoning with one of them.

My son, you are young, and advancing age will cause you to reverse many of your present opinions. Wait till that time comes before you set up to judge the highest matters. The highest of all is that which you now make no account of—a good life with a right belief about the gods, or the opposite. And first I can tell you one thing concerning them without fear of contradiction. It is this: you are not the only one to hold this opinion about the gods, nor were your friends the first to conceive it. There is at all times a greater or less number of men who suffer from this disease. I have known many, and I can tell you this: not one of those who in his youth has taken up the belief that the gods do not exist, ever persists in that way of thinking to his old age. The other two notions do persist—not in many cases, but in some—namely that, though the gods exist, they have no regard to human things, and also the notion that they have some regard to human things, but can be easily propitiated by sacrifices and prayers. If you take my advice, you will wait for the belief which, according to your powers, may become clear to you, keeping the question before your mind and learning from others, above all from the lawgiver. Meanwhile, do not venture upon any impiety towards the gods. It will be the lawgiver's business, now and in the future, to do his best to instruct you in the truth of these things.

Here we suddenly encounter a remarkable theory, reputed by many to be the cleverest of all theories: that all things, at every time, come into existence either by nature, or by design, or by chance. No doubt wise men are likely to be right; but let us follow up their thought and ask what it means. They say that the greatest and best things are the work of nature and chance, lesser things of design. Art takes over from nature the great primary works of creation, and moulds or fabricates all those lesser things we call artificial. To put it more plainly: the existence of fire, water, air, and earth is due to nature and chance, not to design; while the secondary bodies, in earth and sun and moon and stars, have come into being through the agency of these elements, which are altogether without soul. The elements, each moving with the chance motion of its peculiar property, and meeting casually with something proper to combine with it—hot with cold, dry with wet, and soft with hard, and all the other necessary mixtures of opposite qualities blended by chance—have in this manner given birth to the whole heaven and all things in it and also to all animals and plants, all the seasons having arisen from these elements, not thanks to Mind, or to any god or design, but merely, as I say, to nature and chance. Design, or art, they say, came into existence later, a mortal thing and of mortal origin, and gave birth to a certain kind of toys, that have little truth or reality in them, but are rather unsubstantial images like their parent, such as the creations of painting, music, and the arts that are fellows to these. There are other arts which produce something of serious value, namely those, and those only, which co-operate with nature, like medicine, husbandry, and gymnastic. Further they hold that statecraft has little common ground with nature, and is nearly all a matter of art; consequently all law-making is unnatural and artificial, and based on false assumptions.

Cleinias. In what sense?

Athenian. In the first place they say that gods do not exist in nature, but are the product of deliberate conventions, which, moreover, vary from place to place, according as each set of men agreed together to make laws for themselves; also that what is naturally honourable is not the same as what is legally enjoined as such; while the principles of justice have no natural existence at all, but mankind is always disputing about them and changing them, and each alteration has no natural validity, but is valid as a matter of deliberate convention just at the time and place where it is made.

All these statements are made by men whom young people think wise, poets and prose-writers, who declare that the perfection of right is any claim that violence can make good. Hence our young men are afflicted with impiety, for they think that gods such as those which the law bids us to believe in, do not exist; and there arises a faction who invite them to live the true life according to nature, which really means to escape from the slavery of legal subjection to others, and to live in dominion over them.

(After agreeing that atheism should be met by persuasion and not merely by threats of punishment, the Athenian proceeds to his argument, 891 c.)

The opinions I have described imply a belief that fire, water, earth, and air are the primary things, called 'nature,' and that soul is a later thing, derived from them; indeed, that is the plain meaning of the theory. Have we not here laid bare the source of the unwise belief held by all these inquirers in the science of nature? The argument should be carefully examined at every point. It is a matter of great importance, if it can be shown that the leaders of irreligious thought have gone astray in their reasoning. I must pursue a line of thought that is perhaps unfamiliar. This philosophy which manufactures irreligious minds inverts the natural order, placing last what should be first, namely the primary cause of the generation and destruction of all things. Hence their error about the true nature of the gods. Nearly all betray their ignorance of the character

and significance of soul, and especially of its origin.
They do not know that soul is one of the first things,
older than any kind of body, whose changes and trans-
positions it certainly controls. And if soul is older than
body, it follows that the order of things to which soul
belongs must be prior to the things of the body. So belief,
attention, intelligence, art, and law will be prior to hard
and soft or heavy and light. And the great and primary
works and processes, since they belong to the primary
order of things, will be effects of design; while the things
they wrongly call 'natural things' or 'nature' will
be secondary and subject to the government of design
and intelligence. By 'nature' they mean the way in
which the primary things come into existence; [1] and if
it turns out that soul is primary, then, not fire or air, but
soul, as being among the first things to come into existence, might with perfect justice be called pre-eminently
natural.' This conclusion can be established by showing
that soul is older than body, but not otherwise.

(The Athenian then analyses motion into ten kinds. The
most important distinction is between (1) self-originating motion,
of a thing which moves itself as well as other things, and (2)
transmitted motion, of a thing which, though it moves others,
is only passing on a motion received from something else. The
former is characteristic of living things, and indeed the power
of self-motion is what we mean by "life" or "soul." It follows
that, as the only original source of motion, soul must be older
than body, which has only transmitted motion. Soul is superior
and master, body is servant; and the things of the soul are prior
to bodily properties. He continues, 896 D:)

We must acknowledge the further consequence that
soul is the cause of good and evil, beauty and ugliness,
justice and injustice, and all other such contraries, if

[1] The original meaning of *physis* (Nature) is "growth"; then
meant what "grows," as opposed to anything made by art,
and especially the ultimate irreducible elements of existing things.

we are to maintain that it is the cause of all things. And
if soul dwells in all things that have any kind of motion
and orders them, we must assert that the heavens are
ordered by soul. By one soul or more than one? I will
answer that question for you: more than one. We cannot
assume less than two, the one beneficent, the other having
the contrary effect.[1]

(The orderly motions of the heavens show that they are
governed by a wise and rational soul; and the same argument
applies to each of the heavenly bodies. The sun, for instance,
must have a soul, either dwelling in its fiery body or having a
body of its own and pushing the sun from outside, or having
no body at all. Such a soul must be recognised as a god. Thus
all the heavenly bodies are shown to be divine, and "all things
are full of gods."

The Athenian next turns to the objection that the gods,
though they exist, have no care for human things—an objection
based on the observation of the apparent prosperity of the
wicked. It is first argued that the admitted wisdom and virtue
of the gods are inconsistent with their neglecting small things.
But this argument, though declared to be cogent, is supple-
mented by the persuasive charm of a "myth," as follows, 903 B :

Let us persuade our young man that the power which
cares for the universe has disposed all things with a
view to the preservation and excellence of the whole
system, in which each part, according to the measure of
its capacity, does and suffers what properly belongs to
it. Over each set of things rulers are appointed to determine, down to the smallest detail, what shall be done
and suffered, rulers who have achieved perfection in the

[1] This famous passage was too hastily understood by Christian
Fathers as a recognition of the Devil. Modern scholars will not
admit that Plato even asserts that there are two world-souls.
In Xenophon's *Education of Cyrus*, Araspas, who has yielded
to temptation, says to Cyrus: "Clearly I must have two souls,
for one soul cannot at the same time be both good and bad, and
desire right and wrong, and want and not want to do the same
thing. Clearly there are two souls, and we do right or wrong
according as the good or the bad soul prevails." (VI. i. 41.)

minutest fraction of their work.[1] Your part in this system, stubborn man, is only one part, which, tiny as it is, contributes to the whole and keeps it always in view; and what you do not see is that every individual thing comes into existence for the sake of that whole, to the end that the life of the universe may exist in blessedness; you exist for its sake, not it for yours. Any physician or skilful workman, it is true, always has an eye to the perfection of every part of his work; but he makes the perfection of the part contribute to the general good of the whole; he does not make the whole for the sake of the part. Yet you are discontented, because you cannot see how what is best for the whole in your case is also best for you, so far as the whole common process permits. A soul is appointed now to this body, and now to that, and is constantly undergoing every sort of change, either on its own account or because of some other soul; and all the master of the game has to do is to shift the pieces on his draught-board, moving each character, as it grows better or worse, to a better or a worse position, to the end that it may receive its proper portion. . . .

Since our King perceived that all actions are animated by soul and contain much virtue and much vice, and that soul and body together make a thing which, though not eternal, like the gods of established religion, is indestructible (for if either should perish, no living creature could ever be born); and since he reflected also that what is good in soul is always of a beneficent nature, and what is bad, harmful—taking all this into consideration, he contrived that every portion of soul should be posted in that place where it shall most easily and perfectly promote in the whole universe the triumph of virtue

[1] Meaning not certain.

R

and the defeat of vice. He contrived, in fact, for this general end, that there should always be a right place for every character to fill as it develops from time to time, a proper region for it to inhabit; but he left to the will of each one the acts that are responsible for his becoming such as he is. For, speaking generally, the manner of every man's birth is determined by his desires, and the character he is born with corresponds to the character his soul has already acquired.

Whatever, then, has a living soul changes by virtue of an inward principle, and, as it changes, moves according to the order and law of Destiny. When the alteration of character is slight, it merely journeys to another place upon the surface of the ground; but when it is great and much wrong has been done, it falls into that underworld known as Hades and by other names whose terrors haunt us in waking life and in the visions of the soul set free from the body in sleep. And when a soul, by its own will and confirmed by the conversation of its associates, comes to partake of virtue and vice in yet larger measure, then, if its conversation has been with divine virtue and it has become in surpassing measure divine, so surely does it travel into a surpassing region of perfect purity being carried into another and a better place; while, if its conversation has been with evil, the region to which its life is removed is correspondingly evil.[1]

This, my son, you who think you are neglected by

[1] In this paragraph Plato distinguishes several classes, which may be compared with Pindar's classification in *Olympian* II: (1) Slight changes of character, leading to reincarnation on earth, with promotion or degradation in the scale of existence; (2) greater offences, atoned for in Hades between two incarnations (the corresponding reward of the more meritorious in Elysium, described by Pindar, is omitted); (3) the final escape of the pure soul to the divine life (Pindar's Isles of the Blest) and the final banishment of the impure. See p. 62.

eaven, ' this,' as Homer says, ' is the justice of the gods who hold Olympus '—that according as you grow better or worse, the better or the worse will be the souls to whose company your journey takes you, receiving, both in life and in all your deaths, such treatment as like must mete to like. Neither you nor any other unfortunate shall ever boast of having outwitted this divine justice, which has been set above every other ordinance. You will do well to take good heed of it, for it will not fail to take heed of you. Be you never so small, you shall not creep into the depths of the earth; be you never so high, you shall not take wings and fly up into the heavens; but you shall be duly punished, either remaining here on earth, or when you have gone to Hades, or have been conveyed to some yet more forbidding place. The same holds true of those whom you have seen raised from low to high estate by impious deeds and other acts of wickedness. You thought they had risen from misery to happiness, and that their fortunes were like a mirror in which you had discerned the universal negligence of the gods, because you did not know in what manner the lives of such men contribute to the total sum. Surely it behoves you to know this, you who are so bold; for without this knowledge no man can ever discern the pattern of life or make any pronouncement upon good or evil fortune.

If you listen to us old men, who tell you that you know not what you are saying about the gods, God himself will be your helper; but if you still need further persuasion, hear our argument with the third opponent, who holds that the wrong-doer can placate the gods with bribes.

The gods must surely be rulers; but to what sort of rulers can they be likened? To the charioteer in a race,

or to the pilot of a ship, or to the captains of an army
Or perhaps to the cautious physician in his battle with
disease; or to the husbandman looking anxiously for the
hard season that threatens the growth of his plants; or
to the herdsman of a flock ? For as we have agreed that
the world is full of good and of evil, and that the evil
is more than the good, so now we affirm that a battle
between such antagonists is undying and calls for extra
ordinary vigilance, and that the gods and spirits, whose
chattels we are, fight upon our side. Destruction for us
lies in injustice and insolence combined with foolishness
salvation, in justice and temperance, united with wisdom
which dwell in the living powers of heaven, and to some
small measure may be seen in ourselves.

But certain souls dwelling upon the earth and rejoicing
like savage beasts in their unlawful prey, pay homage
to the souls of the guardians (whether we liken these to
watch-dogs, or to shepherds, or to masters and lord
supreme over all), and with flattering addresses and
magical prayers win from them licence to seek their
own advantage among mankind and yet suffer no harm
Such is the rumour spread by the wicked. But we declare
that this grasping spirit of self-seeking is the same evil
that is called disease in bodies of flesh, pestilence in the
temperature of the seasons, and in cities and government
injustice—the same thing under another name. To say
that the gods are indulgent to unjust men who give
them a share of the spoils of injustice, would be to
compare the gods to sheep-dogs who should suffer the
flock to be ravaged, if the wolves gave them a share of
the prey; to a pilot, beguiled by the vapour of wine to
make shipwreck of his vessel and its company; or to a
charioteer betraying for a bribe the victory to another

eam. All such comparisons are outrageous. The gods are the greatest of all guardians and watch over the greatest things. They cannot be worse than dogs or common men, who would never betray their trust for bribes dishonestly offered. Of all impious men, the worst and most impious is he who holds to this belief.

So we may say that we have sufficiently demonstrated the three theses proposed to us: that the gods exist; that they are mindful of us; and that they are deaf to the appeals of injustice.

XVI. ARISTOTLE

On primitive Religion

ARISTOTLE, *Metaphysics* xii. 8, 1074*b* 1.

The ancients have handed down from remote antiquity a tradition in mythical form that these (the heavenl
bodies) are gods and that the divine encompasses the whol
natural world. The rest is a later addition in mythica
language, designed for the persuasion of the multitud
and for its expediency, including the maintenance o
social institutions. The gods are said to have the form
of men or to resemble other living creatures, and to hav
other attributes that go with these. If we separate fror
these additions the original belief that the primary sub
stances are gods, this may be taken as an inspired utteranc
—a relic preserved to our own day from former civilisa
tions, in which the arts and speculation have perishec
and very likely been rediscovered and perished agai
more than once. This is all that can be clearly made ou
about the belief of our ancestors and of primitive time

The Divine in the Region outside the Heaven

ARISTOTLE, *On the Heavens* I. ix. 12, 279*a* 6.

From what has been said it is clear that there is no
and cannot be, a mass of any kind of body outside th
heaven; for the cosmos as a whole contains all the matte
that properly belongs to it, namely physical body pe
ceptible by the senses. Consequently there are not nov
and never have been, nor can be more heavens than on
but our heaven is one, unique, and complete.

Also it is plain that outside the heaven is neither place, nor void, nor time. No place or void, for in any place it is possible for body to exist, and void is defined as that in which body does not exist, but might come to be; no time, because time is the number of motion, and motion cannot exist apart from a physical body. But we have shown that there is not, and cannot be, body outside the heaven. Clearly then there is neither place nor void nor time outside it.

Consequently, the things there are of such a nature as not to be in any place, nor does time make them grow old, nor is there any kind of change that affects anything that is set above the outermost sphere of spatial motion. They cannot change nor be affected in any way, but they live the best and most self-sufficing life throughout all their duration (*aion*). This term "duration," used by the ancients, expresses their inspired insight. "Duration" is the name given to the fulfilment comprising the complete span of time during which anything lives, and beyond which there is no natural development. On the same principle the end of the entire heaven, the end which comprises all time and indefinity, is "duration,"—*aion* being derived from *aiei on*, "being for ever,"—immortal and divine. From it are derived, with divers degrees of clear expression or of dimness, the being and life of all other things. In popular philosophical discourse about divine things we are often told that the divine—anything that is primary and supreme—must be unchangeable. This is true and bears out what has been said. For there is nothing superior to it that might cause it to move (such a thing, if it existed, would be more divine), nor has it any imperfection or lack of any good proper to it. Its unceasing motion is, moreover, easily accounted for, since a thing ceases to move only when it comes to its proper place; but for a body that moves in a circle, the place where its motion begins is the same as the place where it ends.

The First and Unmoved Cause of Motion

ARISTOTLE, *Metaphysics* xii. 6 (abridged).

Since there are three kinds of substance, two of them physical, the third immovable,[1] with regard to the last we must assert that there must be an eternal unmoved substance. For substances are prior to all other things, and if all substances are perishable, all things are so. Motion, however, cannot have begun to exist, nor can it cease to be: it must always have been. The same is true of Time, for if Time were not, there could be no before or after. . . .

Further, if there is something merely capable of moving things or of acting upon them, but not actually doing so, there will not necessarily be motion; for a thing can have power without exercising it. Nothing then is gained by supposing eternal substances, like the (Platonic) Ideas, unless they contain a principle capable of causing change; and even this is not enough, nor will a further substance over and above the Ideas suffice: it must act, or there will not necessarily be motion. Even this will not suffice, if its essence is mere potency; for there will not necessarily be *eternal* motion, since a mere potentiality may not be realised. There must, then, be a principle whose essence is actuality.

[1] Substances are classified as (A) perceptible and physical (*i.e.* subject to motion), of which (1) some are perishable, *e.g.* plants and animals, (2) some eternal, viz. the heavenly bodies; (B) (3) eternal and immovable, and imperceptible.—*Metaphysics* xii. 1, 1069a 30.

Further these substances must be immaterial; for they must be eternal, at least if anything else is eternal. Therefore they must be actuality.

Yet there is a difficulty; for it is thought that, whereas anything that acts must be capable of acting, what is capable of acting does not always act, and that consequently potency is prior. But if that is so, it would be possible that nothing at all should exist; for all things might be capable of existing without ever having come into existence. This involves the same impossibility as the mythological doctrine that the world arose out of "Night," or the physical philosophers' theory of an original state in which all things were confused. How is motion to arise, unless there is some cause actually existing? . . .

It follows that there cannot have been a chaos or "Night" for an indefinite time; but the same things have always existed (either in periodical recurrence or in some other way), since actuality is prior to potency. If then the same thing always exists, there must be something permanently acting in the same way.[1] And again, if there is to be generation and perishing, there must also be something else which is always acting in different ways.[2] This second thing must have an inherent motion of its own, and also a motion derived from something else. The cause of this derived motion must either be the agent first mentioned (the sphere of the fixed stars) or some third thing. It must be the agent first mentioned, since otherwise we should have to attribute to this further agent both the motion of the second agent and that of the third. So it is better to say it is the agent

---

[1] The sphere of the fixed stars.
[2] The spheres of the sun, moon, and planets.

first mentioned. That agent caused eternal movement, the second caused variety: both together consequently cause eternal variety. Such is in fact the character of the motions; so why seek for other principles?

Since this is a possible account of the matter, and the alternative would be that the world should have arisen out of Night or a primitive confusion or not-being, these difficulties may be taken as solved.

There is, then, something (viz. the sphere of the fixed stars) which is always moved with a motion that is unceasing, and therefore circular. This is no less plain in fact than in theory. Accordingly, the first heaven is eternal.

There is then also something which causes it to move. And since that which both is moved and causes other things to move is intermediate, there is a cause of motion which is not itself moved, an eternal thing which is substance and actuality.

Now motion is caused in this way by the object of desire and the object of thought; these cause motion without being themselves moved. The primary objects of desire and of thought are the same. For the object of appetite is what seems good, and the object of rational desire is what really is good; and the belief is the cause, rather than the effect, of the desire: the thinking is the starting-point. And thought is moved by its object. . .

(The primary object of thought, namely simple actual substance, is identified with the primary object of desire, namely "the best," *i.e.* the final cause.)

That the final cause may be something immovable, is shown by the distinction of its meanings. By the final cause may be meant either something for whose good the action is done or the good for the sake of which it is done. Of these the latter may be immovable, though the former is not.[1] The final cause then causes motion, as being the object of desire; and by that which it moves, it moves all other things.

Now if a thing is moved, it is capable of changing. Consequently, if the actuality of the first heaven is primary motion, then, in so far as it is moved, it is capable of change—of place, although not of substance. But since there is something that causes motion without being itself moved and actually exists, this cannot change in any way. Motion in space is the primary species of change, and circular motion is prior to all other kinds of motion in space; and circular motion is produced by the mover which is itself unmoved.

The existence of this first mover is then necessary, and, in so far, good, and in this sense a principle. . . .

It is then on a principle of this kind that the heavens and the world of nature depend. Its life is like the best activity of which we are capable, though we can enjoy it only for a little while at a time, whereas this principle is always in that state, since its activity is also pleasure. . . .

Absolute thought in the fullest sense has for its object the absolutely best in the fullest sense. The thinking mind, by taking part in the nature of its object, thinks itself; for it becomes its object in the act of comprehending and thinking it, so that the thinking mind and its object are the same. For that which is capable of receiving the object of thought, namely the essence, is a thinking mind. And when it possesses this object it is active. This activity, rather than the receptivity, is what is held to

---

[1] Thus the final cause of healing is either (1) the person to be cured (who is not "immovable," since his state is to be changed) or (2) the good, viz. health, that is aimed at.

be the divine characteristic of mind, and the act of contemplation is what is supremely pleasant and good.

That God should be always in that good state in which we sometimes are, is a wonderful thing; still more wonderful, if his state is better than ours. And it is better. And life belongs to God; for the activity of thought is life, and God is that activity: his essential activity is an eternal life that is the best possible life.

We say then that God is a living being, eternal and most good, so that life and duration continuous and eternal belong to God; for this *is* God.

The Nature of Happiness

ARISTOTLE, *Ethics* X. vii. 7. In the concluding part of the *Ethics*, Aristotle describes the nature of human happiness It is not a mere state of being good, but an activity, and one of those activities which are desirable for their own sake, not as a means, and so self-sufficient. It is not amusement or re-laxation, but the activity of the divine part of our nature, the speculative intellect.

If, then, among the forms of virtuous activity, war and politics, although they stand out as pre-eminent in nobility and grandeur, are yet unleisured and directed towards a further end instead of being desired for their own sakes, while the activity of reason, on the other hand, when it is speculative, appears to be superior in serious worth, to aim at no end beyond itself, and to contain a pleasure which is peculiar to it and so enhances the activity; and if self-sufficiency, leisured-ness, and such freedom from weariness as is possible to humanity, together with all the other attributes of felicity, are found to go with this activity;—then, per-fect well-being for man will lie in this, provided it be granted a complete span of life; for nothing that belongs to well-being is incomplete.

Such a life as this, however, is higher than the measure of humanity; not in virtue of his humanity will man lead this life, but in virtue of something within him that is divine; and by as much as this something is superior to his composite nature, by so much is its activity superior to the rest of virtue. If, then, Reason is divine in comparison with man, so is the life of Reason divine in comparison with human life. We ought not to listen to those who exhort man to keep to man's thoughts, or a mortal to the thoughts of mortality, but, so far as may be, to achieve immortality and do what man may to live according to the highest thing that is in him; for little though it be in bulk, in power and worth it is far above all the rest.

XVII. POPULAR THOUGHT

This section contains miscellaneous specimens of popular thought from the orators and comedians, together with a few passages for which no other place could be found.

EPICHARMUS

Death is not to be feared

EPICHARMUS, the Sicilian comic poet, is said to have died at an advanced age shortly after 467 B.C. *Frags.* 9; 22.

It comes together and is dispersed and goes back whence it came: earth to earth, and the breath on high. What hardship is in that? None!

If you have a pious mind, no harm will come to you when you die. Your living breath (*pneuma*) will always remain aloft in the sky.

Heaven sees all

EPICHARMUS, *frag.* 23.

Nothing escapes the divine; that is a thing you ought to know. God himself is our overseer, and there is no limit to his power.

PERICLES

On religious Festivals

THUCYDIDES ii. 38. The funeral speech which Thucydides puts into the mouth of Pericles about two years before his death in 429, contains, in the course of a panegyric of Athenian life and institutions, the following reference to religious festivals:

Moreover we have provided many occasions for the refreshment of our spirit from toil, in the regular observance, throughout the year, of sacrifices and festivals at which contests are held and in the refinement of private hospitality, where the enjoyment of each day banishes sadness.

On Immortality

PLUTARCH, *Pericles* 8.

Stesimbrotus tells us that Pericles, pronouncing a panegyric over those who had fallen at Samos, said that they had become immortal like the gods. " For, though we do not see the gods themselves, yet from the honours they enjoy and the good things they bestow we infer their immortality. The same is true also of those who die for their country."

The Soul to Air, the Body to Earth

C.I.A. i. 442. Epitaph on the Athenians slain in battle at Potidaea, 432 B.C.

Their souls were received into the air of heaven; their bodies into earth. By the gates of Potidaea they were slain.

EURIPIDES, *Suppliants* 531.

Now let the dead be laid in earth, and each part return hither whence it came into the light of day—the breath into the air of heaven, the body into earth. For the body is not ours in fee; we are but lifelong tenants; and after that, Earth that nursed it must take it back again.

IOPHON

The Gods are not to be known

IOPHON (son of Sophocles), *Bacchae, frag.* 2.

I am but a woman, yet of this I am sure: the more man seeks to know about the gods, the less he will know.

THEODECTES

Divine Vengeance

THEODECTES, *frag.* 8 (from a lost tragedy).

If any man find fault with the divine vengeance because
it is late in overtaking the unjust and comes not immediately, let him hear the reason. If punishment came
at once, many would pray to the gods because they were
afraid, and not in pious mood; but as it is, while punishment is far off, men indulge their nature; then later,
when they are caught in wrong-doing, they pay the penalty

ANDOCIDES

Divine Vengeance

ANDOCIDES, *On the Mysteries* 137. Andocides, accused of
impiety in regard to the mysteries, had gone into exile, but on
his return was put on his defence by Cephisius.

My accusers argue that the gods preserved me from
danger in order that, upon my return, a Cephisius might
bring about my ruin. I cannot approve this way of
thinking about the gods. If they conceived that I had
done them an injury, would they not have caught me in
the extremity of danger and taken their revenge? There
is no greater peril than a sea-voyage in the winter season.
My person was in their hands, they were masters of my
life and my goods, and they preserved me. They could
have secured that my very body should be denied burial. .
We are to believe that the gods rescued me from all these
perils, and, instead of taking vengeance themselves, found
a champion in Cephisius, the vilest man in Athens,
whose claim to citizenship is false, whom not a man of
you would trust with anything that belonged to him
if you knew what kind of man he is!

For my part, I think we should recognise that my present predicament is a peril of human origin, while the perils of the sea are divine. If, then, it is right to speculate upon the ways of heaven, I think the gods would look with anger and indignation upon the destruction by other hands of one whom they themselves had preserved.

EUCLEIDES OF MEGARA

Evil does not exist

DIOGENES LAERTIUS ii. 106. Eucleides was a pupil of Socrates, and founder of the Socratic school at Megara.

Eucleides of Megara declared that the good was one thing called by many names, sometimes " Wisdom," sometimes " God," or again " Mind," and so on. He altogether denied the existence of things contrary to the good.

ANTISTHENES

There is but one God

PHILODEMUS, *On Piety* 7. Antisthenes founded the Cynic School.

In Antisthenes' book called *Physicus* it is stated that in popular religion there are many gods, but in nature only one.

CLEMENT OF ALEXANDRIA, *Exhortation to the Greeks*, p. 61 P.

Antisthenes says, " God is not like anything: hence no one can understand him by means of an image."

S

Xenophon

On Providence and Design

Xenophon, *Recollections of Socrates* i. 4. The ideas expressed in this imaginary conversation cannot be safely attributed to Socrates.

Socrates had observed that Aristodemus neither sacrificed nor gave heed to divination, but on the contrary was disposed to ridicule those who did.

Tell me, Aristodemus (he began), are there any human beings who have won your admiration for their wisdom?

Ar. In the writing of epic poetry I have the greatest admiration for Homer . . . and as a dithyrambic poet for Melanippides. I admire also Sophocles as a tragedian, Polycleitus as a sculptor, and Zeuxis as a painter.

Socr. Which would you consider the more worthy of admiration, a fashioner of senseless images devoid of motion or one who could fashion living creatures endowed with understanding and activity?

Ar. Decidedly the latter, provided his living creatures owed their birth to design and were not the offspring of some chance.

Socr. But now if you had two sorts of things, the one of which presents no clue as to what it is for, and the other is obviously for some useful purpose—which would you judge to be the result of chance, which of design?

Ar. Clearly that which is produced for some useful end is the work of design.

Socr. Does it not strike you then that he who made man from the beginning did for some useful end furnish him with his several senses—giving him eyes to behold the visible world, and ears to catch the intonations of sound? Or again, what good would there be in odours nostrils had not been bestowed upon us? what perception of sweet things and pungent, and of all the pleasures of the palate, had not a tongue been fashioned in us as an interpreter of the same? And besides all this, do you not think this looks like a matter of foresight, this closing of the delicate orbs of sight with eyelids as with folding doors, which, when there is need to use them for any purpose, can be thrown wide open and firmly closed again in sleep? and, that even the winds of heaven may not visit them too roughly, this planting of the eyelashes like a protecting screen? this coping of the region above the eyes with cornice-work of eyebrow so that no drop of sweat fall from the head and injure them? again, this readiness of the ear to catch all sounds and yet not to be surcharged? this capacity of the front teeth of all animals to cut and of the " grinders " to receive the food and reduce it to pulp? . . . I ask you, when you see all these things constructed with such show of foresight can you doubt whether they are products of chance or intelligence?

Ar. To be sure not! Viewed in this light they would seem to be the handiwork of some wise artificer, full of love for all things living.

Socr. What shall we say of this passion implanted in man to beget offspring, this passion in the mother to bear her babe, and in the creature itself, once born, this deep desire of life and fear of death?

Ar. No doubt these do look like the contrivances of someone deliberately planning the existence of living creatures.

Socr. Well, and doubtless you feel to have a spark of wisdom yourself?

Ar. Put your questions, and I will answer.

Socr. And yet you imagine that elsewhere no spark
wisdom is to be found? And that, too, when you kno
that you have in your body a tiny fragment only of t
mighty earth, a little drop of the great waters, and of t
other elements, vast in their extent, you got, I presume,
particle of each towards the compacting of your bodi
frame. Mind alone, it would seem, which is nowhere
be found, you had the lucky chance to snatch up and ma
off with, you cannot tell how. And these things aroun
and about us, enormous in size, infinite in number, ov
their orderly arrangement, as you suppose, to son
vacuity of wit?

Ar. It may be, for my eyes fail to see the master agen
of these, as one sees the fabricators of things produc
on earth.

Socr. No more do you see your own soul, which
the master agent of your body; so that, as far as that go
you may maintain, if you like, that you do nothing wi
intelligence, but everything by chance. . . .

Again, do you suppose that the gods could have in
planted in the heart of man the belief in their capaci
to work him weal or woe had they not the power? Wou
not men have discovered the imposture in all this lap
of time? Do you not perceive that the wisest and mo
perdurable of human institutions—be they cities or trib
of men—are ever the most God-fearing; and in the ind
vidual man the riper his age and judgment, the deep
his religiousness? Ah, my good sir (he broke forth), la
to heart and understand that even as your own mind with
you can turn and dispose of your body as it lists, so oug
we to think that the wisdom which abides within t
universal frame does so dispose of all things as it fin
agreeable to itself; for hardly may it be that your eye

ble to range over many a league, but that the eye of
God is powerless to embrace all things at a glance; or
that to your soul it is given to dwell in thought on matters
here or far away in Egypt or in Sicily, but that the wisdom and thought of God is not sufficient to include all
things at one instant under His care. . . . If you will
but make trial of the gods by acts of service, whether
they will choose to give you counsel in matters obscure
to mortal vision, you shall discover the nature and the
greatness of Godhead to be such that they are able at
once to see all things and to hear all things and to be
present everywhere, nor does the least thing escape their
watchful care.   H. G. DAKYNS.

The Death of Cyrus

XENOPHON, *The Education of Cyrus* viii, 7. This work is a
romance. The ideas expressed are those of Xenophon.

When his life was far spent amid such achievements
and Cyrus was now a very old man, he came back for
the seventh time in his reign to Persia. His father and
mother were in the course of nature long since dead;
so Cyrus performed the customary sacrifice and led the
Persians in their national dance and distributed presents
among them all, as had been his custom.

As he slept in the palace he saw a vision: a figure of
more than human majesty appeared to him in a dream
and said: " Make ready, Cyrus; for thou shalt soon
depart to the gods." When the vision was past, he awoke
and seemed almost to know that the end of his life was
at hand. Accordingly, he at once took victims and offered
sacrifice in the high places to ancestral Zeus, to Helius,
and to the rest of the gods, even as the Persians are wont

to make sacrifice; and as he sacrificed, he prayed, saying
" O ancestral Zeus and Helius and all the gods, accep
these offerings as tokens of gratitude for help in achievin
many glorious enterprises; for in omens in the sacrific
in signs from heaven, in the flight of birds, and in ominou
words, ye ever showed me what I ought to do and wha
I ought not to do. And I render heartfelt thanks to yo
that I have never failed to recognise your fostering car
and never in my successes entertained proud though
transcending human bounds. And I beseech of you tha
ye will now also grant prosperity and happiness to m
children, my wife, my friends, and my country, and to m
myself an end befitting the life that ye have given me.

(Cyrus summons his sons, his friends, and the Persian magis
trates, to hear his last words. After defining the succession
he exhorts his sons:)

" Nay, by our fathers' gods, I implore you, my sons
honour one another, if you care at all to give me pleasure
For assuredly, this one thing, so it seems to me, you d
not know clearly, that I shall have no further being whe
I have finished this earthly life; for not even in this li
have you seen my soul, but you have detected its existenc
by what it accomplished. Have you never yet observe
what terror the souls of those who have been foull
dealt with strike into the hearts of those who have she
their blood, and what avenging deities they send upo
the track of the wicked? And do you think that th
honours paid to the dead would continue, if their soul
had no part in any of them? I am sure I do not; nor ye
my sons, have I ever convinced myself of this—that onl
as long as it is contained in a mortal body is the soul alive
but when it has been freed from it, is dead; for I se
that it is the soul that endues mortal bodies with life, a

long as it is in them. Neither have I been able to convince myself of this—that the soul will want intelligence just when it is separated from this unintelligent body; but when the spirit is set free, pure and untrammelled by matter,[1] then it is likely to be most intelligent. And when man is resolved into his primal elements, it is clear that every part returns to kindred matter, except the soul; that alone cannot be seen, either when present or when departing.

"Consider again," he continued, "that there is nothing in the world more nearly akin to death than is sleep; and the soul of man at just such times is revealed in its most divine aspect, and at such times, too, it looks forward into the future; for then, it seems, it is most untrammelled by the bonds of the flesh.

"Now if this be true, as I think it is, and if the soul does leave the body, then do what I request of you and show reverence for my soul. But if it is not so, and if the soul remains in the body and dies with it, then at least fear the gods, eternal, all-seeing, omnipotent, who keep this ordered universe together, unimpaired, ageless, unerring, indescribable in its beauty and its grandeur; and never allow yourselves to do or purpose anything wicked or unholy.

"Next to the gods, however, show respect also to all the race of men as they continue in perpetual succession; for the gods do not hide you away in darkness, but your works must ever live on in the sight of all men; and if they are pure and untainted with unrighteousness, they will make your power manifest among all mankind. But if you conceive any unrighteous schemes against

---

[1] Literally "when the Mind is separated out, unmixed and pure." Compare Anaxagoras, above, p. 124.

each other, you will forfeit in the eyes of all men your right to be trusted. . . .

" Now as to my body, when I am dead, my sons, lay it away neither in gold nor in silver nor in anything else, but commit it to the earth as soon as may be. For what is more blessed than to be united with the earth, which brings forth and nourishes all things beautiful and all things good? I have always been a friend to man, and I think I should gladly now become a part of that which does him so much good. . . .

" Invite, however, all the Persians and our allies to my burial, to joy with me in that I shall henceforth be in security such that no evil can ever again come nigh me, whether I shall be in the divine presence or whether I shall no longer have any being. . . .

" Remember also this last word of mine," he said: " if you do good to your friends, you will also be able to punish your enemies. And now farewell, my children, and say farewell to your mother as from me. And to all my friends, both present and absent, I bid farewell."

After these words, he shook hands with them all, covered himself over, and so died.

W. MILLER.

LYCURGUS

The Providence of Heaven

LYCURGUS, *Speech Against Leocrates* 93. Leocrates was indicted for treason as having fled from Athens on the day when the news came of the defeat at Chaeronea (338 B.C.).

The first thing that the gods do is to lead astray the minds of wicked men. These verses from the old poets sound like an oracle that they had taken down and left as an heirloom to posterity:

When the first blinding stroke of heaven's wrath
Falls, it roots out the good will from the heart,
That, turned to evil purpose, man may sin
And know not that he sins.

Every elderly man must remember, every young man must have heard, the story of Callistratus. Condemned to death, he took to flight and was told by the oracle at Delphi, that if he returned to Athens he would be given his lawful rights. He came and took sanctuary at the altar of the Twelve Gods, but none the less he was put to death—and justly, for the lawful right of the wrong-doer is punishment. The god was right to give those whom Callistratus had wronged their due opportunity of chastising the guilty. It would be strange if he should give as clear a sign to the wicked as to the pious.

Sirs, it is my belief that the divine care keeps watch over all human conduct—especially over conduct towards parents and the dead and over piety towards the gods themselves. With good reason; for it is the worst of impieties not to spend our lives in the service of those to whom we owe life itself and most of its good things, much more to offend against them. In Sicily they tell a story—not strictly historical, perhaps, but it will do the younger members of this audience good to hear it— of an eruption of Mount Etna, in which the burning lava flowed over the country and up to one of the towns. The inhabitants fled to save themselves, all except one young man, who, seeing that his father was too old to escape and was being overtaken, lifted him up and carried him. With the added burden, he was overtaken himself. The sequel illustrates the divine benevolence towards the good. It is related that the fire flowed all round the spot where they were, and they alone were saved. The place is still called after them the Saints' Field. The

men who fled in all haste and left their parents to thei
fate, perished.

HYPEREIDES

From a Funeral Oration

HYPEREIDES, *Funeral Oration* over Leosthenes and hi
comrades slain in the Lamian War, 322 B.C. Jebb writes: "Th
closing sentences are addressed to the kinsfolk of the dead. . .
It should be remembered that these words were spoken, ove
almost the last martyrs of Greek freedom, by one who himse
was very soon to suffer torture and death in that cause." (*Atti
Orators* ii, 392.)

It is hard perhaps to comfort those who are in such
sorrow; grief is not laid to rest by speech or by observance; rather is it for the nature of the mourner, an
the nearness of the lost, to determine the boundaries o
anguish. Still, we must take heart, and lighten pain a
we may, and remember not only the death of the departe
but the good name also that they have left behind them
We owe not tears to their fate, but rather great praise
to their deeds. If they came not to old age among men
they have got the glory that never grows old, and hav
been made blessed perfectly. Those among them wh
died childless shall have as their inheritors the immorta
eulogies of Greece; and those of them who have lef
children behind them have bequeathed a trust of whic
their country's love will assume the guardianship. Mor
than this,—if to die is to be as though we had neve
been, then these have passed away from sickness and pai
and from all the accidents of the earthly life; or, if ther
is feeling in the underworld, and if, as we conjecture
the care of the Divine Power is over it, then it may we
be that they who rendered aid to the worship of the god

in the hour of its imminent desolation are most precious
to that Power's providence.   R. C. JEBB.

DEMOSTHENES

The Altars in the Soul

DEMOSTHENES, *Speech against Aristogeiton* 34.

There are in every city altars and temples to all the
gods, and among them to Forethought, under which
title Athena is revered as a great and beneficent power.
At Delphi, at the very entrance of the precinct of Apollo,
who as a god and a prophet knows what is best, there
is a magnificent shrine of the goddess of Forethought;
there is no temple to Folly or Pitilessness. Ay, and all
mankind have altars dedicated to Justice, to Law-abiding-
ness, and to Mercy—the fairest and holiest being those
that are in the inmost soul and nature of every man, while
others are set up outwardly for the common worship
of all. There are no altars to Shamelessness or Slander
or Perjury or Ingratitude—Aristogeiton's attributes!

FOURTH CENTURY COMEDY

Let us eat and drink, for to-morrow we die

AMPHIS, *Gynaecocratia*.

Drink and play: death ends our life, and short is our
time on earth. But, once we are dead, there is no end
of death.

AMPHIS, *Ialemus* 2.

One who is born to die and does not seek to add some
pleasure to life and let everything else go, is a fool and
under heaven's curse. So I think, and every wise man
will judge the same.

Mourning

ANTIPHANES, *Aphrodisius, frag.* 2.

We should not mourn overmuch for those who are dear to us. They are not dead; they have only gone before upon the road that all must travel. Some day we too shall come to the same inn, to spend the rest of time in their society.

We know nothing

ANAXANDRIDES, *Canephorus.*

We are all dullards in divinity; we know nothing.

INDEX OF PERSONS AND AUTHORS